Copyright 2020 by David Clark -All rights reserved.

No part of this book may be reproduced or transmitted in any form or by any means, electronic or mechanical, including photocopying and recording, or by any information storage and retrieval system, without permission in writing from the publisher. This is a work of fiction. Names, places, characters and incidents are either the product of the author's imagination or are used fictitiously, and any resemblance to any actual persons, living or dead, organizations, events or locales is entirely coincidental. The unauthorized reproduction or distribution of this copyrighted work is ilegal.

Disclaimer Notice:

Please note the information contained within this document is for educational and entertainment purposes only. All effort has been executed to present accurate, up to date, reliable, complete information. No warranties of any kind are declared or implied. Readers acknowledge that the author is not engaged in the rendering of legal, financial, medical, or professional advice. The content within this book has been derived from various sources. Please consult a licensed professional before attempting any techniques outlined in this book.

By reading this document, the reader agrees that under no circumstances is the author responsible for any losses, direct or indirect, that are incurred as a result of the use of the information contained within this document, including, but not limited to, errors, omissions, or inaccuracies.

CONTENTS

Introduction 7
Slow Cooker Breakfast Recipes for 2 8
    Cinnamon Oatmeal 8
    Sausage and Potato Mix 8
    Flavorful Coconut Quinoa 8
    Veggie Hash Brown Mix 8
    Hash Brown with Bacon 8
    Cinnamon French Toast 9
    Delish Carrots Oatmeal 9
    Thyme Hash Browns 9
    Banana Oatmeal 9
    Chia Oatmeal 9
    Easy Buttery Oatmeal 9
    Ginger Raisins Oatmeal 10
    Apple with Chia Mix 10
    Pumpkin and Quinoa Mix 10
    Berries Quinoa 10
    Quinoa and Veggies Casserole 10
    Cauliflower with Eggs 11
    Sausage and Eggs Mix 11
    Parmesan Quinoa 11
    Broccoli Casserole 11
    Shrimp Bowls 11
    Peach, Vanilla and Oats Mix 12
    Eggs Mix 12
    Potato and Ham Mix 12
    Flavorful Spinach Frittata 12
    Chili Eggs Mix 12
    Cheesy Eggs 13
    Tomato and Zucchini Eggs Mix 13
    Chocolate Bread 13
    Almond and Quinoa Bowls 13
    Carrots Casserole 13
    Cranberry Oatmeal 14
    Mushroom Casserole 14
    Ginger Bowls 14
    Granola Bowls 14
    Squash Bowls 14
    Lamb and Eggs 14
    Cauliflower Casserole 15
    Yummy Beef Meatloaf 15
    Leek Casserole 15
    Eggs and Sweet Potato 15
    Pork and Eggplant 15
    Apple Spread 16
    Cocoa Oats 16
    Beans Salad 16
    Peppers Rice 16
    Cashew Butter 16
    Pumpkin and Berries 17
    Quinoa and Chia Pudding 17
    Beans Bowls 17
    Basil Sausage and Broccoli Mix 17
    Zucchini and Cauliflower Eggs 17
    Mushroom Quiche 18
    Scallions Quinoa and Carrots 18
    Ham Omelet 18
    Peppers and Eggs 18
    Baby Spinach Rice Mix 19
    Egg Scramble 19
    Peas and Rice Bowls 19
    Asparagus Casserole 19
Slow Cooker Lunch Recipes for 2 20
    Seafood Soup 20
    Sesame Salmon 20
    Shrimp Stew 20
    Shrimp and Spinach 20
    Ginger Salmon 20
    Cod Stew 21
    Sweet Potato and Clam Chowder 21
    Maple Chicken 21
    Salsa Chicken 21
    Turkey and Mushrooms 21
    Chicken and Tomato Mix 22
    Turkey and Figs 22
    Turkey and Walnuts 22
    Thyme Chicken 22
    Beef and Cauliflower 22
    Soy Pork Chops 23
    Pork and Cranberries 23
    Lamb and Onion 23
    Pork Roast and Olives 23
    Beef Stew 23
    Beef and Celery 24
    Tomato Pasta Mix 24
    Honey Lamb Roast 24
    Worcestershire Beef 24
    Chickpeas Stew 24
    Savory Lentils Soup 25
    Chicken Soup 25
    Lime Chicken 25
    Shrimp Gumbo 25
    Chicken Soup 25
    Pork Soup 26
    Mushroom Stew 26
    Beans Chili 26
    Parsley Chicken 26
    Mustard Short Ribs 26
    Piquant Creamy Brisket 27
    Mushroom Soup 27
    Potato Soup 27
    Chicken with Corn 27
    Mixed Pork and Beans 27
    Pork Chops 28
    Chicken and Peach Mix 28
    Chicken Drumsticks 28
    Mustard Pork Chops 28
    Fennel Soup 28
    Artichoke Soup 28
    Beans and Mushroom 29
    Chicken and Eggplant Stew 29
    Turmeric Stew 29
    Pork Chili 29
    Cinnamon Pork Ribs 29
    Pork and Mushroom 30
    Pork and Tomatoes Mix 30

Pork Shanks	30
Potato Stew	30
Chicken and Rice	30
Salmon Stew	31
Pork and Chickpeas	31
Beef and Cabbage	31
Beef Stew	31
Beef Curry	31
Chicken and Brussels Sprouts	32
Chickpeas Stew	32
Eggplant Curry	32
Beef and Artichokes	32
Beef Soup	32
Veggie Soup	33
Turkey Stew	33
Masala Beef Mix	33
Slow Cooker Side Dish Recipes for 2	**34**
Cheddar Potatoes	34
Balsamic Cauliflower	34
Black Beans Mix	34
Butter Green Beans	34
Appetizing Corn Sauté	34
Sage Peas	35
Tomato and Corn	35
Dill Mushroom Sauté	35
Appetizing Zucchini Mix	35
Squash and Eggplant Mix	35
Carrots and Spinach Mix	36
Coconut Potatoes	36
Sage Sweet Potatoes	36
Cauliflower and Almonds	36
Garlic Risotto	36
Curry Savory Veggie Mix	36
Rosemary Leeks	37
Spicy Brussels Sprouts	37
Potatoes and Leeks Mix	37
Black Beans Mix	37
Orange Carrots Mix	37
Hot Lentils	37
Marjoram Rice Mix	38
Mashed Potatoes	38
Barley Mix	38
Beans Mix	38
Creamy Beans	38
Spinach Mix	38
BBQ-Beans	39
White Beans Mix	39
Sweet Potato and Cauliflower	39
Cabbage Mix	39
Parsley Mushroom	39
Cinnamon Squash	39
Appetizing Zucchini Mix	40
Kale Mix	40
Buttery Spinach	40
Bacon Potatoes	40
Cauliflower Mash	40
Savory Veggie Mix	40
Farro Mix	41
Cumin Quinoa Pilaf	41
Saffron Risotto	41
Mint Farro Pilaf	41
Parmesan Rice	41
Spinach Rice	41
Mango Rice	42
Lemony Artichokes	42
Coconut Bok Choy	42
Italian Eggplant	42
Cabbage and Onion	42
Balsamic Okra Mix	42
Garlic Carrots	43
Curry Broccoli Mix	43
Rice and Corn	43
Cauliflower and Potatoes	43
Asparagus Mix	43
Garlic Squash Mix	43
Carrots and Parsnips	44
Lemony Kale	44
Brussels Sprouts and Cauliflower	44
Cabbage and Kale Mix	44
Thyme Mushrooms	44
Veggie Medley	45
Green Beans and Zucchinis	45
Tarragon Sweet Potatoes	45
Spicy Brussels Sprouts	45
Parmesan Spinach Mix	45
Peas and Tomatoes	46
Savoy Cabbage Mix	46
Slow Cooker Snack Recipes for 2	**47**
Delish Spinach Spread	47
Artichoke Dip	47
Crab Dip	47
Lemony Shrimp Dip	47
Squash Salsa	47
Flavory Beans Spread	48
Rice Bowls	48
Cauliflower Spread	48
Flavory Mushroom Dip	48
Chickpeas Spread	48
Spinach Dip	49
Potato Salad	49
Stuffed Peppers	49
Corn Dip	49
Tomato and Mushroom	49
Salsa Beans Dip	49
Pineapple and Tofu	50
Chickpeas Salsa	50
Mushroom Spread	50
Bulgur and Beans Salsa	50
Appetizing Beets Salad	50
Lentils Salsa	51
Tacos	51
Appetizing Almond Bowls	51
Eggplant Salsa	51
Appetizing Almond Spread	51
Onion Dip	51
Yummy Nuts Bowls	52
Eggplant Salad	52
Yummy Lentils Dip	52
Turkey Meatballs	52
Easy Stuffed Mushrooms	52

Paprika Cod Sticks 53	Turkey with Rice 65
Nuts Snack 53	Italian Turkey 65
Salmon Bites 53	Duck with Mushrooms 65
Spinach and Nuts Dip 53	Turkey and Tomato Sauce 65
Curry Pork Meatballs 53	Tomato Chicken 66
Calamari Rings 53	Turkey with Leeks 66
Shrimp Salad 54	Coconut Turkey 66
Easy Chicken Salad 54	Chicken and Zucchinis 66
Apple and Carrot Dip 54	Turkey with Radishes 66
Easy Sweet Potato Dip 54	Simple Chives Duck 67
Spinach, Walnuts and Calamari Salad 54	Cilantro Chicken and Eggplant Mix 67
Delightful Chicken Meatballs 55	Chicken and Brussels Sprouts 67
Cinnamon Pecans Snack 55	Chicken and Mango Mix 67
Almonds and Shrimp Bowls 55	Turkey with Avocado 67
Broccoli Dip 55	Chicken and Peppers 68
WalYummy Nuts Bowls 55	Chicken and Cabbage 68
Cauliflower Bites 55	Lime Turkey and Chard 68
Appetizing Beef Dip 56	BBQ Turkey 68
Zucchini Spread 56	Chicken and Asparagus 68
Appetizing Beef Dip 56	Lemony Turkey and Potatoes 69
Eggplant Salsa 56	Turkey and Okra 69
Appetizing Carrots Spread 56	Spicy Duck Mix 69
Cauliflower Dip 57	Orange Chicken Mix 69
Yummy Lentils Hummus 57	Turkey with Carrots 69
Spinach Dip 57	Flavorful Rosemary Chicken Thighs ... 70
Yummy Peppers Salsa 57	Turkey with Kidney Beans 70
Artichoke Dip 57	Coriander and Turmeric Chicken 70
Yummy Mushroom Salsa 58	Garlic Turkey 70
Slow Cooker Poultry Recipes for 2 59	Cumin Chicken 70
Chicken and Green Beans 59	Slow Cooker Meat Recipes for 2 71
Oregano Turkey and Tomatoes 59	Pork Chops and Mango 71
Mustard Chicken Mix 59	Beef and Zucchinis Mix 71
Lemony Turkey and Spinach 59	Pork and Olives 71
Paprika Chicken and Artichokes 59	Pork and Soy Sauce Mix 71
Chicken Wings 60	Beef with Sauce 71
Lime Chicken Mix 60	Pork and Beans Mix 72
Chicken and Olives 60	Beef and Spinach 72
Turkey and Fennel Mix 60	Pork and Chilies Mix 72
Chicken with Tomatoes 60	Hot Ribs 72
Chicken and Onions Mix 61	Beef and Corn Mix 72
Pesto Chicken 61	Cider Beef Mix 73
Ginger Turkey Mix 61	Tarragon Pork Chops 73
Turkey and Plums 61	Honey Pork Chops 73
Creamy Turkey Mix 61	Turmeric Lamb 73
Chicken and Apples 62	Chili Lamb 73
Chicken and Endives 62	Beef and Red Onions 73
Basil Chicken 62	Pork and Okra 74
Chicken and Broccoli 62	Easy Chives Lamb 74
Flavorful Rosemary Chicken 62	Oregano Beef 74
Chicken Curry 63	Pork with Green Beans 74
Flavorful Balsamic Turkey 63	Lamb Chops 74
Turkey and Scallions Mix 63	Beef and Artichokes 75
Parsley Chicken 63	Lamb with Potatoes 75
Turkey Chili 63	Lamb and Tomatoes Mix 75
Spicy Masala Turkey 64	Pork and Eggplant 75
Chicken and Beans 64	Lemon Lamb 75
Turkey and Corn 64	Lamb with Olives 76
Coriander Turkey 64	Nutmeg Lamb and Squash 76
Turkey with Olives and Corn 64	Lamb and Fennel 76
Turkey and Peas 65	Creamy Lamb 76

Beef and Capers	76
Masala Beef with Sauce	77
Lamb and Cabbage	77
Pork with Lentils	77
Balsamic Lamb Mix	77
Beef with Endives	77
Lamb and Lime Zucchinis	77
Beef with Peas	78
Maple Beef	78
Rosemary Beef	78
Chili Lamb	78
Cumin Pork Chops	78
Paprika Lamb	78
Beef and Corn	79
Lime Pork Chops	79
Lamb and Capers	79
Lamb and Appetizing Zucchini Mix	79
Beef with Peppers	79
Cayenne Lamb	80
Cinnamon Lamb	80
Lamb and Kale	80
Beef with Sprouts	80
Pork Chops and Spinach	80
Curry Lamb	81
Oregano Lamb	81
Pesto Lamb	81
Beef with Green Beans	81
Balsamic Lamb	81
Creamy Beef	82
Coconut Beef	82

Slow Cooker Fish and Seafood Recipes for 2 83

Tasty Lime Shrimp	83
Chili Salmon	83
Herbed Shrimp	83
Paprika Cod	83
Spicy Tuna	83
Herbed Ginger Tuna	84
Chives Shrimp	84
Coriander Salmon	84
Tuna and Green Beans	84
Cod and Corn	84
Turmeric Salmon	84
Sea Bass with Chickpeas	85
Creamy Shrimp	85
Parsley Cod	85
Cod and Tomatoes	85
Orange Cod	85
Garlic Sea Bass	85
Tuna with Brussels Sprouts	86
Shrimp with Spinach	86
Shrimp with Avocado	86
Chives Mackerel	86
Dill Cod	86
Shrimp and Mango	87
Balsamic Tuna	87
Lime Trout	87
Creamy Tuna and Scallions	87
Mustard Cod	87
Shrimp with Pineapple Bowls	87
Lime Crab	88
Salmon and Carrots	88
Shrimp and Eggplant	88
Sea Bass with Squash	88
Coconut Mackerel	88
Salmon with Peas	88
Chili Shrimp with Zucchinis	89
Italian Shrimp	89
Basil Cod with Olives	89
Tuna and Fennel	89
Shrimp with Mushrooms	89
Salmon and Berries	89
Cod with Artichokes	90
Salmon, Tomatoes and Green Beans	90
Shrimp and Rice	90
Shrimp with Red Chard	90
Chives Mussels	90
Calamari with Sauce	91
Salmon Salad	91
Walnut Tuna	91
Almond Shrimp and Cabbage	91
Spicy Shrimp	91
Tomatoes and Kale	92
Trout Bowls	92
Curry Calamari	92
Balsamic Trout	92
Oregano Shrimp	92
Salmon and Strawberries Mix	93
Salmon and Tomatoes	93
Shrimp and Cauliflower Bowls	93
Cod with Broccoli	93
Cinnamon Trout	93

Slow Cooker Dessert Recipes for 2 94

Apples with Cinnamon	94
Vanilla Pears	94
Easy Avocado Cake	94
Coconut Cream	94
Rice Pudding	94
Cherry Bowls	94
Flavorful Berry Cream	95
Simple Maple Pudding	95
Chia and Orange Pudding	95
Berries Mix	95
Apple Compote	95
Easy Plums Stew	95
Cinnamon Peach	96
Strawberry Cake	96
Ginger Pears	96
Raisin Cookies	96
Easy Blueberries Jam	96
Orange Bowls	96
Quinoa Pudding	97
Chia with Avocado Pudding	97
Almond and Cherries Pudding	97
Peach Cream	97
Cinnamon Plums	97
Delightful Cardamom Apples	97
Cherry and Rhubarb Mix	98
Peaches and Wine Sauce	98
Apricot and Peaches Cream	98
Vanilla Grapes Mix	98

Pomegranate and Mango Bowls	98
Mandarin Cream	98
Cranberries Cream	99
Buttery Pineapple	99
Strawberry and Orange Mix	99
Maple Plums and Mango	99
Cantaloupe Cream	99
Yogurt Cheesecake	99
Chocolate Mango	100
Lemon Jam	100
Lemon Peach	100
Rhubarb Stew	100
Strawberry with Blackberry Jam	100
Pear Cream	100
Simple Rhubarb Jam	101
Apricot Marmalade	101
Avocado and Mango Bowls	101
Tomato Jam	101
Cinnamon Peaches	101
Coconut Jam	101
Bread Pudding	102
Tapioca and Chia Pudding	102
Dates Pudding	102
Walnuts and Mango Bowls	102
Berries Salad	102
Pears and Apples	102
Creamy Rhubarb and Plums Bowls	103
Cheese Pudding	103
Greek Cream	103
Easy Ginger Cream	103
Quinoa Pudding	103
Melon Pudding	103
Appendix : Recipes Index	104

Introduction

Recipes made with everyday ingredients are a guarantee you will have everything necessary on hand right away. Push the limits of what slow cooker can do – after all, it's not so hard to follow a couple of instructions. Being simple to follow and understandable this cookbook will raise the bar for slow cooker recipes for beginners and more experienced home cooks. Spend more time enjoying your meal and less time cleaning up the mess every tasty dinner can bring to your kitchen.

Deciding what to cook for dinner does not have to be a scary and tiring decision. This slow cooker cookbook is designed specially to make this choice an easy one. Say YES to no-fuss cooking even if you have never experienced anything like it in your lifetime! Peek at Look Inside breakfast options; discover how simple home cooking can be. Leave aside the hassle of mixing and supervising your meals on the stove and the slow cooker will do the hardest part. Each recipe here is straightforward, requires very basic cooking skills and gives you a chance to make a quality change to those meals you consume daily.

A delicious collection of daily recipes that will easily become your family's favorites – that's what makes this cookbook so great. Soups, stews, roasts, chilis, breakfast and snack recipes, delectable desserts – there's a lot for you to experience for the first time! Get the ingredients, get in the mood and let the cooking begin!

Slow Cooker Breakfast Recipes for 2

Cinnamon Oatmeal
Preparation time: 10 minutes
Cooking time: 6 hours
Servings: 2
Ingredients:
- 1 cup old fashioned oats
- 3 cups almond milk
- 1 cup blackberries
- ½ cup Greek yogurt
- ½ teaspoon cinnamon powder
- ½ teaspoon vanilla extract

Directions:
1. In your slow cooker, mix the oats with the milk, berries and the other ingredients, toss, put the lid on and cook on Low for 6 hours.
2. Divide into bowls and serve for breakfast.

Nutrition: calories 932, fat 43, fiber 16.7, carbs 82.2, protein 24.3

Sausage and Potato Mix
Preparation time: 10 minutes
Cooking time: 6 hours
Servings: 2
Ingredients:
- 2 sweet potatoes, peeled and roughly cubed
- 1 green bell pepper, minced
- ½ yellow onion, chopped
- 4 ounces smoked andouille sausage, sliced
- 1 cup cheddar cheese, shredded
- ¼ cup Greek yogurt
- ¼ teaspoon basil, dried
- 1 cup chicken stock
- Salt and black pepper to the taste
- 1 tablespoon parsley, chopped

Directions:
1. In your slow cooker, combine the potatoes with the bell pepper, sausage and the other ingredients, toss, put the lid on and cook on Low for 6 hours.
2. Divide between plates and serve for breakfast.

Nutrition: calories 623, fat 35.7, fiber 7.6, carbs 53.1, protein 24.8

Flavorful Coconut Quinoa
Preparation time: 10 minutes
Cooking time: 8 hours
Servings: 2
Ingredients:
- ½ cup quinoa
- 2 cups coconut milk
- 1 tablespoon maple syrup
- 1 teaspoon vanilla extract
- 2 tablespoons raisins
- ¼ cup blackberries

Directions:
1. In your slow cooker, mix the quinoa with the milk, maple syrup and the other ingredients, toss, put the lid on and cook on Low for 8 hours.
2. Divide into 2 bowls and serve for breakfast.

Nutrition: calories 775, fat 60, fiber 9.7, carbs 56.5, protein 12

Veggie Hash Brown Mix
Preparation time: 10 minutes
Cooking time: 6 hours and 5 minutes
Servings: 2
Ingredients:
- 1 tablespoon olive oil
- ½ cup white mushrooms, chopped
- ½ yellow onion, chopped
- ¼ teaspoon garlic powder
- ¼ teaspoon onion powder
- ¼ cup sour cream
- 10 ounces hash browns
- ¼ cup cheddar cheese, shredded
- Salt and black pepper to the taste
- ½ tablespoon parsley, chopped

Directions:
1. Heat up a pan with the oil over medium heat, add the onion and mushrooms, stir and cook for 5 minutes.
2. Transfer this to the slow cooker, add hash browns and the other ingredients, toss, put the lid on and cook on Low for 6 hours.
3. Divide between plates and for breakfast.

Nutrition: calories 571, fat 35.6, fiber 5.4, carbs 54.9, protein 9.7

Hash Brown with Bacon
Preparation time: 10 minutes
Cooking time: 3 hours
Servings: 2
Ingredients:
- 5 ounces hash browns, shredded
- 2 bacon slices, cooked and chopped
- ¼ cup mozzarella cheese, shredded
- 2 eggs, whisked
- ¼ cup sour cream
- 1 tablespoon cilantro, chopped
- 1 tablespoon olive oil
- A pinch of salt and black pepper

Directions:
1. Grease your slow cooker with the oil, add the hash browns mixed with the eggs, sour cream and the other ingredients, toss, put the lid on and cook on High for 4 hours.
2. Divide the casserole into bowls and serve.

Nutrition: calories 383, fat 26.9, fiber 2.3, carbs 26.6, protein 9.6

Cinnamon French Toast
Preparation time: 10 minutes
Cooking time: 4 hours
Servings: 2
Ingredients:
- ½ French baguette, sliced
- 2 ounces cream cheese
- 1 tablespoon brown sugar
- 1 egg, whisked
- 3 tablespoons almond milk
- 2 tablespoons honey
- ½ teaspoon cinnamon powder
- 1 tablespoon butter, melted
- Cooking spray

Directions:
1. Spread the cream cheese on all bread slices, grease your slow cooker with the cooking spray and arrange the slices in the pot.
2. In a bowl, mix the egg with the cinnamon, almond milk and the remaining ingredients, whisk and pour over the bread slices.
3. Put the lid on, cook on High for 4 hours, divide the mix between plates and serve for breakfast.

Nutrition: calories 316, fat 23.5, fiber 0.5, carbs 23.9, protein 5.6

Delish Carrots Oatmeal
Preparation time: 10 minutes
Cooking time: 8 hours
Servings: 2
Ingredients:
- ½ cup old fashioned oats
- 1 cup almond milk
- 2 carrots, peeled and grated
- ½ teaspoon cinnamon powder
- 2 tablespoons brown sugar
- ¼ cup walnuts, chopped
- Cooking spray

Directions:
1. Grease your slow cooker with cooking spray, add the oats, milk, carrots and the other ingredients, toss, put the lid on and cook on Low for 8 hours.
2. Divide the oatmeal into 2 bowls and serve.

Nutrition: calories 590, fat 40.7, fiber 9.1, carbs 49.9, protein 12

Thyme Hash Browns
Preparation time: 10 minutes
Cooking time: 4 hours
Servings: 2
Ingredients:
- Cooking spray
- 10 ounces hash browns
- 2 eggs, whisked
- ¼ cup heavy cream
- ¼ teaspoon thyme, dried
- ¼ teaspoon garlic powder
- A pinch of salt and black pepper
- ½ cup mozzarella, shredded
- 1 tablespoon chives, chopped
- 1 tablespoon parsley, chopped

Directions:
1. Grease your slow cooker with cooking spray, spread the hash browns on the bottom, add the eggs, cream and the other ingredients except the cheese and toss.
2. Sprinkle the cheese on top, put the lid on and cook on High for 4 hours.
3. Divide the mix between plates and serve for breakfast.

Nutrition: calories 516, fat 29.2, fiber 4.7, carbs 51.3, protein 12.3

Banana Oatmeal
Preparation time: 10 minutes
Cooking time: 6 hours
Servings: 2
Ingredients:
- 1/2 cup old fashioned oats
- 1 banana, mashed
- ½ teaspoon cinnamon powder
- 2 tablespoons maple syrup
- 2 cups almond milk
- Cooking spray

Directions:
1. Grease your slow cooker with the cooking spray, add the oats, banana and the other ingredients, stir, put the lid on and cook on Low for 6 hours.
2. Divide into 2 bowls and serve for breakfast.

Nutrition: calories 815, fat 60.3, fiber 10.7, carbs 67, protein 11.1

Chia Oatmeal
Preparation time: 10 minutes
Cooking time: 8 hours
Servings: 2
Ingredients:
- 2 cups almond milk
- 1 cup steel cut oats
- 2 tablespoons butter, soft
- ½ teaspoon almond extract
- 2 tablespoons chia seeds

Directions:
1. In your slow cooker, mix the oats with the chia seeds and the other ingredients, toss, put the lid on and cook on Low for 8 hours.
2. Stir the oatmeal one more time, divide into 2 bowls and serve.

Nutrition: calories 812, fat 71.4, fiber 9.4, carbs 41.1, protein 11

Easy Buttery Oatmeal
Preparation time: 10 minutes
Cooking time: 3 hours
Servings: 2
Ingredients:
- Cooking spray
- 2 cups coconut milk
- 1 cup old fashioned oats
- 1 pear, cubed
- 1 apple, cored and cubed
- 2 tablespoons butter, melted

Directions:
1. Grease your slow cooker with the cooking spray, add the milk, oats and the other ingredients, toss, put the lid on and cook on High for 3 hours.
2. Divide the mix into bowls and serve for breakfast.

Nutrition: calories 1002, fat 74, fiber 18, carbs 93, protein 16.2

Ginger Raisins Oatmeal

Preparation time: 10 minutes
Cooking time: 8 hours
Servings: 2
Ingredients:
- 1 cup almond milk
- ½ cup steel cut oats
- ¼ cup raisins
- ½ teaspoon ginger, ground
- 1 tablespoon orange zest, grated
- 1 tablespoon orange juice
- ½ teaspoon vanilla extract
- ½ tablespoon honey

Directions:
1. In your slow cooker, combine the milk with the oats, raisins and the other ingredients, toss, put the lid on and cook on Low for 8 hours.
2. Divide into 2 bowls and serve for breakfast.

Nutrition: calories 435, fat 30.1, fiber 5.8, carbs 41.2, protein 6.2

Apple with Chia Mix

Preparation time: 10 minutes
Cooking time: 8 hours
Servings: 2
Ingredients:
- ¼ cup chia seeds
- 2 apples, cored and roughly cubed
- 1 cup almond milk
- 2 tablespoons maple syrup
- 1 teaspoon vanilla extract
- ½ tablespoon cinnamon powder
- Cooking spray

Directions:
1. Grease your slow cooker with the cooking spray, add the chia seeds, milk and the other ingredients, toss, put the lid on and cook on Low for 8 hours.
2. Divide the mix into bowls and serve for breakfast.

Nutrition: calories 453, fat 29.3, fiber 8, carbs 51.1, protein 3.4

Pumpkin and Quinoa Mix

Preparation time: 10 minutes
Cooking time: 8 hours
Servings: 2
Ingredients:
- Cooking spray
- ½ cup quinoa
- 1 cup almond milk
- 1 tablespoon honey
- ¼ cup pumpkin puree
- ½ teaspoon vanilla extract
- ¼ teaspoon cinnamon powder

Directions:
1. Grease your slow cooker with the cooking spray, add the quinoa, milk, honey and the other ingredients, stir, put the lid on and cook on Low for 7 hours.
2. Divide the mix into bowls and serve for breakfast.

Nutrition: calories 242, fat 3, fiber 8, carbs 20, protein 7

Berries Quinoa

Preparation time: 10 minutes
Cooking time: 8 hours
Servings: 2
Ingredients:
- Cooking spray
- 1 cup quinoa
- 2 cups almond milk
- ¼ cup heavy cream
- ¼ cup blueberries
- 2 tablespoons cocoa powder
- 1 tablespoon brown sugar

Directions:
1. Grease your slow cooker with the cooking spray, add the quinoa, berries and the other ingredients, toss, put the lid on and cook on Low for 8 hours.
2. Divide into 2 bowls and serve for breakfast.

Nutrition: calories 200, fat 4, fiber 5, carbs 17, protein 5

Quinoa and Veggies Casserole

Preparation time: 10 minutes
Cooking time: 6 hours
Servings: 2
Ingredients:
- ¼ cup quinoa
- 1 cup almond milk
- 2 eggs, whisked
- 1 tablespoon parsley, chopped
- 1 tablespoon chives, chopped
- A pinch of salt and black pepper
- ¼ cup baby spinach
- ¼ cup cherry tomatoes, halved
- 2 tablespoons parmesan, shredded
- Cooking spray

Directions:
1. Grease your slow cooker with the cooking spray, add the quinoa mixed with he milk, eggs and the other ingredients except the parmesan, toss and spread into the pot.
2. Sprinkle the parmesan on top, put the lid on and cook on Low for 6 hours.
3. Divide between plates and serve.

Nutrition: calories 251, fat 5, fiber 7, carbs 19, protein 11

Cauliflower with Eggs
Preparation time: 10 minutes
Cooking time: 7 hours
Servings: 2
Ingredients:
- Cooking spray
- 4 eggs, whisked
- A pinch of salt and black pepper
- ¼ teaspoon thyme, dried
- ½ teaspoon turmeric powder
- 1 cup cauliflower florets
- ½ small yellow onion, chopped
- 3 ounces breakfast sausages, sliced
- ½ cup cheddar cheese, shredded

Directions:
1. Grease your slow cooker with cooking spray and spread the cauliflower florets on the bottom of the pot.
2. Add the eggs mixed with salt, pepper and the other ingredients and toss.
3. Put the lid on, cook on Low for 7 hours, divide between plates and serve for breakfast.

Nutrition: calories 261, fat 6, fiber 7, carbs 22, protein 6

Sausage and Eggs Mix
Preparation time: 10 minutes
Cooking time: 8 hours and 10 minutes
Servings: 2
Ingredients:
- 4 eggs, whisked
- 1 red onion, chopped
- ¼ teaspoon rosemary, dried
- ½ teaspoon turmeric powder
- ½ pound pork sausage, sliced
- ½ tablespoon garlic powder
- 1 teaspoon basil, dried
- A pinch of salt and black pepper
- Cooking spray

Directions:
1. Grease a pan with the cooking spray, heat it up over medium-high heat, add the onion and the pork sausage, toss and cook for 10 minutes.
2. Transfer this to the slow cooker, also add the eggs mixed with the remaining ingredients, toss everything, put the lid on and cook on Low for 8 hours.
3. Divide between plates and serve right away for breakfast.

Nutrition: calories 271, fat 7, fiber 8, carbs 20, protein 11

Parmesan Quinoa
Preparation time: 10 minutes
Cooking time: 6 hours
Servings: 2
Ingredients:
- 1 cup quinoa
- 2 cups veggie stock
- 1 tablespoon chives, chopped
- 1 carrot, peeled and grated
- ½ cup parmesan, grated
- ¼ cup heavy cream
- Salt and black pepper to the taste
- Cooking spray

Directions:
1. Grease your slow cooker with the cooking spray, add the quinoa mixed with the stock and the other ingredients except the parmesan and the cream, toss, put the lid on and cook on High for 3 hours.
2. Add the remaining ingredients, toss the mix again, cook on High for 3 more hours, divide into bowls and serve for breakfast.

Nutrition: calories 261, fat 6, fiber 8, carbs 26, protein 11

Broccoli Casserole
Preparation time: 10 minutes
Cooking time: 6 hours
Servings: 2
Ingredients:
- 2 eggs, whisked
- 1 cup broccoli florets
- 2 cups hash browns
- ½ teaspoon coriander, ground
- ½ teaspoon rosemary, dried
- ½ teaspoon turmeric powder
- ½ teaspoon mustard powder
- A pinch of salt and black pepper
- 1 small red onion, chopped
- ½ red bell pepper, chopped
- 1 ounce cheddar cheese, shredded
- Cooking spray

Directions:
1. Grease your slow cooker with the cooking spray, and spread hash browns, broccoli, bell pepper and the onion on the bottom of the pan.
2. In a bowl, mix the eggs with the coriander and the other ingredients, whisk and pour over the broccoli mix in the pot.
3. Put the lid on, cook on Low for 6 hours, divide between plates and serve for breakfast.

Nutrition: calories 261, fat 7, fiber 8, carbs 20, protein 11

Shrimp Bowls
Preparation time: 10 minutes
Cooking time: 2 hours
Servings: 2
Ingredients:
- ½ cup chicken stock
- ½ pound shrimp, peeled and deveined
- 1 carrot, peeled and cubed
- ½ cup baby spinach
- ¼ cup heavy cream
- ¼ tablespoon garlic powder
- ¼ tablespoon onion powder
- ¼ teaspoon rosemary, dried
- A pinch of salt and black pepper
- ¼ cup cheddar cheese, shredded
- 1 ounce cream cheese
- 1 tablespoon chives, chopped

Directions:
1. In your slow cooker, mix the shrimp with the stock, cream and the other ingredients, toss, put the lid on and cook on Low for 2 hours.
2. Divide into bowls, and serve for breakfast.

Nutrition: calories 300, fat 7, fiber 12, carbs 20, protein 10

Peach, Vanilla and Oats Mix

Preparation time: 10 minutes
Cooking time: 8 hours
Servings: 2
Ingredients:
- ½ cup steel cut oats
- 2 cups almond milk
- ½ cup peaches, pitted and roughly chopped
- ½ teaspoon vanilla extract
- 1 teaspoon cinnamon powder

Directions:
1. In your slow cooker, mix the oats with the almond milk, peaches and the other ingredients, toss, put the lid on and cook on Low for 8 hours.
2. Divide into bowls and serve for breakfast right away.

Nutrition: calories 261, fat 5, fiber 8, carbs 18, protein 6

Eggs Mix

Preparation time: 10 minutes
Cooking time: 2 hours
Servings: 2
Ingredients:
- Cooking spray
- 4 eggs, whisked
- ¼ cup sour cream
- A pinch of salt and black pepper
- ½ teaspoon chili powder
- ½ teaspoon hot paprika
- ½ red bell pepper, chopped
- ½ yellow onion, chopped
- 2 cherry tomatoes, cubed
- 1 tablespoon parsley, chopped

Directions:
1. In a bowl, mix the eggs with the cream, salt, pepper and the other ingredients except the cooking spray and whisk well.
2. Grease your slow cooker with cooking spray, pour the eggs mix inside, spread, stir, put the lid on and cook on High for 2 hours.
3. Divide the mix between plates and serve.

Nutrition: calories 162, fat 5, fiber 7, carbs 15, protein 4

Potato and Ham Mix

Preparation time: 10 minutes
Cooking time: 6 hours
Servings: 2
Ingredients:
- Cooking spray
- 4 eggs, whisked
- ½ cup red potatoes, peeled and grated
- ¼ cup heavy cream
- ¼ cup ham, chopped
- 1 tablespoon cilantro, chopped
- ½ teaspoon turmeric powder
- Salt and black pepper to the taste

Directions:
1. Grease your slow cooker with cooking spray, add the eggs, potatoes and the other ingredients, whisk, put the lid on and cook on High for 6 hours.
2. Divide between plates and serve for breakfast.

Nutrition: calories 200, fat 4, fiber 6, carbs 12, protein 6

Flavorful Spinach Frittata

Preparation time: 10 minutes
Cooking time: 5 hours and 10 minutes
Servings: 2
Ingredients:
- Cooking spray
- 1 cup baby spinach
- 1 cup cherry tomatoes, halved
- 3 spring onions, chopped
- 3 ounces roasted red peppers, drained and chopped
- 2 ounces mozzarella, shredded
- 4 eggs, whisked
- ½ teaspoon allspice, ground
- A pinch of salt and black pepper

Directions:
1. Grease a pan with the cooking spray, heat up over medium heat, add the spring onions and roasted peppers and cook for 10 minutes.
2. Transfer the mix to the slow cooker, add the eggs mixed with the rest of the ingredients, toss, spread into the pot, put the lid on and cook on Low for 5 hours.
3. Divide the frittata between plates and serve.

Nutrition: calories 251, fat 4, fiber 6, carbs 12, protein 5

Chili Eggs Mix

Preparation time: 10 minutes
Cooking time: 3 hours
Servings: 2
Ingredients:
- Cooking spray
- 3 spring onions, chopped
- 2 tablespoons sun dried tomatoes, chopped
- 1 ounce canned and roasted green chili pepper, chopped
- ½ teaspoon rosemary, dried
- Salt and black pepper to the taste
- 3 ounces cheddar cheese, shredded
- 4 eggs, whisked
- ¼ cup heavy cream
- 1 tablespoon chives, chopped

Directions:
1. Grease your slow cooker with cooking spray and mix the eggs with the chili peppers and the other ingredients except the cheese.
2. Toss everything into the pot, sprinkle the cheese on top, put the lid on and cook on High for 3 hours.
3. Divide between plates and serve.

Nutrition: calories 224, fat 4, fiber 7, carbs 18, protein 11

Cheesy Eggs

Preparation time: 10 minutes
Cooking time: 3 hours
Servings: 2
Ingredients:
- 4 eggs, whisked
- ¼ cup spring onions, chopped
- 1 tablespoon oregano, chopped
- 1 cup milk
- 2 ounces feta cheese, crumbled
- A pinch of salt and black pepper
- Cooking spray

Directions:
1. In a bowl, combine the eggs with the spring onions and the other ingredients except the cooking spray and whisk.
2. Grease your slow cooker with cooking spray, add eggs mix, stir, put the lid on and cook on Low for 3 hours.
3. Divide between plates and serve for breakfast.

Nutrition: calories 214, fat 4, fiber 7, carbs 18, protein 5

Tomato and Zucchini Eggs Mix

Preparation time: 10 minutes
Cooking time: 3 hours
Servings: 2
Ingredients:
- Cooking spray
- 4 eggs, whisked
- 2 spring onions, chopped
- 1 tablespoon basil, chopped
- ½ teaspoon turmeric powder
- ½ cup tomatoes, cubed
- 1 zucchini, grated
- ¼ teaspoon sweet paprika
- A pinch of salt and black pepper
- 1 tablespoon parsley, chopped
- 2 tablespoons parmesan, grated

Directions:
1. Grease your slow cooker with cooking spray, add the eggs mixed with the zucchini, tomatoes and the other ingredients except the cheese and stir well.
2. Sprinkle the cheese, put the lid on and cook on High for 3 hours.
3. Divide between plates and serve for breakfast right away.

Nutrition: calories 261, fat 5, fiber 7, carbs 19, protein 6

Chocolate Bread

Preparation time: 10 minutes
Cooking time: 3 hours
Servings: 2
Ingredients:
- Cooking spray
- 1 cup almond flour
- ½ teaspoon baking soda
- ½ teaspoon cinnamon powder
- 1 tablespoon avocado oil
- 2 tablespoons maple syrup
- 2 eggs, whisked
- 1 tablespoon butter
- ½ tablespoon milk
- ½ teaspoon vanilla extract
- ½ cup dark chocolate, melted
- 2 tablespoons walnuts, chopped

Directions:
1. In a bowl, mix the flour with the baking soda, cinnamon, oil and the other ingredients except the cooking spray and stir well.
2. Grease a loaf pan that fits the slow cooker with the cooking spray, pour the bread batter into the pan, put the pan in the slow cooker after you've lined it with tin foil, put the lid on and cook on High for 3 hours.
3. Cool the sweet bread down, slice, divide between plates and serve for breakfast.

Nutrition: calories 200, fat 3, fiber 5, carbs 8, protein 4

Almond and Quinoa Bowls

Preparation time: 10 minutes
Cooking time: 5 hours
Servings: 2
Ingredients:
- 1 cup quinoa
- 2 cups almond milk
- 2 tablespoons butter, melted
- 2 tablespoons brown sugar
- A pinch of cinnamon powder
- A pinch of nutmeg, ground
- ¼ cup almonds, sliced
- Cooking spray

Directions:
1. Grease your slow cooker with the cooking spray, add the quinoa, milk, melted butter and the other ingredients, toss, put the lid on and cook on Low for 5 hours.
2. Divide the mix into bowls and serve for breakfast.

Nutrition: calories 211, fat 3, fiber 6, carbs 12, protein 5

Carrots Casserole

Preparation time: 10 minutes
Cooking time: 3 hours
Servings: 2
Ingredients:
- 1 teaspoon ginger, ground
- ½ pound carrots, peeled and grated
- 2 eggs, whisked
- ½ teaspoon garlic powder
- ½ teaspoon rosemary, dried
- Salt and black pepper to the taste
- 1 red onion, chopped
- 1 tablespoons parsley, chopped
- 2 garlic cloves, minced
- ½ tablespoon olive oil

Directions:
1. Grease your slow cooker with the oil and mix the carrots with the eggs, ginger and the other ingredients inside.
2. Toss, put the lid on, cook High for 3 hours, divide between plates and serve.

Nutrition: calories 218, fat 6, fiber 6, carbs 14, protein 5

Cranberry Oatmeal
Preparation time: 10 minutes
Cooking time: 6 hours
Servings: 2
Ingredients:
- 1 cup almond milk
- ½ cup steel cut oats
- ½ cup cranberries
- ½ teaspoon vanilla extract
- 1 tablespoon maple syrup
- 1 tablespoon sugar

Directions:
1. In your slow cooker, mix the oats with the berries, milk and the other ingredients, toss, put the lid on and cook on Low for 6 hours.
2. Divide into bowls and serve for breakfast.

Nutrition: calories 200, fat 5, fiber 7, carbs 14, protein 4

Mushroom Casserole
Preparation time: 10 minutes
Cooking time: 5 hours
Servings: 2
Ingredients:
- ½ cup mozzarella, shredded
- 2 eggs, whisked
- ½ tablespoon balsamic vinegar
- ½ tablespoon olive oil
- 4 ounces baby kale
- 1 red onion, chopped
- ¼ teaspoon oregano
- ½ pound white mushrooms, sliced
- Salt and black pepper to the taste
- Cooking spray

Directions:
1. In a bowl, mix the eggs with the kale, mushrooms and the other ingredients except the cheese and cooking spray and stir well.
2. Grease your slow cooker with cooking spray, add the mushroom mix, spread, sprinkle the mozzarella all over, put the lid on and cook on Low for 5 hours.
3. Divide between plates and serve for breakfast.

Nutrition: calories 216, fat 6, fiber 8, carbs 12, protein 4

Ginger Bowls
Preparation time: 10 minutes
Cooking time: 6 hours
Servings: 2
Ingredients:
- 2 apples, cored, peeled and cut into medium chunks
- 1 tablespoon sugar
- 1 tablespoon ginger, grated
- 1 cup heavy cream
- ¼ teaspoon cinnamon powder
- ½ teaspoon vanilla extract
- ¼ teaspoon cardamom, ground

Directions:
1. In your slow cooker, combine the apples with the sugar, ginger and the other ingredients, toss, put the lid on and cook on Low for 6 hours.
2. Divide into bowls and serve for breakfast.

Nutrition: calories 201, fat 3, fiber 7, carbs 19, protein 4

Granola Bowls
Preparation time: 10 minutes
Cooking time: 4 hours
Servings: 2
Ingredients:
- ½ cup granola
- ¼ cup coconut cream
- 2 tablespoons brown sugar
- 2 tablespoons cashew butter
- 1 teaspoon cinnamon powder
- ½ teaspoon nutmeg, ground

Directions:
1. In your slow cooker, mix the granola with the cream, sugar and the other ingredients, toss, put the lid on and cook on Low for 4 hours.
2. Divide into bowls and serve for breakfast.

Nutrition: calories 218, fat 6, fiber 9, carbs 17, protein 6

Squash Bowls
Preparation time: 10 minutes
Cooking time: 6 hours
Servings: 2
Ingredients:
- 2 tablespoons walnuts, chopped
- 2 cups squash, peeled and cubed
- ½ cup coconut cream
- ½ teaspoon cinnamon powder
- ½ tablespoon sugar

Directions:
1. In your slow cooker, mix the squash with the nuts and the other ingredients, toss, put the lid on and cook on Low for 6 hours.
2. Divide into bowls and serve.

Nutrition: calories 140, fat 1, fiber 2, carbs 2, protein 5

Lamb and Eggs
Preparation time: 10 minutes
Cooking time: 6 hours
Servings: 2
Ingredients:
- 1 pound lamb meat, ground
- 4 eggs, whisked
- 1 tablespoon basil, chopped
- ½ teaspoon cumin powder
- 1 tablespoon chili powder
- 1 red onion, chopped
- 1 tablespoon olive oil
- A pinch of salt and black pepper

Directions:
1. Grease the slow cooker with the oil and mix the lamb with the eggs, basil and the other ingredients inside.
2. Toss, put the lid on, cook on Low for 6 hours, divide into bowls and serve for breakfast.

Nutrition: calories 220, fat 2, fiber 2, carbs 6, protein 2

Cauliflower Casserole
Preparation time: 10 minutes
Cooking time: 5 hours
Servings: 2
Ingredients:
- 1 pound cauliflower florets
- 3 eggs, whisked
- 1 red onion, sliced
- ½ teaspoon sweet paprika
- ½ teaspoon turmeric powder
- 1 garlic clove, minced
- A pinch of salt and black pepper
- Cooking spray

Directions:
1. Spray your slow cooker with the cooking spray, and mix the cauliflower with the eggs, onion and the other ingredients inside.
2. Put the lid on, cook on Low for 5 hours, divide between 2 plates and serve for breakfast.

Nutrition: calories 200, fat 3, fiber 6, carbs 13, protein 8

Yummy Beef Meatloaf
Preparation time: 10 minutes
Cooking time: 4 hours
Servings: 2
Ingredients:
- 1 red onion, chopped
- 1 pound beef stew meat, ground
- ½ teaspoon chili powder
- 1 egg, whisked
- ½ teaspoon olive oil
- ½ teaspoon sweet paprika
- 2 tablespoons white flour
- ½ teaspoon oregano, chopped
- ½ tablespoon basil, chopped
- A pinch of salt and black pepper
- ½ teaspoon marjoram, dried

Directions:
1. In a bowl, mix the beef with the onion, chili powder and the other ingredients except the oil, stir well and shape your meatloaf.
2. Grease a loaf pan that fits your slow cooker with the oil, add meatloaf mix into the pan, put it in your slow cooker, put the lid on and cook on Low for 4 hours.
3. Slice and serve for breakfast.

Nutrition: calories 200, fat 6, fiber 12, carbs 17, protein 10

Leek Casserole
Preparation time: 10 minutes
Cooking time: 4 hours
Servings: 2
Ingredients:
- 1 cup leek, chopped
- Cooking spray
- ½ cup mozzarella, shredded
- 1 garlic clove, minced
- 4 eggs, whisked
- 1 cup beef sausage, chopped
- 1 tablespoon cilantro, chopped

Directions:
1. Grease the slow cooker with the cooking spray and mix the leek with the mozzarella and the other ingredients inside.
2. Toss, spread into the pot, put the lid on and cook on Low for 4 hours.
3. Divide between plates and serve for breakfast.

Nutrition: calories 232, fat 4, fiber 8, carbs 17, protein 4

Eggs and Sweet Potato
Preparation time: 10 minutes
Cooking time: 6 hours
Servings: 2
Ingredients:
- ½ red onion, chopped
- ½ green bell pepper, chopped
- 2 sweet potatoes, peeled and grated
- ½ red bell pepper, chopped
- 1 garlic clove, minced
- ½ teaspoon olive oil
- 4 eggs, whisked
- 1 tablespoon chives, chopped
- A pinch of red pepper, crushed
- A pinch of salt and black pepper

Directions:
1. In a bowl, mix the eggs with the onion, bell peppers and the other ingredients except the oil and whisk well.
2. Grease your slow cooker with the oil, add the eggs and potato mix, spread, put the lid on and cook on Low for 6 hours.
3. Divide everything between plates and serve.

Nutrition: calories 261, fat 6, fiber 6, carbs 16, protein 4

Pork and Eggplant
Preparation time: 10 minutes
Cooking time: 6 hours
Servings: 2
Ingredients:
- 1 red onion, chopped
- 1 eggplant, cubed
- ½ pound pork stew meat, ground
- 3 eggs, whisked
- ½ teaspoon chili powder
- ½ teaspoon garam masala
- 1 tablespoon sweet paprika
- 1 teaspoon olive oil

Directions:
1. In a bowl, mix the eggs with the meat, onion, eggplant and the other ingredients except the oil and stir well.
2. Grease your slow cooker with oil, add the Pork and Eggplant, spread into the pot, put the lid on and cook on Low for 6 hours.
3. Divide the mix between plates and serve for breakfast.

Nutrition: calories 261, fat 7, fiber 6, carbs 16, protein 7

Apple Spread

Preparation time: 10 minutes
Cooking time: 4 hours
Servings: 2
Ingredients:
- 2 apples, cored, peeled and pureed
- ½ cup coconut cream
- 2 tablespoons apple cider
- 2 tablespoons sugar
- ¼ teaspoon cinnamon powder
- ½ teaspoon lemon juice
- ¼ teaspoon ginger, grated

Directions:
1. In your slow cooker, mix the apple puree with the cream, sugar and the other ingredients, whisk, put the lid on and cook on High for 4 hours.
2. Blend using an immersion blender, cool down and serve for breakfast.

Nutrition: calories 172, fat 3, fiber 3, carbs 8, protein 3

Cocoa Oats

Preparation time: 10 minutes
Cooking time: 7 hours
Servings: 2
Ingredients:
- 1 cup almond milk
- ½ cup steel cut oats
- 1 tablespoon cocoa powder
- ½ cup cherries, pitted
- 2 tablespoons sugar
- ¼ teaspoon vanilla extract

Directions:
1. In your slow cooker, mix the almond milk with the cherries and the other ingredients, toss, put the lid on and cook on Low for 7 hours.
2. Divide into 2 bowls and serve for breakfast.

Nutrition: calories 150, fat 1, fiber 2, carbs 6, protein 5

Beans Salad

Preparation time: 10 minutes
Cooking time: 6 hours
Servings: 2
Ingredients:
- 1 cup canned black beans, drained
- 1 cup canned red kidney beans, drained
- 1 cup baby spinach
- 2 spring onions, chopped
- ½ red bell pepper, chopped
- ¼ teaspoon turmeric powder
- ½ teaspoon garam masala
- ¼ cup veggie stock
- A pinch of cumin, ground
- A pinch of chili powder
- A pinch of salt and black pepper
- ½ cup salsa

Directions:
1. In your slow cooker, mix the beans with the spinach, onions and the other ingredients, toss, put the lid on and cook on High for 6 hours.
2. Divide the mix into bowls and serve for breakfast.

Nutrition: calories 130, fat 4, fiber 2, carbs 5, protein 4

Peppers Rice

Preparation time: 10 minutes
Cooking time: 3 hours
Servings: 2
Ingredients:
- ½ cup brown rice
- 1 cup chicken stock
- 2 spring onions, chopped
- ½ orange bell pepper, chopped
- ½ red bell pepper, chopped
- ½ green bell pepper, chopped
- 2 ounces canned green chilies, chopped
- ½ cup canned black beans, drained
- ½ cup mild salsa
- ½ teaspoon sweet paprika
- ½ teaspoon lime zest, grated
- A pinch of salt and black pepper

Directions:
1. In your slow cooker, mix the rice with the stock, spring onions and the other ingredients, toss, put the lid on and cook on High for 3 hours.
2. Divide the mix into bowls and serve for breakfast.

Nutrition: calories 140, fat 2, fiber 2, carbs 5, protein 5

Cashew Butter

Preparation time: 10 minutes
Cooking time: 4 hours
Servings: 2
Ingredients:
- 1 cup cashews, soaked overnight, drained and blended
- ½ cup coconut cream
- ¼ teaspoon cinnamon powder
- 1 teaspoon lemon zest, grated
- 2 tablespoons sugar
- A pinch of ginger, ground

Directions:
1. In your slow cooker, mix the cashews with the cream and the other ingredients, whisk, put the lid on and cook on High for 4 hours.
2. Blend using an immersion blender, divide into jars, and serve for breakfast cold.

Nutrition: calories 143, fat 2, fiber 3, carbs 3, protein 4

Pumpkin and Berries
Preparation time: 10 minutes
Cooking time: 4 hours
Servings: 2
Ingredients:
- ½ cup coconut cream
- 1 and ½ cups pumpkin, peeled and cubed
- 1 cup blackberries
- 2 tablespoons maple syrup
- ¼ teaspoon nutmeg, ground
- ½ teaspoon vanilla extract

Directions:
1. In your slow cooker, combine the pumpkin with the berries, cream and the other ingredients, toss, put the lid on and cook on Low for 4 hours.
2. Divide into bowls and serve for breakfast!

Nutrition: calories 120, fat 2, fiber 2, carbs 4, protein 2

Quinoa and Chia Pudding
Preparation time: 10 minutes
Cooking time: 6 hours
Servings: 2
Ingredients:
- 1 cup coconut cream
- 2 tablespoons chia seeds
- ½ cup almond milk
- 1 tablespoon sugar
- ½ cup quinoa, rinsed
- ½ teaspoon vanilla extract

Directions:
1. In your slow cooker, mix the cream with the chia seeds and the other ingredients, toss, put the lid on and cook on Low for 6 hours.
2. Divide into 2 bowls and serve for breakfast.

Nutrition: calories 120, fat 2, fiber 1, carbs 6, protein 4

Beans Bowls
Preparation time: 10 minutes
Cooking time: 3 hours and 10 minutes
Servings: 2
Ingredients:
- 2 spring onions, chopped
- ½ green bell pepper, chopped
- ½ red bell pepper, chopped
- ½ yellow onion, chopped
- 5 ounces canned black beans, drained
- 5 ounces canned red kidney beans, drained
- 5 ounces canned pinto beans, drained
- ½ cup corn
- ½ teaspoon turmeric powder
- 1 teaspoons chili powder
- ½ teaspoon hot sauce
- A pinch of salt and black pepper
- 1 tablespoon olive oil

Directions:
1. Heat up a pan with the oil over medium-high heat, add the spring onions, bell peppers and the onion, sauté for 10 minutes and transfer to the slow cooker.
2. Add the beans and the other ingredients, toss, put the lid on and cook on High for 3 hours.
3. Divide the mix into bowls and serve for breakfast.

Nutrition: calories 240, fat 4, fiber 2, carbs 6, protein 9

Basil Sausage and Broccoli Mix
Preparation time: 10 minutes
Cooking time: 8 hours and 10 minutes
Servings: 2
Ingredients:
- 4 eggs, whisked
- 1 yellow onion, chopped
- 2 spring onions, chopped
- 1 cup pork sausage, chopped
- 1 cup broccoli florets
- 2 teaspoons basil, dried
- A pinch of salt and black pepper
- A drizzle of olive oil

Directions:
1. Heat up a pan with the oil over medium-high heat, add the yellow onion and the sausage, toss, cook for 10 minutes and transfer to the slow cooker.
2. Add the eggs and the other ingredients, toss, put the lid on and cook on Low for 8 hours.
3. Divide between plates and serve for breakfast.

Nutrition: calories 251, fat 4, fiber 4, carbs 6, protein 7

Zucchini and Cauliflower Eggs
Preparation time: 10 minutes
Cooking time: 6 hours
Servings: 2
Ingredients:
- 2 spring onions, chopped
- A pinch of salt and black pepper
- 4 eggs, whisked
- ½ cup cauliflower florets
- 1 zucchini, grated
- ¼ cup cheddar cheese, shredded
- ¼ cup whipping cream
- 1 tablespoon chives, chopped
- Cooking spray

Directions:
1. Grease the slow cooker with the cooking spray and mix the eggs with the spring onions, cauliflower and the other ingredients inside.
2. Put the lid on and cook on Low for 6 hours.
3. Divide the mix between plates and serve for breakfast.

Nutrition: calories 211, fat 7, fiber 4, carbs 5, protein 5

Mushroom Quiche

Preparation time: 10 minutes
Cooking time: 6 hours
Servings: 2
Ingredients:
- 2 cups baby Bella mushrooms, chopped
- ½ cup cheddar cheese, shredded
- 4 eggs, whisked
- ½ cup heavy cream
- 1 tablespoon basil, chopped
- 2 tablespoons chives, chopped
- A pinch of salt and black pepper
- ½ cup almond flour
- ¼ teaspoons baking soda
- Cooking spray

Directions:
1. In a bowl, mix the eggs with the cream, flour and the other ingredients except the cooking spray and stir well.
2. Grease the slow cooker with the cooking spray, pour the quiche mix, spread well, put the lid on and cook on High for 6 hours.
3. Slice the quiche, divide between plates and serve for breakfast.

Nutrition: calories 211, fat 6, fiber 6, carbs 6, protein 10

Scallions Quinoa and Carrots

Preparation time: 10 minutes
Cooking time: 4 hours
Servings: 2
Ingredients:
- 1 cup quinoa
- 2 cups veggie stock
- 4 scallions, chopped
- 2 carrots, peeled and grated
- 1 tablespoon olive oil
- A pinch of salt and black pepper
- 3 eggs, whisked
- 2 tablespoons cheddar cheese, grated
- 2 tablespoons heavy cream

Directions:
1. In a bowl mix the eggs with the cream, cheddar, salt and pepper and whisk.
2. Grease the slow cooker with the oil, add the quinoa, scallions, carrots and the stock, stir, put the lid on and cook on Low for 2 hours.
3. Add the eggs mix, stir the whole thing, cook on Low for 2 more hours, divide into bowls and serve for breakfast.

Nutrition: calories 172, fat 5, fiber 4, carbs 6, protein 8

Ham Omelet

Preparation time: 10 minutes
Cooking time: 3 hours
Servings: 2
Ingredients:
- Cooking spray
- 4 eggs, whisked
- 1 tablespoon sour cream
- 2 spring onions, chopped
- 1 small yellow onion, chopped
- ½ cup ham, chopped
- ½ cup cheddar cheese, shredded
- 1 tablespoon chives, chopped
- A pinch of salt and black pepper

Directions:
1. Grease your slow cooker with the cooking spray and mix the eggs with the sour cream, spring onions and the other ingredients inside.
2. Toss the mix, spread into the pot, put the lid on and cook on High for 3 hours.
3. Divide the mix between plates and serve for breakfast right away.

Nutrition: calories 192, fat 6, fiber 5, carbs 6, protein 12

Peppers and Eggs

Preparation time: 10 minutes
Cooking time: 4 hours
Servings: 2
Ingredients:
- 4 eggs, whisked
- ½ teaspoon coriander, ground
- ½ teaspoon rosemary, dried
- 2 spring onions, chopped
- 1 red bell pepper, cut into strips
- 1 green bell pepper, cut into strips
- 1 yellow bell pepper, cut into strips
- ¼ cup heavy cream
- ½ teaspoon garlic powder
- A pinch of salt and black pepper
- 1 teaspoon sweet paprika
- Cooking spray

Directions:
1. Grease your slow cooker with the cooking spray, and mix the eggs with the coriander, rosemary and the other ingredients into the pot.
2. Put the lid on, cook on Low for 4 hours, divide between plates and serve for breakfast.

Nutrition: calories 172, fat 6, fiber 3, carbs 6, protein 7

Baby Spinach Rice Mix

Preparation time: 10 minutes
Cooking time: 6 hours
Servings: 4
Ingredients:
- ¼ cup mozzarella, shredded
- ½ cup baby spinach
- ½ cup wild rice
- 1 and ½ cups chicken stock
- ½ teaspoon turmeric powder
- ½ teaspoon oregano, dried
- A pinch of salt and black pepper
- 3 scallions, minced
- ¾ cup goat cheese, crumbled

Directions:
1. In your slow cooker, mix the rice with the stock, turmeric and the other ingredients, toss, put the lid on and cook on Low for 6 hours.
2. Divide the mix into bowls and serve for breakfast.

Nutrition: calories 165, fat 1.2, fiber 3.5, carbs 32.6, protein 7.6

Egg Scramble

Preparation time: 10 minutes
Cooking time: 6 hours
Servings: 2
Ingredients:
- 4 eggs, whisked
- ¼ cup heavy cream
- ¼ cup mozzarella, shredded
- 1 tablespoon chives, chopped
- 1 tablespoon oregano, chopped
- 1 tablespoon rosemary, chopped
- A pinch of salt and black pepper
- Cooking spray

Directions:
1. Grease your slow cooker with the cooking spray, and mix the eggs with the cream, herbs and the other ingredients inside.
2. Stir well, put the lid on, cook for 6 hours on Low, stir once again, divide between plates and serve.

Nutrition: calories 203, fat 15.7, fiber 1.7, carbs 3.8, protein 12.8

Peas and Rice Bowls

Preparation time: 10 minutes
Cooking time: 6 hours
Servings: 2
Ingredients:
- ¼ cup peas
- 1 cup wild rice
- 2 cups veggie stock
- ¼ cup heavy cream
- 1 tablespoon dill, chopped
- 3 spring onions, chopped
- ½ teaspoon coriander, ground
- ½ teaspoon allspice, ground
- A pinch of salt and black pepper
- ¼ cup cheddar cheese, shredded
- 1 teaspoon olive oil

Directions:
1. Grease the slow cooker with the oil, add the rice, peas, stock and the other ingredients except the dill and heavy cream, stir, put the lid on and cook on Low for 3 hours.
2. Add the remaining ingredients, stir the mix, put the lid back on, cook on Low for 3 more hours, divide into bowls and serve for breakfast.

Nutrition: calories 442, fat 13.6, fiber 6.8, carbs 66, protein 17.4

Asparagus Casserole

Preparation time: 10 minutes
Cooking time: 5 hours
Servings: 2
Ingredients:
- 1 pound asparagus spears, cut into medium pieces
- 1 red onion, sliced
- 4 eggs, whisked
- ½ cup cheddar cheese, shredded
- ¼ cup heavy cream
- 1 tablespoon chives, chopped
- A drizzle of olive oil
- A pinch of salt and black pepper

Directions:
1. Grease your slow cooker with the oil, and mix the eggs with the asparagus, onion and the other ingredients except the cheese into the pot.
2. Sprinkle the cheese all over, put the lid on and cook on Low for 5 hours.
3. Divide between plates and serve right away for breakfast.

Nutrition: calories 359, fat 24, fiber 6, carbs 15.5, protein 24.1

Slow Cooker Lunch Recipes for 2

Seafood Soup
Preparation time: 10 minutes
Cooking time: 8 hours
Servings: 2
Ingredients:
- 2 cups chicken stock
- 1 cup coconut milk
- 1 sweet potato, cubed
- ½ yellow onion, chopped
- 1 bay leaf
- 1 carrot, peeled and sliced
- ½ tablespoon thyme, dried
- Salt and black pepper to the taste
- ½ pounds salmon fillets, skinless, boneless cubed
- 12 shrimp, peeled and deveined
- 1 tablespoon chives, chopped

Directions:
1. In your slow cooker, mix the carrot with the sweet potato, onion and the other ingredients except the salmon, shrimp and chives, toss, put the lid on and cook on Low for 6 hours.
2. Add the rest of the ingredients, toss, put the lid on and cook on Low for 2 more hours.
3. Divide the soup into bowls and serve for lunch.

Nutrition: calories 354, fat 10, fiber 4, carbs 17, protein 12

Sesame Salmon
Preparation time: 10 minutes
Cooking time: 3 hours
Servings: 2
Ingredients:
- 2 salmon fillets, boneless and roughly cubed
- 1 cup cherry tomatoes, halved
- 3 spring onions, chopped
- 1 cup baby spinach
- ½ cup chicken stock
- Salt and black pepper to the taste
- 2 tablespoons balsamic vinegar
- 2 tablespoons lemon juice
- 1 teaspoon sesame seeds

Directions:
1. In your slow cooker, mix the salmon with the cherry tomatoes, spring onions and the other ingredients, toss gently, put the lid on and cook on Low for 3 hours.
2. Divide everything into bowls and serve.

Nutrition: calories 230, fat 4, fiber 2, carbs 7, protein 6

Shrimp Stew
Preparation time: 10 minutes
Cooking time: 3 hours
Servings: 2
Ingredients:
- 1 garlic clove, minced
- 1 red onion, chopped
- 1 cup canned tomatoes, crushed
- 1 cup veggie stock
- ½ teaspoon turmeric powder
- 1 pound shrimp, peeled and deveined
- ½ teaspoon coriander, ground
- ½ teaspoon thyme, dried
- ½ teaspoon basil, dried
- A pinch of salt and black pepper
- A pinch of red pepper flakes

Directions:
1. In your slow cooker, mix the onion with the garlic, shrimp and the other ingredients, toss, put the lid on and cook on High for 3 hours.
2. Divide the stew into bowls and serve.

Nutrition: calories 313, fat 4.2, fiber 2.5, carbs 13.2, protein 53.3

Shrimp and Spinach
Preparation time: 10 minutes
Cooking time: 2 hours
Servings: 2
Ingredients:
- 1 pound shrimp, peeled and deveined
- 1 cup baby spinach
- ½ teaspoon sweet paprika
- ½ cup chicken stock
- 1 garlic clove, minced
- 2 jalapeno peppers, chopped
- Cooking spray
- 1 teaspoon coriander, ground
- ½ teaspoon rosemary, dried
- A pinch of sea salt and black pepper

Directions:
1. Grease the slow cooker with the oil, add the shrimp, spinach and the other ingredients, toss, put the lid on and cook on High for 2 hours.
2. Divide everything between plates and serve for lunch.

Nutrition: calories 200, fat 4, fiber 6, carbs 16, protein 4

Ginger Salmon
Preparation time: 10 minutes
Cooking time: 3 hours
Servings: 2
Ingredients:
- 2 salmon fillets, boneless
- 1 tablespoon olive oil
- 1 tablespoon balsamic vinegar
- 1 tablespoon ginger, grated
- A pinch of nutmeg, ground
- A pinch of cloves, ground
- A pinch of salt and black pepper
- 1 teaspoon onion powder
- ½ teaspoon cayenne pepper
- ¼ cup chicken stock

Directions:
1. Grease the slow cooker with the oil and arrange the salmon fillets inside.
2. Add the vinegar, ginger and the other ingredients, rub gently, put the lid on and cook on Low for 3 hours.
3. Divide the fish between plates and serve with a side salad for lunch.

Nutrition: calories 315, fat 18.4, fiber 0.6, carbs 3.6, protein 35.1

Cod Stew

Preparation time: 10 minutes
Cooking time: 3 hours
Servings: 2
Ingredients:
- ½ pound cod fillets, boneless and cubed
- 2 spring onions, chopped
- ¼ cup heavy cream
- 1 carrot, sliced
- 1 zucchini, cubed
- 1 tomato, cubed
- 1 cup chicken stock
- 1 tablespoon olive oil
- 1 green bell pepper, chopped
- 1 tablespoon chives, chopped
- A pinch of salt and black pepper

Directions:
1. In your slow cooker, combine the fish with the spring onions, carrot and the other ingredients except the cream, toss gently, put the lid on and cook on High for 2 hours and 30 minutes.
2. Add the cream, toss gently, put the lid back on, cook the stew on Low for 30 minutes more, divide into bowls and serve.

Nutrition: calories 175, fat 13.3, fiber 3.4, carbs 14, protein 3.3

Sweet Potato and Clam Chowder

Preparation time: 10 minutes
Cooking time: 3 hours and 30 minutes
Servings: 2
Ingredients:
- 1 small yellow onion, chopped
- 1 carrot, chopped
- 1 red bell pepper, cubed
- 6 ounces canned clams, chopped
- 1 sweet potato, chopped
- 2 cups chicken stock
- ½ cup coconut milk
- 1 teaspoon Worcestershire sauce

Directions:
1. In your slow cooker, mix the onion with the carrot, clams and the other ingredients, toss, put the lid on and cook on High for 3 hours.
2. Divide the chowder into bowls and serve for lunch.

Nutrition: calories 288, fat 15.3, fiber 5.9, carbs 36.4, protein 5

Maple Chicken

Preparation time: 10 minutes
Cooking time: 6 hours
Servings: 2
Ingredients:
- 2 spring onions, chopped
- 1 pound chicken breast, skinless and boneless
- 2 garlic cloves, minced
- 1 tablespoon maple syrup
- A pinch of salt and black pepper
- ½ cup chicken stock
- ½ cup tomato sauce
- 1 tablespoon chives, chopped
- 1 teaspoon basil, dried

Directions:
1. In your slow cooker mix the chicken with the garlic, maple syrup and the other ingredients, toss, put the lid on and cook on Low for 6 hours.
2. Divide the mix between plates and serve for lunch.

Nutrition: calories 200, fat 3, fiber 3, carbs 17, protein 6

Salsa Chicken

Preparation time: 10 minutes
Cooking time: 8 hours
Servings: 2
Ingredients:
- 7 ounces mild salsa
- 1 pound chicken breast, skinless, boneless and cubed
- 1 small yellow onion, chopped
- ½ teaspoon coriander, ground
- ½ teaspoon rosemary, dried
- 1 green bell pepper, chopped
- Cooking spray
- 1 tablespoon cilantro, chopped
- 1 red bell pepper, chopped
- 1 tablespoon chili powder

Directions:
1. Grease the slow cooker with the cooking spray and mix the chicken with the salsa, onion and the other ingredients inside.
2. Put the lid on, cook on Low for 8 hours, divide into bowls and serve for lunch.

Nutrition: calories 240, fat 3, fiber 7, carbs 17, protein 8

Turkey and Mushrooms

Preparation time: 10 minutes
Cooking time: 7 hours and 10 minutes
Servings: 2
Ingredients:
- 1 red onion, sliced
- 2 garlic cloves, minced
- 1 pound turkey breast, skinless, boneless and cubed
- 1 tablespoon olive oil
- 1 teaspoon oregano, dried
- 1 teaspoon basil, dried
- A pinch of red pepper flakes
- 1 cup mushrooms, sliced
- ¼ cup chicken stock
- ½ cup canned tomatoes, chopped
- A pinch of salt and black pepper

Directions:
1. Heat up a pan with the oil over medium-high heat, add the onion, garlic and the meat, brown for 10 minutes and transfer to the slow cooker.
2. Add the oregano, basil and the other ingredients, toss, put the lid on and cook on Low for 7 hours.
3. Divide into bowls and serve for lunch.

Nutrition: calories 240, fat 4, fiber 6, carbs 18, protein 10

Chicken and Tomato Mix

Preparation time: 10 minutes
Cooking time: 6 hours
Servings: 2
Ingredients:
- 1 cup cherry tomatoes, halved
- 1 pound chicken breast, skinless, boneless and cubed
- 1 red onion, sliced
- 1 tablespoons garam masala
- 1 garlic clove, minced
- ½ small yellow onion, chopped
- ½ teaspoon ginger powder
- A pinch of salt and cayenne pepper
- ½ teaspoon sweet paprika
- 2 tablespoons chives, chopped

Directions:
1. In your slow cooker, mix the chicken with the tomatoes, onion and the other ingredients, toss, put the lid on and cook on Low for 6 hours.
2. Divide into bowls and serve right away.

Nutrition: calories 259, fat 3, fiber 7, carbs 17, protein 14

Turkey and Figs

Preparation time: 10 minutes
Cooking time: 8 hours
Servings: 2
Ingredients:
- 1 pound turkey breast, boneless, skinless and sliced
- ½ cup black figs, halved
- 1 red onion, sliced
- ½ cup tomato sauce
- ½ teaspoon onion powder
- ¼ teaspoon garlic powder
- 1 tablespoon basil, chopped
- ½ teaspoon chili powder
- ¼ cup white wine
- ½ teaspoon thyme, dried
- ¼ teaspoon sage, dried
- ½ teaspoon paprika, dried
- A pinch of salt and black pepper

Directions:
1. In your slow cooker, mix the turkey breast with the figs, onion and the other ingredients, toss, put the lid on and cook on Low for 8 hours.
2. Divide between plates and serve.

Nutrition: calories 220, fat 5, fiber 8, carbs 18, protein 15

Turkey and Walnuts

Preparation time: 10 minutes
Cooking time: 8 hours
Servings: 2
Ingredients:
- 1 pound turkey breast, skinless, boneless and sliced
- ½ cup scallions, chopped
- 2 tablespoons walnuts, chopped
- 1 tablespoon lemon juice
- ¼ cup veggie stock
- ½ teaspoon chili powder
- 1 tablespoon olive oil
- 1 tablespoon rosemary, chopped
- Salt and black pepper to the taste

Directions:
1. In your slow cooker, mix the turkey with the scallions, walnuts and the other ingredients, toss, put the lid on and cook on Low for 8 hours.
2. Divide everything between plates and serve.

Nutrition: calories 264, fat 4, fiber 6, carbs 15, protein 15

Thyme Chicken

Preparation time: 10 minutes
Cooking time: 7 hours
Servings: 2
Ingredients:
- 1 pound chicken legs
- 1 tablespoon thyme, chopped
- 2 garlic cloves, minced
- ½ cup chicken stock
- 1 carrot, chopped
- ½ yellow onion, chopped
- A pinch of salt and white pepper
- Juice of ½ lemon

Directions:
1. In your slow cooker, mix the chicken legs with the thyme, garlic and the other ingredients, toss, put the lid on and cook on Low for 7 hours.
2. Divide between plates and serve.

Nutrition: calories 320, fat 4, fiber 7, carbs 16, protein 6

Beef and Cauliflower

Preparation time: 10 minutes
Cooking time: 8 hours
Servings: 2
Ingredients:
- 1 pound beef chuck roast, sliced
- 1 cup cauliflower florets
- ½ cup tomato sauce
- ½ cup veggie stock
- ½ tablespoon olive oil
- 2 garlic cloves, minced
- ½ carrot, roughly chopped
- 1 celery rib, roughly chopped
- A pinch of salt and black pepper to the taste
- 1 tablespoon parsley, chopped

Directions:
1. In your slow cooker, mix the roast with the cauliflower, tomato sauce and the other ingredients, toss, put the lid on and cook on Low for 8 hours.
2. Divide between plates and serve.

Nutrition: calories 340, fat 5, fiber 7, carbs 18, protein 22

Soy Pork Chops

Preparation time: 10 minutes
Cooking time: 7 hours
Servings: 2
Ingredients:
- 1 pound pork chops
- 2 tablespoons sugar
- 2 tablespoons soy sauce
- ½ cup beef stock
- 1 tablespoon balsamic vinegar
- 1 tablespoon cilantro, chopped

Directions:
1. In your slow cooker, mix the pork chops with the soy sauce and the other ingredients, toss, put the lid on and cook on Low for 7 hours.
2. Divide everything between plates and serve.

Nutrition: calories 345, fat 5, fiber 7, carbs 17, protein 14

Pork and Cranberries

Preparation time: 10 minutes
Cooking time: 8 hours
Servings: 2
Ingredients:
- 1 pound pork tenderloin, roughly cubed
- ½ cup cranberries
- ½ cup red wine
- ½ teaspoon sweet paprika
- ½ teaspoon chili powder
- 1 tablespoon maple syrup

Directions:
1. In your slow cooker, mix the pork with the cranberries, wine and the other ingredients, toss, put the lid on and cook on Low for 8 hours.
2. Divide between plates and serve.

Nutrition: calories 400, fat 12, fiber 8, carbs 18, protein 20

Lamb and Onion

Preparation time: 10 minutes
Cooking time: 8 hours
Servings: 2
Ingredients:
- 1 pound lamb meat, cubed
- 1 red onion, sliced
- 3 spring onions, sliced
- Salt and black pepper to the taste
- 1 tablespoon olive oil
- ½ teaspoon rosemary, dried
- ¼ teaspoon thyme, dried
- 1 cup water
- ½ cup baby carrots, peeled
- ½ cup tomato sauce
- 1 tablespoon cilantro, chopped

Directions:
1. In your slow cooker, mix the lamb with the onion, spring onions and the other ingredients, toss, put the lid on and cook on Low for 8 hours.
2. Divide the stew between plates and serve hot.

Nutrition: calories 350, fat 8, fiber 3, carbs 14, protein 16

Pork Roast and Olives

Preparation time: 10 minutes
Cooking time: 6 hours
Servings: 2
Ingredients:
- 1 pound pork roast, sliced
- ½ cup black olives, pitted and halved
- ½ cup kalamata olives, pitted and halved
- 2 medium carrots, chopped
- ½ cup tomato sauce
- 1 small yellow onion, chopped
- 2 garlic cloves, minced
- 1 bay leaf
- Salt and black pepper to the taste

Directions:
1. In your slow cooker, mix the pork roast with the olives and the other ingredients, toss, put the lid on and cook on High for 6 hours.
2. Divide everything between plates and serve.

Nutrition: calories 360, fat 4, fiber 3, carbs 17, protein 27

Beef Stew

Preparation time: 10 minutes
Cooking time: 6 hours and 10 minutes
Servings: 2
Ingredients:
- 1 tablespoon olive oil
- 1 red onion, chopped
- 1 carrot, peeled and sliced
- 1 pound beef meat, cubed
- ½ cup beef stock
- ½ cup canned tomatoes, chopped
- 2 tablespoons tomato sauce
- 2 tablespoons balsamic vinegar
- 2 garlic cloves, minced
- ½ cup black olives, pitted and sliced
- 1 tablespoon rosemary, chopped
- Salt and black pepper to the taste

Directions:
1. Heat up a pan with the oil over medium-high heat, add the meat, brown for 10 minutes and transfer to your slow cooker.
2. Add the rest of the ingredients, toss, put the lid on and cook on High for 6 hours.
3. Divide between plates and serve right away!

Nutrition: calories 370, fat 14, fiber 6, carbs 26, protein 38

Beef and Celery

Preparation time: 10 minutes
Cooking time: 8 hours
Servings: 2
Ingredients:
- ½ cup beef stock
- 1 pound beef stew meat, cubed
- 1 cup celery, cubed
- ½ cup tomato sauce
- 2 carrots, chopped
- ½ cup mushrooms, halved
- ½ red onion, roughly chopped
- ½ tablespoon olive oil
- Salt and black pepper to the taste
- ¼ cup red wine
- 1 tablespoon parsley, chopped

Directions:
1. In your slow cooker, mix the beef with the stock, celery and the other ingredients, toss, put the lid on and cook on Low for 8 hours.
2. Divide the stew into bowls and serve.

Nutrition: calories 433, fat 20, fiber 4, carbs 14, protein 39

Tomato Pasta Mix

Preparation time: 10 minutes
Cooking time: 6 hours
Servings: 2
Ingredients:
- ½ pound beef stew meat, ground
- 1 red onion, chopped
- ½ teaspoon sweet paprika
- ½ teaspoon chili powder
- Salt and black pepper to the taste
- ½ teaspoon basil, dried
- ½ teaspoon parsley, dried
- 14 ounces canned tomatoes, chopped
- 1 cup chicken stock
- 1 cup short pasta

Directions:
1. In your slow cooker, mix the beef with the onion, paprika and the other ingredients except the pasta, toss, put the lid on and cook on Low for 5 hours and 30 minutes.
2. Add the pasta, stir, put the lid on again and cook on Low for 30 minutes more.
3. Divide everything between plates and serve.

Nutrition: calories 300, fat 6, fiber 8, carbs 18, protein 17

Honey Lamb Roast

Preparation time: 10 minutes
Cooking time: 7 hours
Servings: 2
Ingredients:
- 1 pound lamb roast, sliced
- 3 tablespoons honey
- ½ tablespoon basil, dried
- ½ tablespoons oregano, dried
- 1 tablespoon garlic, minced
- 1 tablespoon olive oil
- Salt and black pepper to the taste
- ½ cup beef stock

Directions:
1. In your slow cooker, mix the lamb roast with the honey, basil and the other ingredients, toss well, put the lid on and cook on Low for 7 hours.
2. Divide everything between plates and serve.

Nutrition: calories 374, fat 6, fiber 8, carbs 29, protein 6

Worcestershire Beef

Preparation time: 10 minutes
Cooking time: 8 hours
Servings: 2
Ingredients:
- 1 pound beef stew meat, cubed
- 1 teaspoon chili powder
- Salt and black pepper to the taste
- 1 cup beef stock
- 1 and ½ tablespoons Worcestershire sauce
- 1 teaspoon garlic, minced
- 2 ounces cream cheese, soft
- Cooking spray

Directions:
1. Grease your slow cooker with the cooking spray, and mix the beef with the stock and the other ingredients inside.
2. Put the lid on, cook on Low for 8 hours, divide between plates and serve.

Nutrition: calories 372, fat 6, fiber 9, carbs 18, protein 22

Chickpeas Stew

Preparation time: 10 minutes
Cooking time: 6 hours
Servings: 2
Ingredients:
- ½ tablespoon olive oil
- 1 red onion, chopped
- 2 garlic cloves, minced
- 1 red chili pepper, chopped
- ¼ cup carrots, chopped
- 6 ounces canned tomatoes, chopped
- 6 ounces canned chickpeas, drained
- ½ cup chicken stock
- 1 bay leaf
- ½ teaspoon coriander, ground
- A pinch of red pepper flakes
- ½ tablespoon parsley, chopped
- Salt and black pepper to the taste

Directions:
1. In your slow cooker, mix the chickpeas with the onion, garlic and the other ingredients, toss, put the lid on and cook on Low for 6 hours.
2. Divide into bowls and serve.

Nutrition: calories 462, fat 7, fiber 9, carbs 30, protein 17

Savory Lentils Soup

Preparation time: 10 minutes
Cooking time: 4 hours
Servings: 2
Ingredients:
- 2 garlic cloves, minced
- 1 carrot, chopped
- 1 red onion, chopped
- 3 cups veggie stock
- 1 cup brown lentils
- ½ teaspoon cumin, ground
- 1 bay leaf
- 1 tablespoon lime juice
- 1 tablespoon cilantro, chopped
- Salt and black pepper to the taste

Directions:
1. In your slow cooker, mix the lentils with the garlic, carrot and the other ingredients, toss, put the lid on and cook on High for 4 hours.
2. Ladle the soup into bowls and serve.

Nutrition: calories 361, fat 7, fiber 7, carbs 16, protein 5

Chicken Soup

Preparation time: 10 minutes
Cooking time: 7 hours
Servings: 2
Ingredients:
- ½ pound chicken breast, skinless, boneless and cubed
- 3 cups chicken stock
- 1 red onion, chopped
- 1 garlic clove, minced
- ½ celery stalk, chopped
- ¼ teaspoon chili powder
- ¼ teaspoon sweet paprika
- A pinch of salt and black pepper
- A pinch of cayenne pepper
- 1 tablespoon lemon juice
- ½ tablespoon chives, chopped

Directions:
1. In your slow cooker, mix the chicken with the stock, onion and the other ingredients, toss, put the lid on and cook on Low for 7 hours.
2. Divide into bowls and serve right away.

Nutrition: calories 351, fat 6, fiber 7, carbs 17, protein 16

Lime Chicken

Preparation time: 10 minutes
Cooking time: 6 hours
Servings: 2
Ingredients:
- 1 pound chicken thighs, boneless and skinless
- Juice of 1 lime
- 1 tablespoon lime zest, grated
- 2 teaspoons olive oil
- ½ cup tomato sauce
- 2 garlic cloves, minced
- 1 tablespoon thyme, chopped
- Salt and black pepper to the taste

Directions:
1. In your slow cooker, mix the chicken with the lime juice, zest and the other ingredients, toss, put the lid on and cook on High for 6 hours.
2. Divide between plates and serve right away.

Nutrition: calories 324, fat 7, fiber 8, carbs 20, protein 17

Shrimp Gumbo

Preparation time: 10 minutes
Cooking time: 2 hours
Servings: 2
Ingredients:
- 1 pound shrimp, peeled and deveined
- ½ pound pork sausage, sliced
- 1 red onion, chopped
- ½ green bell pepper, chopped
- 1 red chili pepper, minced
- ½ teaspoon cumin, ground
- ½ teaspoon coriander, ground
- Salt and black pepper to the taste
- 1 cup tomato sauce
- ½ cup chicken stock
- ½ tablespoon Cajun seasoning
- ½ teaspoon oregano, dried

Directions:
1. In your slow cooker, mix the shrimp with the sausage, onion and the other ingredients, toss, put the lid on and cook on High for 2 hours.
2. Divide into bowls and serve.

Nutrition: calories 721, fat 36.7, fiber 3.7, carbs 18.2, protein 76.6

Chicken Soup

Preparation time: 10 minutes
Cooking time: 6 hours
Servings: 2
Ingredients:
- ½ pound chicken thighs, skinless, boneless and cubed
- ½ small yellow onion, chopped
- ½ red bell pepper, chopped
- ½ green bell pepper, chopped
- 3 cups chicken stock
- ½ cup butternut squash, peeled and cubed
- 2 ounces canned green chilies, chopped
- ½ teaspoon oregano, dried
- A pinch of salt and black pepper
- ½ tablespoon lime juice
- 1 tablespoon cilantro, chopped

Directions:
1. In your slow cooker, mix the chicken with the onion, bell pepper and the other ingredients, toss, put the lid on and cook on High for 6 hours.
2. Ladle the soup into bowls and serve.

Nutrition: calories 365, fat 11.2, fiber 10.2, carbs 31.4, protein 38

Pork Soup

Preparation time: 10 minutes
Cooking time: 6 hours
Servings: 2
Ingredients:
- ½ cup canned black beans, drained and rinsed
- 1 pound pork stew meat, cubed
- 3 cups beef stock
- 1 small red bell pepper, chopped
- 1 yellow onion, chopped
- 1 teaspoon Italian seasoning
- ½ tablespoon olive oil
- Salt and black pepper to the taste
- ½ cup canned tomatoes, crushed
- 1 tablespoon basil, chopped

Directions:
1. In your slow cooker, mix the pork with the beans, stock and the other ingredients, toss, put the lid on and cook on Low for 6 hours.
2. Divide into bowls and serve.

Nutrition: calories 758, fat 27.9, fiber 9.9, carbs 42.1, protein 82.6

Mushroom Stew

Preparation time: 10 minutes
Cooking time: 6 hours
Servings: 2
Ingredients:
- 1 pound white mushrooms, sliced
- 2 carrots, peeled and cubed
- 1 red onion, chopped
- 1 tablespoon olive oil
- 1 tablespoon balsamic vinegar
- ½ cup tomato sauce
- Salt and black pepper to the taste
- 1 cup veggie stock
- 1 tablespoon basil, chopped

Directions:
1. In your slow cooker, mix the mushrooms with the onion and the other ingredients, toss, put the lid on and cook on Low for 6 hours.
2. Divide the stew into bowls and serve.

Nutrition: calories 400, fat 15, fiber 4, carbs 25, protein 14

Beans Chili

Preparation time: 10 minutes
Cooking time: 3 hours
Servings: 2
Ingredients:
- ½ red bell pepper, chopped
- ½ green bell pepper, chopped
- 1 garlic clove, minced
- ½ cup yellow onion, chopped
- ½ cup roasted tomatoes, crushed
- 1 cup canned red kidney beans, drained
- 1 cup canned white beans, drained
- 1 cup canned black beans, drained
- ½ cup corn
- Salt and black pepper to the taste
- 1 tablespoon chili powder
- 1 cup veggie stock

Directions:
1. In your slow cooker, mix the peppers with the beans and the other ingredients, toss, put the lid on and cook on High for 3 hours.
2. Divide into bowls and serve right away.

Nutrition: calories 400, fat 14, fiber 5, carbs 29, protein 22

Parsley Chicken

Preparation time: 10 minutes
Cooking time: 4 hours
Servings: 2
Ingredients:
- 1 tablespoon olive oil
- Salt and black pepper to the taste
- 2 spring onions, chopped
- 1 carrot, peeled and sliced
- ¼ cup chicken stock
- 1 pound chicken breast, skinless, boneless sand cubed
- ½ cup tomato sauce
- 1 tablespoon parsley, chopped

Directions:
1. In your slow cooker, mix the chicken with the spring onions and the other ingredients, toss, put the lid on and cook on High for 4 hours.
2. Divide into bowls and serve.

Nutrition: calories 453, fat 15, fiber 5, carbs 20, protein 20

Mustard Short Ribs

Preparation time: 10 minutes
Cooking time: 8 hours
Servings: 2
Ingredients:
- 2 beef short ribs, bone in and cut into individual ribs
- Salt and black pepper to the taste
- ½ cup BBQ sauce
- 1 tablespoon mustard
- 1 tablespoon green onions, chopped

Directions:
1. In your slow cooker, mix the ribs with the sauce and the other ingredients, toss, put the lid on and cook on Low for 8 hours.
2. Divide the mix between plates and serve.

Nutrition: calories 284, fat 7, 4, carbs 18, protein 20

Piquant Creamy Brisket

Preparation time: 10 minutes
Cooking time: 8 hours
Servings: 2
Ingredients:
- 1 tablespoon olive oil
- 1 shallot, chopped
- 2 garlic cloves, mined
- 1 pound beef brisket
- Salt and black pepper to the taste
- ¼ cup beef stock
- 3 tablespoons heavy cream
- 1 tablespoon parsley, chopped

Directions:
1. In your slow cooker, mix the brisket with the oil and the other ingredients, toss, put the lid on and cook on Low for 8 hours.
2. Transfer the beef to a cutting board, slice, divide between plates and serve with the sauce drizzled all over.

Nutrition: calories 400, fat 10, fiber 4, carbs 15, protein 20

Mushroom Soup

Preparation time: 10 minutes
Cooking time: 4 hours
Servings: 2
Ingredients:
- 1 small yellow onion, chopped
- 1 carrot, chopped
- 1 small red bell pepper, chopped
- 1 green bell pepper, chopped
- 1 pound mushrooms, sliced
- 1 garlic clove, minced
- ½ teaspoon Italian seasoning
- Salt and black pepper to the taste
- 3 cups chicken stock
- ½ cup half and half
- 1 tablespoon chives, chopped

Directions:
1. In your slow cooker, mix the mushrooms with the onion, carrot and the other ingredients, toss, put the lid on and cook on High for 4 hours.
2. Divide into bowls and serve.

Nutrition: calories 453, fat 14, fiber 6, carbs 28, protein 33

Potato Soup

Preparation time: 10 minutes
Cooking time: 5 hours
Servings: 2
Ingredients:
- 1 small yellow onion, chopped
- 3 cups chicken stock
- ½ pound red potatoes, peeled and cubed
- 1 teaspoon turmeric powder
- ½ cup heavy whipping cream
- 2 ounces cream cheese, cubed
- 1 tablespoon chives, chopped

Directions:
1. In your slow cooker, mix the potatoes with the stock, onion and the other ingredients, toss, put the lid on and cook on High for 5 hours.
2. Divide into bowls and serve.

Nutrition: calories 372, fat 15, fiber 4, carbs 20, protein 22

Chicken with Corn

Preparation time: 10 minutes
Cooking time: 6 hours
Servings: 2
Ingredients:
- 1 pound chicken breast, skinless, boneless and cubed
- 1 cup wild rice
- 1 cup chicken stock
- 1 tablespoon tomato paste
- Salt and black pepper to the taste
- ¼ teaspoon cumin, ground
- 3 ounces canned roasted tomatoes, chopped
- ¼ cup corn
- 2 tablespoons cilantro, chopped

Directions:
1. In your slow cooker, mix the chicken with the rice, stock and the other ingredients, toss, put the lid on and cook on Low for 6 hours.
2. Divide everything between plates and serve.

Nutrition: calories 372, fat 12, fiber 5, carbs 20, protein 25

Mixed Pork and Beans

Preparation time: 10 minutes
Cooking time: 8 hours
Servings: 2
Ingredients:
- 1 cup canned black beans, drained
- 1 cup green beans, trimmed and halved
- ½ pound pork shoulder, cubed
- Salt and black pepper to the taste
- 3 garlic cloves, minced
- ½ yellow onion, chopped
- ½ cup beef stock
- ¼ tablespoon balsamic vinegar
- 1 tablespoon olive oil

Directions:
1. In your slow cooker, mix the beans with the pork and the other ingredients, toss, put the lid on and cook on Low for 8 hours.
2. Divide everything between plates and serve.

Nutrition: calories 453, fat 10, fiber 12, carbs 20, protein 36

Pork Chops

Preparation time: 10 minutes
Cooking time: 7 hours
Servings: 2
Ingredients:
- ½ pound pork loin chops
- 2 tablespoons butter
- 2 scallions, chopped
- 1 cup beef stock
- 1 garlic clove, minced
- ¼ teaspoon thyme, dried
- Salt and black pepper to the taste
- ¼ cup heavy cream
- ¼ tablespoon cornstarch
- ½ teaspoon basil, dried

Directions:
1. In your slow cooker, mix the pork chops with the butter, scallions and the other ingredients, toss, put the lid on and cook on Low for 7 hours.
2. Divide everything between plates and serve.

Nutrition: calories 453, fat 16, fiber 8, carbs 7, protein 27

Chicken and Peach Mix

Preparation time: 10 minutes
Cooking time: 6 hours
Servings: 2
Ingredients:
- 1 pound chicken breast, skinless and boneless
- 1 cup peaches, cubed
- ½ tablespoon avocado oil
- ½ cup chicken stock
- 1 tablespoon balsamic vinegar
- ½ teaspoon garlic, minced
- ¼ cup cherry tomatoes, halved
- 1 tablespoon basil, chopped

Directions:
1. In your slow cooker, mix the chicken with the peaches, oil and the other ingredients, toss, put the lid on and cook on Low for 6 hours.
2. Divide everything between plates and serve.

Nutrition: calories 300, fat 7, fiber 8, carbs 20, protein 39

Chicken Drumsticks

Preparation time: 10 minutes
Cooking time: 8 hours
Servings: 2
Ingredients:
- 1 pound chicken drumsticks
- 2 tablespoons buffalo wing sauce
- ½ cup chicken stock
- 2 tablespoons honey
- 1 teaspoon lemon juice
- Salt and black pepper to the taste

Directions:
1. In your slow cooker, mix the chicken with the sauce and the other ingredients, toss, put the lid on and cook on Low for 8 hours.
2. Divide everything between plates and serve.

Nutrition: calories 361, fat 7, fiber 8, carbs 18, protein 22

Mustard Pork Chops

Preparation time: 10 minutes
Cooking time: 4 hours
Servings: 2
Ingredients:
- 1 tablespoon butter
- 1 pound pork chops, bone in
- 2 carrots, sliced
- 1 cup beef stock
- ½ tablespoon honey
- ½ tablespoon lime juice
- 1 tablespoon lime zest, grated

Directions:
1. In your slow cooker, mix the pork chops with the butter and the other ingredients, toss, put the lid on and cook on High for 4 hours.
2. Divide between plate sand serve.

Nutrition: calories 300, fat 8, fiber 10, carbs 16, protein 16

Fennel Soup

Preparation time: 10 minutes
Cooking time: 4 hours
Servings: 2
Ingredients:
- 2 fennel bulbs, sliced
- ½ cup tomatoes, crushed
- 1 red onion, sliced
- 1 leek, chopped
- 2 cups veggie stock
- ½ teaspoon cumin, ground
- 1 tablespoon dill, chopped
- ½ tablespoon olive oil
- Salt and black pepper to the taste

Directions:
1. In your slow cooker, mix the fennel with the tomatoes, onion and the other ingredients, toss, put the lid on and cook on High for 4 hours.
2. Ladle into bowls and serve hot.

Nutrition: calories 132, fat 2, fiber 5, carbs 11, protein 3

Artichoke Soup

Preparation time: 10 minutes
Cooking time: 5 hours
Servings: 2
Ingredients:
- 2 cups canned artichoke hearts, drained and halved
- 1 small carrot, chopped
- 1 small yellow onion, chopped
- 1 garlic clove, minced
- ¼ teaspoon oregano, dried
- ¼ teaspoon rosemary, dried
- A pinch of red pepper flakes
- A pinch of garlic powder
- A pinch of salt and black pepper
- 3 cups chicken stock
- 1 tablespoon tomato paste
- 1 tablespoon cilantro, chopped

Directions:
1. In your slow cooker, mix the artichokes with the carrot, onion and the other ingredients, toss, put the lid on and cook on Low for 5 hours.
2. Ladle into bowls and serve.

Nutrition: calories 362, fat 3, fiber 5, carbs 16, protein 5

Beans and Mushroom
Preparation time: 10 minutes
Cooking time: 8 hours
Servings: 2
Ingredients:
- Cooking spray
- ½ green bell pepper, chopped
- ½ red bell pepper, chopped
- ½ red onion, chopped
- 2 garlic cloves, minced
- 1 cup tomatoes, cubed
- 1 cup veggie stock
- Salt and black pepper to the taste
- 1 cup white mushrooms, sliced
- 1 cup canned kidney beans, drained
- ½ teaspoon turmeric powder
- ½ teaspoon coriander, ground
- 1 tablespoon parsley, chopped
- ½ tablespoon Cajun seasoning

Directions:
1. Grease the slow cooker with the cooking spray and mix the bell peppers with the onion, garlic and the other ingredients into the pot.
2. Put the lid on, cook on Low for 8 hours, divide into bowls and serve.

Nutrition: calories 272, fat 4, fiber 7, carbs 19, protein 7

Chicken and Eggplant Stew
Preparation time: 10 minutes
Cooking time: 8 hours
Servings: 2
Ingredients:
- 1 cup tomato paste
- ½ cup chicken stock
- 1 pound chicken breast, skinless, boneless and cubed
- 2 eggplants, cubed
- 1 small red onion, chopped
- 1 red bell pepper, chopped
- ½ teaspoon rosemary, dried
- ½ tablespoon smoked paprika
- 1 teaspoon cumin, ground
- Cooking spray
- Salt and black pepper to the taste
- Juice of ½ lemon
- ½ tablespoon parsley, chopped

Directions:
1. In your slow cooker, mix the chicken with the stock, tomato paste and the other ingredients, toss, put the lid on and cook on Low for 8 hours.
2. Divide into bowls and serve for lunch.

Nutrition: calories 261, fat 4, fiber 6, carbs 14, protein 7

Turmeric Stew
Preparation time: 10 minutes
Cooking time: 5 hours
Servings: 2
Ingredients:
- 2 cups veggie stock
- ½ cup canned red lentils, drained
- 1 carrot, sliced
- 1 eggplant, cubed
- ½ cup tomatoes, chopped
- 1 red onion, chopped
- 1 garlic clove, minced
- 1 teaspoon turmeric powder
- ¼ tablespoons ginger, grated
- ½ teaspoons mustard seeds
- ¼ teaspoon sweet paprika
- ½ cup tomato paste
- 1 tablespoon dill, chopped
- Salt and black pepper to the taste

Directions:
1. In your slow cooker, combine the lentils with the stock, tomatoes, eggplant and the other ingredients, toss, put the lid on, cook on High for 5 hours, divide into bowls and serve.

Nutrition: calories 303, fat 4, fiber 8, carbs 12, protein 4

Pork Chili
Preparation time: 10 minutes
Cooking time: 10 hours
Servings: 2
Ingredients:
- 1 pound pork stew meat, cubed
- 1 red onion, sliced
- 1 carrot, sliced
- 1 teaspoon sweet paprika
- ½ teaspoon cumin, ground
- 1 cup tomato paste
- 1 cup veggie stock
- 2 tablespoons chili powder
- 2 teaspoons cayenne pepper
- 1 tablespoon red pepper flakes
- A pinch of salt and black pepper
- 1 red bell pepper, chopped
- 1 yellow bell pepper, chopped
- 1 tablespoon chives, chopped

Directions:
1. In your slow cooker, mix the pork meat with the onion, carrot and the other ingredients, toss, put the lid on and cook on Low for 10 hours.
2. Divide the mix into bowls and serve.

Nutrition: calories 261, fat 7, fiber 4, carbs 8, protein 18

Cinnamon Pork Ribs
Preparation time: 10 minutes
Cooking time: 8 hours
Servings: 2
Ingredients:
- 2 pounds baby back pork ribs
- 1 tablespoon cinnamon powder
- 2 tablespoons olive oil
- ½ teaspoon allspice, ground
- A pinch of salt and black pepper
- ½ teaspoon garlic powder
- 1 tablespoon balsamic vinegar
- ½ cup beef stock
- 1 tablespoon tomato paste

Directions:
1. In your slow cooker, mix the pork ribs with the cinnamon, the oil and the other ingredients, toss, put the lid on and cook on Low for 8 hours.
2. Divide ribs between plates and serve for lunch with a side salad.

Nutrition: calories 312, fat 7, fiber 7, carbs 8, protein 18

Pork and Mushroom

Preparation time: 10 minutes
Cooking time: 7 hours
Servings: 2
Ingredients:
- 2 tablespoons olive oil
- 1 garlic clove, minced
- 1 red onion, sliced
- 2 pounds pork stew meat, cubed
- 1 cup mushrooms, sliced
- 1 cup tomato paste
- A pinch of salt and black pepper
- 1 teaspoon oregano, dried
- 1 teaspoon rosemary, dried
- ½ teaspoon nutmeg, ground
- 1 and ½ cups veggie stock
- 1 tablespoon chives, chopped

Directions:
1. Grease the slow cooker with the oil, add the meat, onion, garlic and the other ingredients, toss, put the lid on and cook on Low for 7 hours.
2. Divide into bowls and serve for lunch.

Nutrition: calories 345, fat 7, fiber 5, carbs 14, protein 32

Pork and Tomatoes Mix

Preparation time: 10 minutes
Cooking time: 8 hours
Servings: 2
Ingredients:
- 1 and ½ pounds pork stew meat, cubed
- 1 cup cherry tomatoes, halved
- 1 cup tomato paste
- 1 tablespoon rosemary, chopped
- ½ teaspoon sweet paprika
- ½ teaspoon coriander, ground
- A pinch of salt and black pepper
- 1 tablespoon chives, chopped

Directions:
1. In your Crockpot, combine the meat with the tomatoes, tomato paste and the other ingredients, toss, put the lid on and cook on Low for 8 hours.
2. Divide between plates and serve for lunch.

Nutrition: calories 352, fat 8, fiber 4, carbs 10, protein 27

Pork Shanks

Preparation time: 10 minutes
Cooking time: 7 hours
Servings: 2
Ingredients:
- 1 and ½ pounds pork shanks
- 1 tablespoon olive oil
- 2 tablespoons basil pesto
- 1 red onion, sliced
- 1 cup beef stock
- ½ cup tomato paste
- 4 garlic cloves, minced
- 1 tablespoon oregano, chopped
- Zest and juice of 1 lemon
- A pinch of salt and black pepper

Directions:
1. In your slow cooker, mix the pork shanks with the oil, pesto and the other ingredients, toss, put the lid on and cook on Low for 7 hours.
2. Divide everything between plates and serve for lunch.

Nutrition: calories 372, fat 7, fiber 5, carbs 12, protein 37

Potato Stew

Preparation time: 10 minutes
Cooking time: 5 hours and 5 minutes
Servings: 4
Ingredients:
- ½ tablespoon olive oil
- 1 pound gold potatoes, peeled and cut into wedges
- 1 red onion, sliced
- 1 cup tomato paste
- ½ cup beef stock
- 1 carrot, sliced
- 1 red bell pepper, cubed
- 4 garlic cloves, minced
- 1 teaspoon sweet paprika
- 1 tablespoon chives, chopped

Directions:
1. Heat up a pan with the oil over medium-high heat, add the onion and garlic, sauté for 5 minutes and transfer to the slow cooker.
2. Add the potatoes and the other ingredients, toss, put the lid on and cook on Low for 5 hours.
3. Divide the stew into bowls and serve for lunch.

Nutrition: calories 273, fat 6, fiber 7, carbs 10, protein 17

Chicken and Rice

Preparation time: 10 minutes
Cooking time: 6 hours
Servings: 2
Ingredients:
- 1 pound chicken breast, skinless, boneless and cubed
- 1 red onion, sliced
- 2 spring onions, chopped
- Cooking spray
- 1 cup wild rice
- 2 cups chicken stock
- ½ teaspoon garam masala
- ½ teaspoon turmeric powder
- 1 tablespoon cilantro, chopped
- A pinch of salt and black pepper

Directions:
1. Grease the slow cooker with the cooking spray, add the chicken, rice, onion and the other ingredients, toss, put the lid on and cook on Low for 6 hours.
2. Divide the mix into bowls and serve for lunch.

Nutrition: calories 362, fat 8, fiber 8, carbs 10, protein 26

Salmon Stew

Preparation time: 10 minutes
Cooking time: 2 hours
Servings: 4
Ingredients:
- 1 pound salmon fillets, boneless and roughly cubed
- 1 cup chicken stock
- ½ cup tomato paste
- ½ red onion, sliced
- 1 carrot, sliced
- 1 sweet potato, peeled and cubed
- 1 tablespoon cilantro, chopped
- Cooking spray
- ½ cup mild salsa
- 2 garlic cloves, minced
- A pinch of salt and black pepper

Directions:
1. In your slow cooker, mix the fish with the stock, tomato paste, onion and the other ingredients, toss gently, put the lid on and cook on Low for 2 hours
2. Divide the mix into bowls and serve for lunch.

Nutrition: calories 292, fat 6, fiber 7, carbs 12, protein 22

Pork and Chickpeas

Preparation time: 10 minutes
Cooking time: 10 hours
Servings: 2
Ingredients:
- 1 red onion, sliced
- 1 pound pork stew meat, cubed
- 1 cup canned chickpeas, drained
- 1 cup beef stock
- 1 cup tomato paste
- ½ teaspoon sweet paprika
- ½ teaspoon turmeric powder
- A pinch of salt and black pepper
- 1 tablespoon hives, chopped

Directions:
1. In your slow cooker, mix the onion with the meat, chickpeas, stock and the other ingredients, toss, put the lid on and cook on Low for 10 hours.
2. Divide the mix between plates and serve for lunch.

Nutrition: calories 322, fat 6, fiber 6, carbs 9, protein 22

Beef and Cabbage

Preparation time: 10 minutes
Cooking time: 8 hours
Servings: 2
Ingredients:
- 1 pound beef stew meat, cubed
- 1 cup green cabbage, shredded
- 1 cup red cabbage, shredded
- 1 carrot, grated
- ½ cup water
- 1 cup tomato paste
- ½ teaspoon sweet paprika
- 1 tablespoon chives, chopped
- A pinch of salt and black pepper

Directions:
1. In your slow cooker, mix the beef with the cabbage, carrot and the other ingredients, toss, put the lid on and cook on Low for 8 hours.
2. Divide the mix between plates and serve for lunch.

Nutrition: calories 251, fat 6, fiber 7, carbs 12, protein 6

Beef Stew

Preparation time: 10 minutes
Cooking time: 6 hours
Servings: 2
Ingredients:
- 1 pound beef stew meat, cubed
- 1 teaspoon sweet paprika
- 1 red onion, sliced
- ½ cup mushrooms, sliced
- 1 carrot, peeled and cubed
- ½ cup tomatoes, cubed
- 1 tablespoon balsamic vinegar
- A pinch of salt and black pepper
- 1 teaspoon onion powder
- 1 teaspoon thyme, dried
- 1 cup beef stock
- 1 tablespoon cilantro, chopped

Directions:
1. In your slow cooker, mix the beef with the paprika, onion, mushrooms and the other ingredients except the cilantro, toss, put the lid on and cook on Low for 6 hours.
2. Divide into bowls and serve with the cilantro, sprinkled on top.

Nutrition: calories 322, fat 5, fiber 7, carbs 9, protein 16

Beef Curry

Preparation time: 10 minutes
Cooking time: 6 hours
Servings: 2
Ingredients:
- 1 pound beef stew meat
- 4 garlic cloves, minced
- 1 red onion, sliced
- 2 carrots, grated
- 1 tablespoon ginger, grated
- 2 tablespoons yellow curry paste
- 2 cups coconut milk
- A pinch of salt and black pepper

Directions:
1. In your slow cooker, mix the beef with the garlic, onion and the other ingredients, toss, put the lid on and cook on Low for 6 hours.
2. Divide the curry into bowls and serve for lunch.

Nutrition: calories 352, fat 6, fiber 7, carbs 9, protein 18

Chicken and Brussels Sprouts
Preparation time: 10 minutes
Cooking time: 6 hours
Servings: 2
Ingredients:
- 1 pound chicken breast, skinless, boneless and cubed
- 1 red onion, sliced
- 1 cup Brussels sprouts, trimmed and halved
- 1 cup chicken stock
- ½ cup tomato paste
- A pinch of salt and black pepper
- 1 garlic clove, crushed
- 1 tablespoon thyme, chopped
- 1 tablespoon rosemary, chopped

Directions:
1. In your slow cooker, mix the chicken with the onion, sprouts and the other ingredients, toss, put the lid on and cook on Low for 6 hours.
2. Divide the mix between plates and serve for lunch.

Nutrition: calories 261, fat 7, fiber 6, carbs 8, protein 26

Chickpeas Stew
Preparation time: 10 minutes
Cooking time: 3 hours
Servings: 4
Ingredients:
- 2 cups canned chickpeas, drained and rinsed
- 1 cup tomato sauce
- ½ cup chicken stock
- 1 red onion, sliced
- 2 garlic cloves, minced
- 1 tablespoon thyme, chopped
- ½ teaspoon turmeric powder
- ½ teaspoon garam masala
- 2 carrots, chopped
- 3 celery stalks, chopped
- 2 tablespoons parsley, chopped
- A pinch of salt and black pepper

Directions:
1. In your slow cooker, mix the chickpeas with the tomato sauce, chicken stock and the other ingredients, toss, put the lid on and cook on High for 3 hours.
2. Divide into bowls and serve for lunch.

Nutrition: calories 300, fat 4, fiber 7, carbs 9, protein 22

Eggplant Curry
Preparation time: 10 minutes
Cooking time: 3 hours
Servings: 2
Ingredients:
- 2 tablespoons olive oil
- 1 pound eggplant, cubed
- 2 tablespoons red curry paste
- 1 cup coconut milk
- ½ cup veggie stock
- 1 teaspoon turmeric powder
- ½ teaspoon rosemary, dried
- 4 kaffir lime leaves

Directions:
1. In your slow cooker, mix the eggplant with the oil, curry paste and the other ingredients, toss, put the lid on and cook on High for 3 hours.
2. Discard lime leaves, divide the curry into bowls and serve for lunch.

Nutrition: calories 281, fat 7, fiber 6, carbs 8, protein 22

Beef and Artichokes
Preparation time: 10 minutes
Cooking time: 4 hours
Servings: 2
Ingredients:
- 1 pound beef stew meat, cubed
- 1 cup canned artichoke hearts, halved
- 1 cup beef stock
- 1 red onion, sliced
- 1 cup tomato sauce
- ½ teaspoon rosemary, dried
- ½ teaspoon coriander, ground
- 1 teaspoon garlic powder
- A drizzle of olive oil
- A pinch of salt and black pepper
- 1 tablespoon chives, chopped

Directions:
1. Grease the slow cooker with the oil and mix the beef with the artichokes, stock and the other ingredients inside.
2. Toss, put the lid on and cook on High for 4 hours.
3. Divide the stew into bowls and serve.

Nutrition: calories 322, fat 5, fiber 4, carbs 12, protein 22

Beef Soup
Preparation time: 10 minutes
Cooking time: 5 hours
Servings: 2
Ingredients:
- 1 pound beef stew meat, cubed
- 3 cups beef stock
- ½ cup tomatoes, cubed
- 1 red onion, chopped
- 1 green bell pepper, chopped
- 1 carrot, cubed
- A pinch of salt and black pepper
- ½ tablespoon oregano, dried
- ¼ teaspoon chili pepper
- 2 tablespoon tomato paste
- 1 jalapeno, chopped
- 1 tablespoon cilantro, chopped

Directions:
1. In your slow cooker, mix the beef with the stock, tomatoes and the other ingredients, toss, put the lid on and cook on Low for 5 hours.
2. Divide the soup into bowls and serve for lunch.

Nutrition: calories 391, fat 6, fiber 7, carbs 8, protein 27

Veggie Soup

Preparation time: 10 minutes
Cooking time: 4 hours
Servings: 2
Ingredients:
- ½ pound gold potatoes, peeled and roughly cubed
- 1 carrot, sliced
- 1 zucchini, cubed
- 1 eggplant, cubed
- 1 cup tomatoes, cubed
- 4 cups veggie stock
- A pinch of salt and black pepper
- 3 tablespoons tomato paste
- 1 sweet onion, chopped
- 1 tablespoon lemon juice
- 1 tablespoon chives, chopped

Directions:
1. In your slow cooker, mix the potatoes with the carrot, zucchini and the other ingredients, toss, put the lid on and cook on Low for 4 hours.
2. Divide the soup into bowls and serve.

Nutrition: calories 392, fat 7, fiber 8, carbs 12, protein 28

Turkey Stew

Preparation time: 10 minutes
Cooking time: 8 hours
Servings: 2
Ingredients:
- 1 pound turkey breast, skinless, boneless and cubed
- 1 carrot, peeled and sliced
- 3 tomatoes, cubed
- 1 red onion, chopped
- 2 garlic cloves, minced
- ½ teaspoon sweet paprika
- ½ teaspoon chili powder
- 1 cup chicken stock
- 2 tablespoons tomato paste
- 1 teaspoon cumin powder
- 1 teaspoon oregano, dried
- A pinch of salt and black pepper

Directions:
1. In your slow cooker, mix the turkey with the carrot, tomatoes, onion and the other ingredients, toss, put the lid on and cook on Low for 8 hours.
2. Divide the stew into bowls and serve for lunch.

Nutrition: calories 328, fat 6, fiber 8, carbs 12, protein 28

Masala Beef Mix

Preparation time: 10 minutes
Cooking time: 5 hours
Servings: 2
Ingredients:
- 1 pound beef roast meat, cubed
- 1 red onion, sliced
- 1 eggplant, cubed
- 2 tablespoons olive oil
- 1 teaspoon black mustard seeds
- A pinch of salt and black pepper
- 1 tablespoon lemon zest, grated
- 2 tablespoons lemon juice
- 1 tablespoon garam masala
- 1 tablespoons coriander powder
- 1 teaspoon turmeric powder
- ½ teaspoon black peppercorns, ground
- ½ cup beef stock

Directions:
1. In your slow cooker, mix the meat with the onion, eggplant, oil, mustard seeds and the other ingredients, toss, put the lid on and cook on High for 5 hours.
2. Divide the mix between plates and serve for lunch with a side salad.

Nutrition: calories 300, fat 4, fiber 6, carbs 9, protein 22

Slow Cooker Side Dish Recipes for 2

Cheddar Potatoes
Preparation time: 10 minutes
Cooking time: 3 hours
Servings: 2
Ingredients:
- ½ pound gold potatoes, peeled and cut into wedges
- 2 ounces heavy cream
- ½ teaspoon turmeric powder
- ½ teaspoon rosemary, dried
- ¼ cup cheddar cheese, shredded
- 1 tablespoon butter, melted
- Cooking spray
- A pinch of salt and black pepper

Directions:
1. Grease your slow cooker with the cooking spray, add the potatoes, cream, turmeric and the other ingredients, toss, put the lid on and cook on High for 3 hours.
2. Divide between plates and serve as a side dish.

Nutrition: calories 300, fat 14, fiber 6, carbs 22, protein 6

Balsamic Cauliflower
Preparation time: 10 minutes
Cooking time: 5 hours
Servings: 2
Ingredients:
- 2 cups cauliflower florets
- ½ cup veggie stock
- 1 tablespoon balsamic vinegar
- 1 tablespoon lemon zest, grated
- 2 spring onions, chopped
- ¼ teaspoon sweet paprika
- Salt and black pepper to the taste
- 1 tablespoon dill, chopped

Directions:
1. In your slow cooker, mix the cauliflower with the stock, vinegar and the other ingredients, toss, put the lid on and cook on Low for 5 hours.
2. Divide the cauliflower mix between plates and serve.

Nutrition: calories 162, fat 11, fiber 2, carbs 11, protein 5

Black Beans Mix
Preparation time: 10 minutes
Cooking time: 5 hours
Servings: 2
Ingredients:
- 2 tablespoons tomato paste
- Cooking spray
- 2 cups black beans
- ¼ cup veggie stock
- 1 red onion, sliced
- Cooking spray
- 1 teaspoon Italian seasoning
- ½ celery rib, chopped
- ½ red bell pepper, chopped
- ½ sweet red pepper, chopped
- ¼ teaspoon mustard seeds
- Salt and black pepper to the taste
- 2 ounces canned corn, drained
- 1 tablespoon cilantro, chopped

Directions:
1. Grease the slow cooker with the cooking spray, and mix the beans with the stock, onion and the other ingredients inside.
2. Put the lid on, cook on Low for 5 hours, divide between plates and serve as a side dish.

Nutrition: calories 255, fat 6, fiber 7, carbs 38, protein 7

Butter Green Beans
Preparation time: 10 minutes
Cooking time: 2 hours
Servings: 2
Ingredients:
- 1 pound green beans, trimmed and halved
- 2 tablespoons butter, melted
- ½ cup veggie stock
- 1 teaspoon rosemary, dried
- 1 tablespoon chives, chopped
- Salt and black pepper to the taste
- ¼ teaspoon soy sauce

Directions:
1. In your slow cooker, combine the green beans with the melted butter, stock and the other ingredients, toss, put the lid on and cook on Low for 2 hours.
2. Divide between plates and serve as a side dish.

Nutrition: calories 236, fat 6, fiber 8, carbs 10, protein 6

Appetizing Corn Sauté
Preparation time: 10 minutes
Cooking time: 2 hours
Servings: 2
Ingredients:
- 3 cups corn
- 2 tablespoon whipping cream
- 1 carrot, peeled and grated
- 1 tablespoon chives, chopped
- 2 tablespoons butter, melted
- Salt and black pepper to the taste
- 2 bacon strips, cooked and crumbled
- 1 tablespoon green onions, chopped

Directions:
1. In your slow cooker, combine the corn with the cream, carrot and the other ingredients, toss, put the lid on and cook on Low for 2 hours.
2. Divide between plates, and serve.

Nutrition: calories 261, fat 11, fiber 3, carbs 17, protein 6

Sage Peas

Preparation time: 10 minutes
Cooking time: 2 hours
Servings: 2
Ingredients:
- 1 pound peas
- 1 red onion, sliced
- ½ cup veggie stock
- ½ cup tomato sauce
- 2 garlic cloves, minced
- ¼ teaspoon sage, dried
- Salt and black pepper to the taste
- 1 tablespoon dill, chopped

Directions:
1. In your slow cooker, combine the peas with the onion, stock and the other ingredients, toss, put the lid on and cook on Low for 2 hours.
2. Divide between plates and serve as a side dish.

Nutrition: calories 100, fat 4, fiber 3, carbs 15, protein 4

Tomato and Corn

Preparation time: 10 minutes
Cooking time: 4 hours
Servings: 2
Ingredients:
- 1 red onion, sliced
- 2 spring onions, chopped
- 1 cup corn
- 1 cup tomatoes, cubed
- 1 tablespoon olive oil
- ½ red bell pepper, chopped
- ½ cup tomato sauce
- ¼ teaspoon sweet paprika
- ½ teaspoon cumin, ground
- 1 tablespoon chives, chopped
- Salt and black pepper to the taste

Directions:
1. Heat up a pan with the oil over medium-high heat, add the onion, spring onions and bell pepper and cook for 10 minutes.
2. Transfer the mix to the slow cooker, add the corn and the other ingredients, toss, put the lid on and cook on Low for 4 hours.
3. Divide the mix between plates and serve as a side dish.

Nutrition: calories 312, fat 4, fiber 6, carbs 12, protein 6

Dill Mushroom Sauté

Preparation time: 10 minutes
Cooking time: 3 hours
Servings: 2
Ingredients:
- 1 pound white mushrooms, halved
- 1 tablespoon olive oil
- 1 red onion, sliced
- 1 carrot, peeled and grated
- 2 green onions, chopped
- 1 garlic clove, minced
- 1 cup beef stock
- ½ cup tomato sauce
- 1 tablespoon dill, chopped

Directions:
1. Grease the slow cooker with the oil and mix the mushrooms with the onion, carrot and the other ingredients inside.
2. Put the lid on, cook on Low for 3 hours, divide between plates and serve as a side dish.

Nutrition: calories 200, fat 6, fiber 4, carbs 28, protein 5

Appetizing Zucchini Mix

Preparation time: 10 minutes
Cooking time: 2 hours
Servings: 2
Ingredients:
- ¼ cup carrots, grated
- 1 pound zucchinis, roughly cubed
- 1 teaspoon hot paprika
- ½ teaspoon chili powder
- 2 spring onions, chopped
- ½ tablespoon olive oil
- ½ teaspoon curry powder
- 1 garlic clove, minced
- ½ teaspoon ginger powder
- A pinch of salt and black pepper
- 1 tablespoon cilantro, chopped

Directions:
1. In your slow cooker, mix the carrots with the zucchinis, paprika and the other ingredients, toss, put the lid on and cook on Low for 2 hours.
2. Divide between plates and serve as a side dish.

Nutrition: calories 200, fat 5, fiber 7, carbs 28, protein 4

Squash and Eggplant Mix

Preparation time: 10 minutes
Cooking time: 4 hours
Servings: 2
Ingredients:
- 1 butternut squash, peeled and roughly cubed
- 1 eggplant, roughly cubed
- 1 red onion, chopped
- Cooking spray
- ½ cup veggie stock
- ¼ cup tomato paste
- ½ tablespoon parsley, chopped
- Salt and black pepper to the taste
- 2 garlic cloves, minced

Directions:
1. Grease the slow cooker with the cooking spray and mix the squash with the eggplant, onion and the other ingredients inside.
2. Put the lid on and cook on Low for 4 hours.
3. Divide between plates and serve as a side dish.

Nutrition: calories 114, fat 4, fiber 4, carbs 18, protein 4

Carrots and Spinach Mix
Preparation time: 10 minutes
Cooking time: 2 hours
Servings: 2
Ingredients:
- 2 carrots, sliced
- 1 small yellow onion, chopped
- Salt and black pepper to the taste
- ¼ teaspoon oregano, dried
- ½ teaspoon sweet paprika
- 2 ounces baby spinach
- 1 cup veggie stock
- 1 tablespoons lemon juice
- 2 tablespoons pistachios, chopped

Directions:
1. In your slow cooker, mix the spinach with the carrots, onion and the other ingredients, toss, put the lid on and cook on Low for 2 hours.
2. Divide everything between plates and serve.

Nutrition: calories 219, fat 8, fiber 14, carbs 15, protein 17

Coconut Potatoes
Preparation time: 10 minutes
Cooking time: 4 hours
Servings: 2
Ingredients:
- ½ pound gold potatoes, halved and sliced
- 2 scallions, chopped
- 1 tablespoon avocado oil
- 2 ounces coconut milk
- ¼ cup veggie stock
- Salt and black pepper to the taste
- 1 tablespoons parsley, chopped

Directions:
1. In your slow cooker, mix the potatoes with the scallions and the other ingredients, toss, put the lid on and cook on High for 4 hours.
2. Divide the mix between plates and serve.

Nutrition: calories 306, fat 14, fiber 4, carbs 15, protein 12

Sage Sweet Potatoes
Preparation time: 10 minutes
Cooking time: 3 hours
Servings: 2
Ingredients:
- ½ pound sweet potatoes, thinly sliced
- 1 tablespoon sage, chopped
- 2 tablespoons orange juice
- A pinch of salt and black pepper
- ½ cup veggie stock
- ½ tablespoon olive oil

Directions:
1. In your slow cooker, mix the potatoes with the sage and the other ingredients, toss, put the lid on and cook on High for 3 hours.
2. Divide between plates and serve as a side dish.

Nutrition: calories 189, fat 4, fiber 4, carbs 17, protein 4

Cauliflower and Almonds
Preparation time: 10 minutes
Cooking time: 3 hours
Servings: 2
Ingredients:
- 2 cups cauliflower florets
- 2 ounces tomato paste
- 1 small yellow onion, chopped
- 1 tablespoon chives, chopped
- Salt and black pepper to the taste
- 1 tablespoon almonds, sliced

Directions:
1. In your slow cooker, mix the cauliflower with the tomato paste and the other ingredients, toss, put the lid on and cook on High for 3 hours.
2. Divide between plates and serve as a side dish.

Nutrition: calories 177, fat 12, fiber 7, carbs 20, protein 7

Garlic Risotto
Preparation time: 10 minutes
Cooking time: 2 hours
Servings: 2
Ingredients:
- 1 small shallot, chopped
- 1 cup wild rice
- 1 cup chicken stock
- 1 tablespoons olive oil
- 2 garlic cloves, minced
- Salt and black pepper to the taste
- 2 tablespoons cilantro, chopped

Directions:
1. In your slow cooker, mix the rice with the stock, shallot and the other ingredients, toss, put the lid on and cook on High for 2 hours
2. Divide between plates and serve as a side dish.

Nutrition: calories 204, fat 7, fiber 3, carbs 17, protein 7

Curry Savory Veggie Mix
Preparation time: 10 minutes
Cooking time: 3 hours
Servings: 2
Ingredients:
- 2 zucchinis, cubed
- 1 eggplant, cubed
- ½ cup button mushrooms, quartered
- 1 small red sweet potatoes, chopped
- ½ cup veggie stock
- 1 garlic cloves, minced
- ¼ tablespoon Thai red curry paste
- ¼ tablespoon ginger, grated
- Salt and black pepper to the taste
- 2 tablespoons coconut milk

Directions:
1. In your slow cooker, mix the zucchinis with the eggplant and the other ingredients, toss, put the lid on and cook on Low for 3 hours.
2. Divide between plates and serve as a side dish.

Nutrition: calories 169, fat 2, fiber 2, carbs 15, protein 6

Rosemary Leeks

Preparation time: 10 minutes
Cooking time: 3 hours
Servings: 2
Ingredients:
- ½ tablespoon olive oil
- ½ leeks, sliced
- ½ cup tomato sauce
- 2 garlic cloves, minced
- Salt and black pepper to the taste
- ¼ tablespoon rosemary, chopped

Directions:
1. In your slow cooker, mix the leeks with the oil, sauce and the other ingredients, toss, put the lid on, cook on High for 3 hours, divide between plates and serve as a side dish.

Nutrition: calories 202, fat 2, fiber 6, carbs 18, protein 8

Spicy Brussels Sprouts

Preparation time: 10 minutes
Cooking time: 3 hours
Servings: 2
Ingredients:
- ½ pounds Brussels sprouts, trimmed and halved
- A pinch of salt and black pepper
- 2 tablespoons mustard
- ½ cup veggie stock
- 1 tablespoons olive oil
- 2 tablespoons maple syrup
- 1 tablespoon thyme, chopped

Directions:
1. In your slow cooker, mix the sprouts with the mustard and the other ingredients, toss, put the lid on and cook on Low for 3 hours.
2. Divide between plates and serve as a side dish.

Nutrition: calories 170, fat 4, fiber 4, carbs 14, protein 6

Potatoes and Leeks Mix

Preparation time: 10 minutes
Cooking time: 4 hours
Servings: 2
Ingredients:
- 2 leeks, sliced
- ½ pound sweet potatoes, cut into medium wedges
- ½ cup veggie stock
- ½ tablespoon balsamic vinegar
- 1 tablespoon chives, chopped
- ½ teaspoon pumpkin pie spice

Directions:
1. In your slow cooker, mix the leeks with the potatoes and the other ingredients, toss, put the lid on and cook on High for 4 hours.
2. Divide between plates and serve as a side dish.

Nutrition: calories 351, fat 8, fiber 5, carbs 48, protein 7

Black Beans Mix

Preparation time: 10 minutes
Cooking time: 6 hours
Servings: 2
Ingredients:
- ½ pound black beans, soaked overnight and drained
- A pinch of salt and black pepper
- ½ cup veggie stock
- ½ tablespoon lime juice
- 2 tablespoons cilantro, chopped
- 2 tablespoons pine nuts

Directions:
1. In your slow cooker, mix the beans with the stock and the other ingredients, toss, put the lid on and cook on Low for 6 hours.
2. Divide everything between plates and serve.

Nutrition: calories 200, fat 3, fiber 4, carbs 7, protein 5

Orange Carrots Mix

Preparation time: 10 minutes
Cooking time: 6 hours
Servings: 2
Ingredients:
- ½ pound carrots, sliced
- A pinch of salt and black pepper
- ½ tablespoon olive oil
- ½ cup orange juice
- ½ teaspoon orange rind, grated

Directions:
1. In your slow cooker, mix the carrots with the oil and the other ingredients, toss, put the lid on and cook on Low for 6 hours.
2. Divide between plates and serve as a side dish.

Nutrition: calories 140, fat 2, fiber 2, carbs 7, protein 6

Hot Lentils

Preparation time: 10 minutes
Cooking time: 6 hours
Servings: 2
Ingredients:
- 1 tablespoon thyme, chopped
- ½ tablespoon olive oil
- 1 cup canned lentils, drained
- ½ cup veggie stock
- 2 garlic cloves, minced
- 1 tablespoon cider vinegar
- 2 tablespoons tomato paste
- 1 tablespoon rosemary, chopped

Directions:
1. In your slow cooker, mix the lentils with the thyme and the other ingredients, toss, put the lid on and cook on Low for 6 hours.
2. Divide between plates and serve as a side dish.

Nutrition: calories 200, fat 2, fiber 4, carbs 7, protein 8

Marjoram Rice Mix
Preparation time: 10 minutes
Cooking time: 6 hours
Servings: 2
Ingredients:
- 1 cup wild rice
- 2 cups chicken stock
- 1 carrot, peeled and grated
- 2 tablespoons marjoram, chopped
- 1 tablespoon olive oil
- A pinch of salt and black pepper
- 1 tablespoon green onions, chopped

Directions:
1. In your slow cooker, mix the rice with the stock and the other ingredients, toss, put the lid on and cook on Low for 6 hours.
2. Divide between plates and serve.

Nutrition: calories 200, fat 2, fiber 3, carbs 7, protein 5

Mashed Potatoes
Preparation time: 10 minutes
Cooking time: 6 hours
Servings: 2
Ingredients:
- 1 pound gold potatoes, peeled and cubed
- 2 garlic cloves, chopped
- 1 cup milk
- 1 cup water
- 2 tablespoons butter
- A pinch of salt and white pepper

Directions:
1. In your slow cooker, mix the potatoes with the water, salt and pepper, put the lid on and cook on Low for 6 hours.
2. Mash the potatoes, add the rest of the ingredients, whisk and serve.

Nutrition: calories 135, fat 4, fiber 2, carbs 10, protein 4

Barley Mix
Preparation time: 10 minutes
Cooking time: 6 hours
Servings: 2
Ingredients:
- 1 red onion, sliced
- ½ teaspoon sweet paprika
- ½ teaspoon turmeric powder
- 1 cup barley
- 1 cup veggie stock
- A pinch of salt and black pepper
- 1 garlic clove, minced

Directions:
1. In your slow cooker, mix the barley with the onion, paprika and the other ingredients, toss, put the lid on and cook on Low for 6 hours.
2. Divide between plates and serve as a side dish.

Nutrition: calories 160, fat 3, fiber 7, carbs 13, protein 7

Beans Mix
Preparation time: 10 minutes
Cooking time: 8 hours
Servings: 2
Ingredients:
- ½ pound lima beans, soaked for 6 hours and drained
- 1 tablespoon olive oil
- 2 scallions, chopped
- 1 carrot, chopped
- 2 tablespoons tomato paste
- 1 garlic cloves, minced
- A pinch of salt and black pepper to the taste
- 3 cups water
- A pinch of red pepper, crushed
- 2 tablespoons parsley, chopped

Directions:
1. In your slow cooker, mix the beans with the scallions, oil and the other ingredients, toss, put the lid on and cook on Low for 8 hours.
2. Divide between plates and serve as a side dish/

Nutrition: calories 160, fat 3, fiber 7, carbs 9, protein 12

Creamy Beans
Preparation time: 10 minutes
Cooking time: 2 hours
Servings: 2
Ingredients:
- 2 ounces green beans, trimmed and halved
- 2 tablespoons hot sauce
- 2 tablespoons heavy cream
- ½ cup coconut milk
- ¼ teaspoon cumin, ground
- ¼ tablespoon chili powder

Directions:
1. In your slow cooker, mix the beans with the hot sauce and the other ingredients, toss, put the lid on and cook on Low for 2 hours.
2. Divide between plates and serve right away as a side dish.

Nutrition: calories 230, fat 4, fiber 6, carbs 8, protein 10

Spinach Mix
Preparation time: 10 minutes
Cooking time: 1 hour
Servings: 2
Ingredients:
- 1 pound baby spinach
- ½ cup cherry tomatoes, halved
- ½ tablespoon olive oil
- ½ cup veggie stock
- 1 small yellow onion, chopped
- ¼ teaspoon coriander, ground
- ¼ teaspoon cumin, ground
- ¼ teaspoon garam masala
- ¼ teaspoon chili powder
- Salt and black pepper to the taste

Directions:
1. In your slow cooker, mix the spinach with the tomatoes, oil and the other ingredients, toss, put the lid on and cook on High for 1 hour.
2. Divide between plates and serve as a side dish.,

Nutrition: calories 270, fat 4, fiber 6, carbs 8, protein 12

BBQ-Beans

Preparation time: 10 minutes
Cooking time: 8 hours
Servings: 2
Ingredients:
- ¼ pound navy beans, soaked overnight and drained
- 1 cup bbq sauce
- 1 tablespoon sugar
- 1 tablespoon ketchup
- 1 tablespoon water
- 1 tablespoon apple cider vinegar
- 1 tablespoon olive oil
- 1 tablespoon soy sauce

Directions:
1. In your slow cooker, mix the beans with the sauce, sugar and the other ingredients, toss, put the lid on and cook on Low for 8 hours.
2. Divide between plates and serve as a side dish.

Nutrition: calories 430, fat 7, fiber 8, carbs 15, protein 19

White Beans Mix

Preparation time: 10 minutes
Cooking time: 6 hours
Servings: 4
Ingredients:
- 1 celery stalk, chopped
- 2 garlic cloves, minced
- 1 carrot, chopped
- 1 cup veggie stock
- ½ cup canned tomatoes, crushed
- ½ teaspoon chili powder
- ½ tablespoon Italian seasoning
- 15 ounces canned white beans, drained
- 1 tablespoon parsley, chopped

Directions:
1. In your slow cooker, mix the beans with the celery, garlic and the other ingredients, toss, put the lid on and cook on Low for 6 hours.
2. Divide the mix between plates and serve.

Nutrition: calories 223, fat 3, fiber 7, carbs 10, protein 7

Sweet Potato and Cauliflower

Preparation time: 10 minutes
Cooking time: 4 hours
Servings: 2
Ingredients:
- 2 sweet potatoes, peeled and cubed
- 1 cup cauliflower florets
- ½ cup coconut milk
- 1 teaspoons sriracha sauce
- A pinch of salt and black pepper
- ½ tablespoon sugar
- 1 tablespoon red curry paste
- 3 ounces white mushrooms, roughly chopped
- 2 tablespoons cilantro, chopped

Directions:
1. In your slow cooker, mix the sweet potatoes with the cauliflower and the other ingredients, toss, put the lid on and cook on Low for 4 hours.
2. Divide between plates and serve as a side dish.

Nutrition: calories 200, fat 3, fiber 5, carbs 15, protein 12

Cabbage Mix

Preparation time: 10 minutes
Cooking time: 6 hours
Servings: 2
Ingredients:
- 1 pound red cabbage, shredded
- 1 apple, peeled, cored and roughly chopped
- A pinch of salt and black pepper to the taste
- ¼ cup chicken stock
- 1 tablespoon mustard
- ½ tablespoon olive oil

Directions:
1. In your slow cooker, mix the cabbage with the apple and the other ingredients, toss, put the lid on and cook on Low for 6 hours.
2. Divide between plates and serve as a side dish.

Nutrition: calories 200, fat 4, fiber 2, carbs 8, protein 6

Parsley Mushroom

Preparation time: 10 minutes
Cooking time: 4 hours
Servings: 2
Ingredients:
- 1 pound brown mushrooms, halved
- 2 garlic cloves, minced
- A pinch of basil, dried
- A pinch of oregano, dried
- ½ cup veggie stock
- Salt and black pepper to the taste
- 1 tablespoon olive oil
- 1 tablespoon parsley, chopped

Directions:
1. In your slow cooker, mix the mushrooms with the garlic, basil and the other ingredients, toss, put the lid on and cook on Low for 4 hours.
2. Divide everything between plates and serve.

Nutrition: calories 122, fat 6, fiber 1, carbs 8, protein 5

Cinnamon Squash

Preparation time: 10 minutes
Cooking time: 4 hours
Servings: 2
Ingredients:
- 1 acorn squash, peeled and cut into medium wedges
- 1 cup coconut cream
- A pinch of cinnamon powder
- A pinch of salt and black pepper

Directions:
1. In your slow cooker, mix the squash with the cream and the other ingredients, toss, put the lid on and cook on Low for 4 hours.
2. Divide between plates and serve as a side dish.

Nutrition: calories 230, fat 3, fiber 3, carbs 10, protein 2

Appetizing Zucchini Mix

Preparation time: 10 minutes
Cooking time: 6 hours
Servings: 2
Ingredients:
- 1 pound zucchinis, sliced
- ½ teaspoon Italian seasoning
- ½ teaspoon sweet paprika
- Salt and black pepper
- ½ cup heavy cream
- ½ teaspoon garlic powder
- 1 tablespoon olive oil

Directions:
1. In your slow cooker, mix the zucchinis with the seasoning, paprika and the other ingredients, toss, put the lid on and cook on Low for 6 hours.
2. Divide between plates and serve as a side dish.

Nutrition: calories 170, fat 2, fiber 4, carbs 8, protein 5

Kale Mix

Preparation time: 10 minutes
Cooking time: 2 hours
Servings: 2
Ingredients:
- 1 pound baby kale
- ½ tablespoon tomato paste
- ½ cup chicken stock
- ½ teaspoon chili powder
- A pinch of salt and black pepper
- 1 tablespoon olive oil
- 1 small yellow onion, chopped
- 1 tablespoon apple cider vinegar

Directions:
1. In your slow cooker, mix the kale with the tomato paste, stock and the other ingredients, toss, put the lid on and cook on Low for 2 hours.
2. Divide between plates and serve as a side dish.

Nutrition: calories 200, fat 4, fiber 7, carbs 10, protein 3

Buttery Spinach

Preparation time: 10 minutes
Cooking time: 2 hours
Servings: 2
Ingredients:
- 1 pound baby spinach
- 1 cup heavy cream
- ½ teaspoon turmeric powder
- A pinch of salt and black pepper
- ½ teaspoon garam masala
- 2 tablespoons butter, melted

Directions:
1. In your slow cooker, mix the spinach with the cream and the other ingredients, toss, put the lid on and cook on Low for 2 hours.
2. Divide between plates and serve as a side dish.

Nutrition: calories 230, fat 12, fiber 2, carbs 9, protein 12

Bacon Potatoes

Preparation time: 10 minutes
Cooking time: 6 hours
Servings: 2
Ingredients:
- 2 sweet potatoes, peeled and cut into wedges
- 1 tablespoon balsamic vinegar
- ½ tablespoon sugar
- A pinch of salt and black pepper
- ¼ teaspoon sage, dried
- A pinch of thyme, dried
- 1 tablespoon olive oil
- ½ cup veggie stock
- 2 bacon slices, cooked and crumbled

Directions:
1. In your slow cooker, mix the potatoes with the vinegar, sugar and the other ingredients, toss, put the lid on and cook on Low for 6 hours
2. Divide between plates and serve as a side dish.

Nutrition: calories 209, fat 4, fiber 4, carbs 29, protein 4

Cauliflower Mash

Preparation time: 10 minutes
Cooking time: 5 hours
Servings: 2
Ingredients:
- 1 pound cauliflower florets
- ½ cup heavy cream
- 1 tablespoon dill, chopped
- 2 garlic cloves, minced
- 1 tablespoons butter, melted
- A pinch of salt and black pepper

Directions:
1. In your slow cooker, mix the cauliflower with the cream and the other ingredients, toss, put the lid on and cook on High for 5 hours.
2. Mash the mix, whisk, divide between plates and serve.

Nutrition: calories 187, fat 4, fiber 5, carbs 7, protein 3

Savory Veggie Mix

Preparation time: 10 minutes
Cooking time: 5 hours
Servings: 2
Ingredients:
- 1 eggplant, cubed
- 1 cup cherry tomatoes, halved
- 1 small zucchini, halved and sliced
- ½ red bell pepper, chopped
- ½ cup tomato sauce
- 1 carrot, peeled and cubed
- 1 sweet potato, peeled and cubed
- A pinch of red pepper flakes, crushed
- 1 tablespoon basil, chopped
- 1 tablespoon parsley, chopped
- A pinch of salt and black pepper
- ½ cup veggie stock
- 1 tablespoon capers
- 1 tablespoon red wine vinegar

Directions:
1. In your slow cooker, mix the eggplant with the tomatoes, zucchini and the other ingredients, toss, put the lid on and cook on Low for 5 hours.
2. Divide between plates and serve as a side dish.

Nutrition: calories 100, fat 1, fiber 2, carbs 7, protein 5

Farro Mix

Preparation time: 10 minutes
Cooking time: 4 hours
Servings: 2
Ingredients:
- 2 scallions, chopped
- 2 garlic cloves, minced
- 1 tablespoon olive oil
- 1 cup whole grain farro
- 2 cups chicken stock
- Salt and black pepper to the taste
- ½ tablespoon parsley, chopped
- 1 tablespoon cherries, dried

Directions:
1. In your slow cooker, mix the farro with the scallions, garlic and the other ingredients, toss, put the lid on and cook on Low for 4 hours.
2. Divide between plates and serve as a side dish.

Nutrition: calories 152, fat 4, fiber 5, carbs 20, protein 4

Cumin Quinoa Pilaf

Preparation time: 10 minutes
Cooking time: 2 hours
Servings: 2
Ingredients:
- 1 cup quinoa
- 2 teaspoons butter, melted
- Salt and black pepper to the taste
- 1 teaspoon turmeric powder
- 2 cups chicken stock
- 1 teaspoon cumin, ground

Directions:
1. Grease your slow cooker with the butter, add the quinoa and the other ingredients, toss, put the lid on and cook on High for 2 hours
2. Divide between plates and serve as a side dish.

Nutrition: calories 152, fat 3, fiber 6, carbs 8, protein 4

Saffron Risotto

Preparation time: 10 minutes
Cooking time: 2 hours
Servings: 2
Ingredients:
- ½ tablespoon olive oil
- ¼ teaspoon saffron powder
- 1 cup Arborio rice
- 2 cups veggie stock
- A pinch of salt and black pepper
- A pinch of cinnamon powder
- 1 tablespoon almonds, chopped

Directions:
1. In your slow cooker, mix the rice with the stock and the other ingredients, toss, put the lid on and cook on High for 2 hours.
2. Divide between plates and serve as a side dish.

Nutrition: calories 251, fat 4, fiber 7, carbs 29, protein 4

Mint Farro Pilaf

Preparation time: 10 minutes
Cooking time: 4 hours
Servings: 2
Ingredients:
- ½ tablespoon balsamic vinegar
- ½ cup whole grain farro
- A pinch of salt and black pepper
- 1 cup chicken stock
- ½ tablespoon olive oil
- 1 tablespoon green onions, chopped
- 1 tablespoon mint, chopped

Directions:
1. In your slow cooker, mix the farro with the vinegar and the other ingredients, toss, put the lid on and cook on Low for 4 hours.
2. Divide between plates and serve.

Nutrition: calories 162, fat 3, fiber 6, carbs 9, protein 4

Parmesan Rice

Preparation time: 10 minutes
Cooking time: 2 hours and 30 minutes
Servings: 2
Ingredients:
- 1 cup rice
- 2 cups chicken stock
- 1 tablespoon olive oil
- 1 red onion, chopped
- 1 tablespoon lemon juice
- Salt and black pepper to the taste
- 1 tablespoon parmesan, grated

Directions:
1. In your slow cooker, mix the rice with the stock, oil and the other ingredients, toss, put the lid on and cook on High for 2 hours and 30 minutes.
2. Divide between plates and serve as a side dish.

Nutrition: calories 162, fat 4, fiber 6, carbs 29, protein 6

Spinach Rice

Preparation time: 10 minutes
Cooking time: 2 hours
Servings: 2
Ingredients:
- 2 scallions, chopped
- 1 tablespoon olive oil
- 1 cup Arborio rice
- 1 cup chicken stock
- 6 ounces spinach, chopped
- Salt and black pepper to the taste
- 2 ounces goat cheese, crumbled

Directions:
1. In your slow cooker, mix the rice with the stock and the other ingredients, toss, put the lid on and cook on High for 2 hours.
2. Divide between plates and serve as a side dish.

Nutrition: calories 300, fat 10, fiber 6, carbs 20, protein 14

Mango Rice
Preparation time: 10 minutes
Cooking time: 2 hours
Servings: 2
Ingredients:
- 1 cup rice
- 2 cups chicken stock
- ½ cup mango, peeled and cubed
- Salt and black pepper to the taste
- 1 teaspoon olive oil

Directions:
1. In your slow cooker, mix the rice with the stock and the other ingredients, toss, put the lid on and cook on High for 2 hours.
2. Divide between plates and serve as a side dish.

Nutrition: calories 152, fat 4, fiber 5, carbs 18, protein 4

Lemony Artichokes
Preparation time: 10 minutes
Cooking time: 3 hours
Servings: 2
Ingredients:
- 1 cup veggie stock
- 2 medium artichokes, trimmed
- 1 tablespoon lemon juice
- 1 tablespoon lemon zest, grated
- Salt to the taste

Directions:
1. In your slow cooker, mix the artichokes with the stock and the other ingredients, toss, put the lid on and cook on Low for 3 hours.
2. Divide artichokes between plates and serve as a side dish.

Nutrition: calories 100, fat 2, fiber 5, carbs 10, protein 4

Coconut Bok Choy
Preparation time: 10 minutes
Cooking time: 1 hour
Servings: 2
Ingredients:
- 1 pound bok choy, torn
- ½ cup chicken stock
- ½ teaspoon chili powder
- 1 garlic clove, minced
- 1 teaspoon ginger, grated
- 1 tablespoon coconut oil
- Salt to the taste

Directions:
1. In your slow cooker, mix the bok choy with the stock and the other ingredients, toss, put the lid on and cook on High for 1 hour.
2. Divide between plates and serve as a side dish.

Nutrition: calories 100, fat 1, fiber 2, carbs 7, protein 4

Italian Eggplant
Preparation time: 10 minutes
Cooking time: 2 hours
Servings: 2
Ingredients:
- 2 small eggplants, roughly cubed
- ½ cup heavy cream
- Salt and black pepper to the taste
- 1 tablespoon olive oil
- A pinch of hot pepper flakes
- 2 tablespoons oregano, chopped

Directions:
1. In your slow cooker, mix the eggplants with the cream and the other ingredients, toss, put the lid on and cook on High for 2 hours.
2. Divide between plates and serve as a side dish.

Nutrition: calories 132, fat 4, fiber 6, carbs 12, protein 3

Cabbage and Onion
Preparation time: 10 minutes
Cooking time: 2 hours
Servings: 2
Ingredients:
- 1 and ½ cups green cabbage, shredded
- 1 cup red cabbage, shredded
- 1 tablespoon olive oil
- 1 red onion, sliced
- 2 spring onions, chopped
- ½ cup tomato paste
- ¼ cup veggie stock
- 2 tomatoes, chopped
- 2 jalapenos, chopped
- 1 tablespoon chili powder
- 1 tablespoon chives, chopped
- A pinch of salt and black pepper

Directions:
1. Grease your slow cooker with the oil and mix the cabbage with the onion, spring onions and the other ingredients inside.
2. Toss, put the lid on and cook on High for 2 hours.
3. Divide between plates and serve as a side dish.

Nutrition: calories 211, fat 3, fiber 3, carbs 6, protein 8

Balsamic Okra Mix
Preparation time: 10 minutes
Cooking time: 2 hours
Servings: 4
Ingredients:
- 2 cups okra, sliced
- 1 cup cherry tomatoes, halved
- 1 tablespoon olive oil
- ½ teaspoon turmeric powder
- ½ cup canned tomatoes, crushed
- 2 tablespoons balsamic vinegar
- 2 tablespoons basil, chopped
- 1 tablespoon thyme, chopped

Directions:
1. In your slow cooker, mix the okra with the tomatoes, crushed tomatoes and the other ingredients, toss, put the lid on and cook on High for 2 hours.
2. Divide between plates and serve as a side dish.

Nutrition: calories 233, fat 12, fiber 4, carbs 8, protein 4

Garlic Carrots

Preparation time: 10 minutes
Cooking time: 4 hours
Servings: 2
Ingredients:
- 1 pound carrots, sliced
- 2 garlic cloves, minced
- 1 red onion, chopped
- 1 tablespoon olive oil
- ½ cup tomato sauce
- A pinch of salt and black pepper
- ½ teaspoon oregano, dried
- 2 teaspoons lemon zest, grated
- 1 tablespoon lemon juice
- 1 tablespoon chives, chopped

Directions:
1. In your slow cooker, mix the carrots with the garlic, onion and the other ingredients, toss, put the lid on and cook on Low for 4 hours.
2. Divide the mix between plates and serve.

Nutrition: calories 219, fat 8, fiber 4, carbs 8, protein 17

Curry Broccoli Mix

Preparation time: 10 minutes
Cooking time: 3 hours
Servings: 2
Ingredients:
- 1 pound broccoli florets
- 1 cup tomato paste
- 1 tablespoon red curry paste
- 1 red onion, sliced
- ½ teaspoon Italian seasoning
- 1 teaspoon thyme, dried
- Salt and black pepper to the taste
- ½ tablespoon cilantro, chopped

Directions:
3. In your slow cooker, mix the broccoli with the curry paste, tomato paste and the other ingredients, toss, put the lid on and cook on Low for 3 hours.
4. Divide the mix between plates and serve as a side dish.

Nutrition: calories 177, fat 12, fiber 2, carbs 7, protein 7

Rice and Corn

Preparation time: 10 minutes
Cooking time: 6 hours
Servings: 2
Ingredients:
- 2 cups veggie stock
- 1 cup wild rice
- 1 cup corn
- 3 spring onions, chopped
- 1 tablespoon olive oil
- 2 teaspoons rosemary, dried
- ½ teaspoon garam masala
- Salt and black pepper to the taste
- 1 tablespoon cilantro, chopped

Directions:
1. In your slow cooker, mix the stock with the rice, corn and the other ingredients, toss, put the lid on and cook on Low for 6 hours.
2. Divide between plates and serve as a side dish.

Nutrition: calories 169, fat 5, fiber 3, carbs 8, protein 5

Cauliflower and Potatoes

Preparation time: 10 minutes
Cooking time: 4 hours
Servings: 2
Ingredients:
- 1 cup cauliflower florets
- ½ pound sweet potatoes, peeled and cubed
- 1 cup veggie stock
- ½ cup tomato sauce
- 1 tablespoon chives, chopped
- Salt and black pepper to the taste
- 1 teaspoon sweet paprika

Directions:
1. In your slow cooker, mix the cauliflower with the potatoes, stock and the other ingredients, toss, put the lid on and cook on High for 4 hours.
2. Divide between plates and serve as a side dish.

Nutrition: calories 135, fat 5, fiber 1, carbs 7, protein 3

Asparagus Mix

Preparation time: 10 minutes
Cooking time: 2 hours
Servings: 2
Ingredients:
- 1 pound asparagus, trimmed and halved
- 1 red onion, sliced
- 2 garlic cloves, minced
- 1 cup veggie stock
- 1 tablespoon lemon juice
- A pinch of salt and black pepper
- ¼ cup parsley, chopped

Directions:
1. In your slow cooker, mix the asparagus with the onion, garlic and the other ingredients, toss, put the lid on and cook on High for 2 hours.
2. Divide between plates and serve as a side dish.

Nutrition: calories 159, fat 4, fiber 4, carbs 6, protein 2

Garlic Squash Mix

Preparation time: 10 minutes
Cooking time: 3 hours
Servings: 2
Ingredients:
- 1 pound butternut squash, peeled and cubed
- 2 spring onions, chopped
- 1 cup veggie stock
- ½ teaspoon red pepper flakes, crushed
- ½ teaspoon turmeric powder
- A pinch of salt and black pepper
- 3 garlic cloves, minced

Directions:
1. In your slow cooker, mix the squash with the garlic, stock and the other ingredients, toss, put the lid on and cook on Low for 3 hours.
2. Divide squash mix between plates and serve as a side dish.

Nutrition: calories 196, fat 3, fiber 7, carbs 8, protein 7

Carrots and Parsnips
Preparation time: 10 minutes
Cooking time: 6 hours
Servings: 2
Ingredients:
- 1 tablespoon avocado oil
- 1 pound baby carrots, peeled
- ½ pound parsnips, peeled and cut into sticks
- 1 teaspoon sweet paprika
- ½ cup tomato paste
- ½ cup veggie stock
- ½ teaspoon chili powder
- A pinch of salt and black pepper
- 2 garlic cloves, minced
- 1 tablespoon dill, chopped

Directions:
1. Grease the slow cooker with the oil and mix the carrots with the parsnips, paprika and the other ingredients inside.
2. Toss, put the lid on and cook on Low for 6 hours.
3. Divide everything between plates and serve as a side dish.

Nutrition: calories 273, fat 7, fiber 5, carbs 8, protein 12

Lemony Kale
Preparation time: 10 minutes
Cooking time: 2 hours
Servings: 2
Ingredients:
- 1 yellow bell pepper, chopped
- 1 red bell pepper, chopped
- 1 tablespoon olive oil
- 1 red onion, sliced
- 4 cups baby kale
- 1 teaspoon lemon zest, grated
- 1 tablespoon lemon juice
- ½ cup veggie stock
- 1 garlic clove, minced
- A pinch of salt and black pepper
- 1 tablespoon basil, chopped

Directions:
1. In your slow cooker, mix the kale with the oil, onion, bell peppers and the other ingredients, toss, put the lid on and cook on Low for 2 hours.
2. Divide the mix between plates and serve as a side dish.

Nutrition: calories 251, fat 9, fiber 6, carbs 7, protein 8

Brussels Sprouts and Cauliflower
Preparation time: 10 minutes
Cooking time: 4 hours
Servings: 2
Ingredients:
- 1 cup Brussels sprouts, trimmed and halved
- 1 cup cauliflower florets
- 1 tablespoon olive oil
- 1 cup veggie stock
- 2 tablespoons tomato paste
- 1 teaspoon chili powder
- ½ teaspoon ginger powder
- A pinch of salt and black pepper
- 1 tablespoon thyme, chopped

Directions:
1. In your slow cooker, mix the Brussels sprouts with the cauliflower, oil, stock and the other ingredients, toss, put the lid on and cook on Low for 4 hours.
2. Divide the mix between plates and serve as a side dish.

Nutrition: calories 100, fat 4, fiber 4, carbs 8, protein 3

Cabbage and Kale Mix
Preparation time: 10 minutes
Cooking time: 2 hours
Servings: 2
Ingredients:
- 1 red onion, sliced
- 1 cup green cabbage, shredded
- 1 cup baby kale
- ½ cup canned tomatoes, crushed
- ½ teaspoon hot paprika
- ½ teaspoon Italian seasoning
- A pinch of salt and black pepper
- 1 tablespoon dill, chopped

Directions:
1. In your slow cooker, mix the cabbage with the kale, onion and the other ingredients, toss, put the lid on and cook on High for 2 hours.
2. Divide between plates and serve right away as a side dish.

Nutrition: calories 200, fat 4, fiber 2, carbs 8, protein 6

Thyme Mushrooms
Preparation time: 10 minutes
Cooking time: 4 hours
Servings: 2
Ingredients:
- 4 garlic cloves, minced
- 1 tablespoon olive oil
- 1 pound white mushroom caps, halved
- 1 cup corn
- 1 cup canned tomatoes, crushed
- ¼ teaspoon thyme, dried
- ½ cup veggie stock
- A pinch of salt and black pepper
- 2 tablespoons parsley, chopped

Directions:
1. Grease your slow cooker with the oil, and mix the garlic with the mushrooms, corn and the other ingredients inside.
2. Toss, put the lid on and cook on Low for 4 hours.
3. Divide between plates and serve as a side dish.

Nutrition: calories 122, fat 6, fiber 1, carbs 8, protein 5

Veggie Medley

Preparation time: 10 minutes
Cooking time: 3 hours
Servings: 2
Ingredients:
- 1 zucchini, cubed
- 1 eggplant, cubed
- ½ cup baby carrots, peeled
- ½ cup baby kale
- 1 cup cherry tomatoes, halved
- 1 teaspoon sweet paprika
- 1 tablespoon olive oil
- 1 cup tomato sauce
- 1 teaspoon Italian seasoning
- A pinch of salt and black pepper
- 1 cup yellow squash, peeled and cut into wedges
- 1 teaspoon garlic powder
- 1 tablespoon cilantro, chopped
- A pinch of salt and black pepper

Directions:
1. Grease your Crockpot with the oil, and mix the zucchini with the eggplant, carrots and the other ingredients inside.
2. Toss, put the lid on and cook on Low for 3 hours.
3. Divide the mix between plates and serve as a side dish.

Nutrition: calories 100, fat 2, fiber 4, carbs 8, protein 5

Green Beans and Zucchinis

Preparation time: 10 minutes
Cooking time: 3 hours
Servings: 2
Ingredients:
- 1 pound green beans, trimmed and halved
- 1 cup zucchinis, cubed
- 1 cup tomato sauce
- 1 teaspoon smoked paprika
- ½ teaspoon cumin, ground
- Salt and black pepper to the taste
- ½ teaspoon garlic powder
- ¼ tablespoon chives, chopped

Directions:
1. In your slow cooker, mix the green beans with the zucchinis, tomato sauce and the other ingredients, toss, put the lid on and cook on Low for 3 hours.
2. Divide the mix between plates and serve as a side dish.

Nutrition: calories 114, fat 5, fiber 6, carbs 8, protein 9

Tarragon Sweet Potatoes

Preparation time: 10 minutes
Cooking time: 3 hours
Servings: 4
Ingredients:
- 1 pound sweet potatoes, peeled and cut into wedges
- 1 cup veggie stock
- ½ teaspoon chili powder
- ½ teaspoon cumin, ground
- Salt and black pepper to the taste
- 1 tablespoon olive oil
- 1 tablespoon tarragon, dried
- 2 tablespoons balsamic vinegar

Directions:
1. In your slow cooker, mix the sweet potatoes with the stock, chili powder and the other ingredients, toss, put the lid on and cook on High for 3 hours.
2. Divide the mix between plates and serve as a side dish.

Nutrition: calories 80, fat 4, fiber 4, carbs 8, protein 4

Spicy Brussels Sprouts

Preparation time: 10 minutes
Cooking time: 3 hours
Servings: 2
Ingredients:
- 1 pound Brussels sprouts, trimmed and halved
- 1 tablespoon olive oil
- 1 tablespoon mustard
- 1 tablespoon balsamic vinegar
- Salt and black pepper to the taste
- ¼ cup veggie stock
- A pinch of red pepper, crushed
- 2 tablespoons chives, chopped

Directions:
1. In your slow cooker, mix the Brussels sprouts with the oil, mustard and the other ingredients, toss, put the lid on and cook on High for 3 hours.
2. Divide the mix between plates and serve as a side dish.

Nutrition: calories 256, fat 12, fiber 6, carbs 8, protein 15

Parmesan Spinach Mix

Preparation time: 10 minutes
Cooking time: 2 hours
Servings: 2
Ingredients:
- 2 garlic cloves, minced
- 1 pound baby spinach
- ¼ cup veggie stock
- A drizzle of olive oil
- Salt and black pepper to the taste
- 4 tablespoons heavy cream
- 2 tablespoons parmesan cheese, grated

Directions:
1. Grease your Crockpot with the oil, and mix the spinach with the garlic and the other ingredients inside.
2. Toss, put the lid on and cook on Low for 2 hours.
3. Divide the mix between plates and serve as a side dish.

Nutrition: calories 133, fat 10, fiber 4, carbs 4, protein 2

Peas and Tomatoes

Preparation time: 10 minutes
Cooking time: 3 hours
Servings: 2
Ingredients:
- 1 pound okra, sliced
- ½ pound tomatoes, cut into wedges
- 1 tablespoon olive oil
- ½ cup veggie stock
- ½ teaspoon chili powder
- Salt and black pepper to the taste
- 1 tablespoon mint, chopped
- 3 green onions, chopped
- 1 tablespoon chives, chopped

Directions:
1. Grease your slow cooker with the oil, and mix the okra with the tomatoes and the other ingredients inside.
2. Put the lid on, cook on Low for 3 hours, divide between plates and serve as a side dish.

Nutrition: calories 70, fat 1, fiber 1, carbs 4, protein 6

Savoy Cabbage Mix

Preparation time: 10 minutes
Cooking time: 2 hours
Servings: 2
Ingredients:
- 1 pound Savoy cabbage, shredded
- 1 red onion, sliced
- 1 tablespoon olive oil
- ½ cup veggie stock
- A pinch of salt and black pepper
- 1 carrot, grated
- ½ cup tomatoes, cubed
- ½ teaspoon sweet paprika
- ½ inch ginger, grated

Directions:
1. In your slow cooker, mix the cabbage with the onion, oil and the other ingredients, toss, put the lid on and cook on High for 2 hours.
2. Divide the mix between plates and serve as a side dish.

Nutrition: calories 100, fat 3, fiber 4, carbs 5, protein 2

Slow Cooker Snack Recipes for 2

Delish Spinach Spread
Preparation time: 10 minutes
Cooking time: 2 hours
Servings: 2
Ingredients:
- 4 ounces baby spinach
- 2 tablespoons mayonnaise
- 2 ounces heavy cream
- ½ teaspoon turmeric powder
- A pinch of salt and black pepper
- 1 ounce Swiss cheese, shredded

Directions:
1. In your slow cooker, mix the spinach with the cream, mayo and the other ingredients, toss, put the lid on and cook on Low for 2 hours.
2. Divide into bowls and serve as a party spread.

Nutrition: calories 132, fat 4, fiber 3, carbs 10, protein 4

Artichoke Dip
Preparation time: 10 minutes
Cooking time: 2 hours
Servings: 2
Ingredients:
- 2 ounces canned artichoke hearts, drained and chopped
- 2 ounces heavy cream
- 2 tablespoons mayonnaise
- ¼ cup mozzarella, shredded
- 2 green onions, chopped
- ½ teaspoon garam masala
- Cooking spray

Directions:
1. Grease your slow cooker with the cooking spray, and mix the artichokes with the cream, mayo and the other ingredients inside.
2. Stir, cover, cook on Low for 2 hours, divide into bowls and serve as a party dip.

Nutrition: calories 100, fat 3, fiber 2, carbs 7, protein 3

Crab Dip
Preparation time: 10 minutes
Cooking time: 1 hour
Servings: 2
Ingredients:
- 2 ounces crabmeat
- 1 tablespoon lime zest, grated
- ½ tablespoon lime juice
- 2 tablespoons mayonnaise
- 2 green onions, chopped
- 2 ounces cream cheese, cubed
- Cooking spray

Directions:
1. Grease your slow cooker with the cooking spray, and mix the crabmeat with the lime zest, juice and the other ingredients inside.
2. Put the lid on, cook on Low for 1 hour, divide into bowls and serve as a party dip.

Nutrition: calories 100, fat 3, fiber 2, carbs 9, protein 4

Lemony Shrimp Dip
Preparation time: 10 minutes
Cooking time: 2 hours
Servings: 2
Ingredients:
- 3 ounces cream cheese, soft
- ½ cup heavy cream
- 1 pound shrimp, peeled, deveined and chopped
- ½ tablespoon balsamic vinegar
- 2 tablespoons mayonnaise
- ½ tablespoon lemon juice
- A pinch of salt and black pepper
- 2 ounces mozzarella, shredded
- 1 tablespoon parsley, chopped

Directions:
1. In your slow cooker, mix the cream cheese with the shrimp, heavy cream and the other ingredients, whisk, put the lid on and cook on Low for 2 hours.
2. Divide into bowls and serve as a dip.

Nutrition: calories 342, fat 4, fiber 3, carbs 7, protein 10

Squash Salsa
Preparation time: 10 minutes
Cooking time: 3 hours
Servings: 2
Ingredients:
- 1 cup butternut squash, peeled and cubed
- 1 cup cherry tomatoes, cubed
- 1 cup avocado, peeled, pitted and cubed
- ½ tablespoon balsamic vinegar
- ½ tablespoon lemon juice
- 1 tablespoon lemon zest, grated
- ¼ cup veggie stock
- 1 tablespoon chives, chopped
- A pinch of rosemary, dried
- A pinch of sage, dried
- A pinch of salt and black pepper

Directions:
1. In your slow cooker, mix the squash with the tomatoes, avocado and the other ingredients, toss, put the lid on and cook on Low for 3 hours.
2. Divide into bowls and serve as a snack.

Nutrition: calories 182, fat 5, fiber 7, carbs 12, protein 5

Flavory Beans Spread

Preparation time: 10 minutes
Cooking time: 6 hours
Servings: 2
Ingredients:
- 1 cup canned black beans, drained
- 2 tablespoons tahini paste
- ½ teaspoon balsamic vinegar
- ¼ cup veggie stock
- ½ tablespoon olive oil

Directions:
1. In your slow cooker, mix the beans with the tahini paste and the other ingredients, toss, put the lid on and cook on Low for 6 hours.
2. Transfer to your food processor, blend well, divide into bowls and serve.

Nutrition: calories 221, fat 6, fiber 5, carbs 19, protein 3

Rice Bowls

Preparation time: 10 minutes
Cooking time: 6 hours
Servings: 2
Ingredients:
- ½ cup wild rice
- 1 red onion, sliced
- ½ cup brown rice
- 2 cups veggie stock
- ½ cup baby spinach
- ½ cup cherry tomatoes, halved
- 2 tablespoons pine nuts, toasted
- 1 tablespoon raisins
- 1 tablespoon chives, chopped
- 1 tablespoon dill, chopped
- ½ tablespoon olive oil
- A pinch of salt and black pepper

Directions:
1. In your slow cooker, mix the rice with the onion, stock and the other ingredients, toss, put the lid on and cook on Low for 6 hours.
2. Divide in to bowls and serve as a snack.

Nutrition: calories 301, fat 6, fiber 6, carbs 12, protein 3

Cauliflower Spread

Preparation time: 10 minutes
Cooking time: 7 hours
Servings: 2
Ingredients:
- 1 cup cauliflower florets
- 1 tablespoon mayonnaise
- ½ cup heavy cream
- 1 tablespoon lemon juice
- ½ teaspoon garlic powder
- ¼ teaspoon smoked paprika
- ¼ teaspoon mustard powder
- A pinch of salt and black pepper

Directions:
1. In your slow cooker, combine the cauliflower with the cream, mayonnaise and the other ingredients, toss, put the lid on and cook on Low for 7 hours.
2. Transfer to a blender, pulse well, into bowls and serve as a spread.

Nutrition: calories 152, fat 13.8, fiber 1.5, carbs 6.2, protein 2

Flavory Mushroom Dip

Preparation time: 10 minutes
Cooking time: 5 hours
Servings: 2
Ingredients:
- 4 ounces white mushrooms, chopped
- 1 eggplant, cubed
- ½ cup heavy cream
- ½ tablespoon tahini paste
- 2 garlic cloves, minced
- A pinch of salt and black pepper
- 1 tablespoon balsamic vinegar
- ½ tablespoon basil, chopped
- ½ tablespoon oregano, chopped

Directions:
1. In your slow cooker, mix the mushrooms with the eggplant, cream and the other ingredients, toss, put the lid on and cook on High for 5 hours.
2. Divide the mushroom mix into bowls and serve as a dip.

Nutrition: calories 261, fat 7, fiber 6, carbs 10, protein 6

Chickpeas Spread

Preparation time: 10 minutes
Cooking time: 8 hours
Servings: 2
Ingredients:
- ½ cup chickpeas, dried
- 1 tablespoons olive oil
- 1 tablespoon lemon juice
- 1 cup veggie stock
- 1 tablespoon tahini
- A pinch of salt and black pepper
- 1 garlic clove, minced
- ½ tablespoon chives, chopped

Directions:
1. In your slow cooker, combine the chickpeas with the stock, salt, pepper and the garlic, stir, put the lid on and cook on Low for 8 hours.
2. Drain chickpeas, transfer them to a blender, add the rest of the ingredients, pulse well, divide into bowls and serve as a party spread.

Nutrition: calories 211, fat 6, fiber 7, carbs 8, protein 4

Spinach Dip

Preparation time: 10 minutes
Cooking time: 1 hour
Servings: 2
Ingredients:
- 2 tablespoons heavy cream
- ½ cup Greek yogurt
- ½ pound baby spinach
- 2 garlic cloves, minced
- Salt and black pepper to the taste

Directions:
1. In your slow cooker, mix the spinach with the cream and the other ingredients, toss, put the lid on and cook on High for 1 hour.
2. Blend using an immersion blender, divide into bowls and serve as a party dip.

Nutrition: calories 221, fat 5, fiber 7, carbs 12, protein 5

Potato Salad

Preparation time: 10 minutes
Cooking time: 8 hours
Servings: 2
Ingredients:
- 1 red onion, sliced
- 1 pound gold potatoes, peeled and roughly cubed
- 2 tablespoons balsamic vinegar
- ½ cup heavy cream
- 1 tablespoons mustard
- A pinch of salt and black pepper
- 1 tablespoon dill, chopped
- ½ cup celery, chopped

Directions:
1. In your slow cooker, mix the potatoes with the cream, mustard and the other ingredients, toss, put the lid on and cook on Low for 8 hours.
2. Divide salad into bowls, and serve as an appetizer.

Nutrition: calories 251, fat 6, fiber 7, carbs 8, protein 7

Stuffed Peppers

Preparation time: 10 minutes
Cooking time: 4 hours
Servings: 2
Ingredients:
- 1 red onion, chopped
- 1 teaspoons olive oil
- ½ teaspoon sweet paprika
- ½ tablespoon chili powder
- 1 garlic clove, minced
- 1 cup white rice, cooked
- ½ cup corn
- A pinch of salt and black pepper
- 2 colored bell peppers, tops and insides scooped out
- ½ cup tomato sauce

Directions:
1. In a bowl, mix the onion with the oil, paprika and the other ingredients except the peppers and tomato sauce, stir well and stuff the peppers the with this mix.
2. Put the peppers in the slow cooker, add the sauce, put the lid on and cook on Low for 4 hours.
3. Transfer the peppers on a platter and serve as an appetizer.

Nutrition: calories 253, fat 5, fiber 4, carbs 12, protein 3

Corn Dip

Preparation time: 10 minutes
Cooking time: 2 hours
Servings: 2
Ingredients:
- 1 cup corn
- 1 tablespoon chives, chopped
- ½ cup heavy cream
- 2 ounces cream cheese, cubed
- ¼ teaspoon chili powder

Directions:
1. In your slow cooker, mix the corn with the chives and the other ingredients, whisk, put the lid on and cook on Low for 2 hours.
2. Divide into bowls and serve as a dip.

Nutrition: calories 272, fat 5, fiber 10, carbs 12, protein 4

Tomato and Mushroom

Preparation time: 10 minutes
Cooking time: 4 hours
Servings: 2
Ingredients:
- 1 cup cherry tomatoes, halved
- 1 cup mushrooms, sliced
- 1 small yellow onion, chopped
- 1 garlic clove, minced
- 12 ounces tomato sauce
- ¼ cup cream cheese, cubed
- 1 tablespoon chives, chopped
- Salt and black pepper to the taste

Directions:
1. In your slow cooker, mix the tomatoes with the mushrooms and the other ingredients, toss, put the lid on and cook on Low for 4 hours.
2. Divide into bowls and serve as a party salsa

Nutrition: calories 285, fat 4, fiber 7, carbs 12, protein 4

Salsa Beans Dip

Preparation time: 10 minutes
Cooking time: 1 hour
Servings: 2
Ingredients:
- ¼ cup salsa
- 1 cup canned red kidney beans, drained and rinsed
- ½ cup mozzarella, shredded
- 1 tablespoon green onions, chopped

Directions:
1. In your slow cooker, mix the salsa with the beans and the other ingredients, toss, put the lid on cook on High for 1 hour.
2. Divide into bowls and serve as a party dip

Nutrition: calories 302, fat 5, fiber 10, carbs 16, protein 6

Pineapple and Tofu

Preparation time: 10 minutes
Cooking time: 6 hours
Servings: 2
Ingredients:
- ½ cup firm tofu, cubed
- 1 cup pineapple, peeled and cubed
- 1 cup cherry tomatoes, halved
- ½ tablespoons sesame oil
- 1 tablespoon soy sauce
- ½ cup pineapple juice
- ½ tablespoon ginger, grated
- 1 garlic clove, minced

Directions:
1. In your slow cooker, mix the tofu with the pineapple and the other ingredients, toss, put the lid on and cook on Low for 6 hours.
2. Divide into bowls and serve as an appetizer.

Nutrition: calories 201, fat 5, fiber 7, carbs 15, protein 4

Chickpeas Salsa

Preparation time: 10 minutes
Cooking time: 6 hours
Servings: 2
Ingredients:
- 1 cup canned chickpeas, drained
- 1 cup veggie stock
- ½ cup black olives, pitted and halved
- 1 small yellow onion, chopped
- ¼ tablespoon ginger, grated
- 4 garlic cloves, minced
- ¼ tablespoons coriander, ground
- ¼ tablespoons red chili powder
- ¼ tablespoons garam masala
- 1 tablespoon lemon juice

Directions:
1. In your slow cooker, mix the chickpeas with the stock, olives and the other ingredients, toss, put the lid on and cook on Low for 6 hours.
2. Divide into bowls and serve as an appetizer.

Nutrition: calories 355, fat 5, fiber 14, carbs 16, protein 11

Mushroom Spread

Preparation time: 10 minutes
Cooking time: 4 hours
Servings: 2
Ingredients:
- 1 pound mushrooms, sliced
- 3 garlic cloves, minced
- 1 cup heavy cream
- 2 teaspoons smoked paprika
- Salt and black pepper to the taste
- 2 tablespoons parsley, chopped

Directions:
1. In your slow cooker, mix the mushrooms with the garlic and the other ingredients, whisk, put the lid on and cook on Low for 4 hours.
2. Whisk, divide into bowls and serve as a party spread.

Nutrition: calories 300, fat 6, fiber 12, carbs 16, protein 6

Bulgur and Beans Salsa

Preparation time: 10 minutes
Cooking time: 8 hours
Servings: 2
Ingredients:
- 1 cup veggie stock
- ½ cup bulgur
- 1 small yellow onion, chopped
- 1 red bell pepper, chopped
- 1 garlic clove, minced
- 5 ounces canned kidney beans, drained
- ½ cup salsa
- 1 tablespoon chili powder
- ¼ teaspoon oregano, dried
- Salt and black pepper to the taste

Directions:
1. In your slow cooker, mix the bulgur with the stock and the other ingredients, toss, put the lid on and cook on Low for 8 hours.
2. Divide into bowls and serve cold as an appetizer.

Nutrition: calories 351, fat 4, fiber 6, carbs 12, protein 4

Appetizing Beets Salad

Preparation time: 10 minutes
Cooking time: 6 hours
Servings: 2
Ingredients:
- 2 cups beets, cubed
- ¼ cup carrots, grated
- 2 ounces tempeh, rinsed and cubed
- 1 cup cherry tomatoes, halved
- ¼ cup veggie stock
- 3 ounces canned black beans, drained
- Salt and black pepper to the taste
- ½ teaspoon nutmeg, ground
- ½ teaspoon sweet paprika
- ½ cup parsley, chopped

Directions:
1. In your slow cooker, mix the beets with the carrots, tempeh and the other ingredients, toss, put the lid on and cook on Low for 6 hours.
2. Divide into bowls and serve cold as an appetizer.

Nutrition: calories 300, fat 6, fiber 6, carbs 16, protein 6

Lentils Salsa
Preparation time: 10 minutes
Cooking time: 3 hours
Servings: 2
Ingredients:
- 1 cup canned lentils, drained
- 1 cup mild salsa
- 3 ounces tomato paste
- 2 tablespoons balsamic vinegar
- 1 small sweet onion, chopped
- 1 garlic clove, minced
- ½ tablespoon sugar
- A pinch of red pepper flakes
- A pinch of salt and black pepper
- 1 tablespoon chives, chopped

Directions:
1. In your slow cooker, mix the lentils with the salsa and the other ingredients, toss, put the lid on and cook on High for 3 hours.
2. Divide into bowls and serve as a party salsa.

Nutrition: calories 260, fat 3, fiber 4, carbs 6, protein 7

Tacos
Preparation time: 10 minutes
Cooking time: 4 hours
Servings: 2
Ingredients:
- 13 ounces canned pinto beans, drained
- ¼ cup chili sauce
- 2 ounces chipotle pepper in adobo sauce, chopped
- ½ tablespoon cocoa powder
- ¼ teaspoon cinnamon powder
- 4 taco shells

Directions:
1. In your slow cooker, mix the beans with the chili sauce and the other ingredients except the taco shells, toss, put the lid on and cook on Low for 4 hours.
2. Divide the mix into the taco shells and serve them as an appetizer.

Nutrition: calories 352, fat 3, fiber 6, carbs 12, protein 10

Appetizing Almond Bowls
Preparation time: 10 minutes
Cooking time: 4 hours
Servings: 2
Ingredients:
- 1 tablespoon cinnamon powder
- 1 cup sugar
- 2 cups almonds
- ½ cup water
- ½ teaspoons vanilla extract

Directions:
1. In your slow cooker, mix the almonds with the cinnamon and the other ingredients, toss, put the lid on and cook on Low for 4 hours.
2. Divide into bowls and serve as a snack.

Nutrition: calories 260, fat 3, fiber 4, carbs 12, protein 8

Eggplant Salsa
Preparation time: 10 minutes
Cooking time: 7 hours
Servings: 2
Ingredients:
- 2 cups eggplant, chopped
- 1 teaspoon capers, drained
- 1 cup black olives, pitted and halved
- ½ cup mild salsa
- 2 garlic cloves, minced
- ½ tablespoon basil, chopped
- 1 teaspoon balsamic vinegar
- A pinch of salt and black pepper

Directions:
1. In your slow cooker, mix the eggplant with the capers and the other ingredients, toss, put the lid on and cook on Low for 7 hours.
2. Divide into bowls and serve as an appetizer.

Nutrition: calories 170, fat 3, fiber 5, carbs 10, protein 5

Appetizing Almond Spread
Preparation time: 10 minutes
Cooking time: 8 hours
Servings: 2
Ingredients:
- ¼ cup almonds
- 1 cup heavy cream
- ½ teaspoon nutritional yeast flakes
- A pinch of salt and black pepper

Directions:
1. In your slow cooker, mix the almonds with the cream and the other ingredients, toss, put the lid on and cook on Low for 8 hours.
2. Transfer to a blender, pulse well, divide into bowls and serve.

Nutrition: calories 270, fat 4, fiber 4, carbs 8, protein 10

Onion Dip
Preparation time: 10 minutes
Cooking time: 8 hours
Servings: 2
Ingredients:
- 2 cups yellow onions, chopped
- A pinch of salt and black pepper
- 1 tablespoon olive oil
- ½ cup heavy cream
- 2 tablespoons mayonnaise

Directions:
1. In your slow cooker, mix the onions with the cream and the other ingredients, whisk, put the lid on and cook on Low for 8 hours.
2. Divide into bowls and serve as a party dip.

Nutrition: calories 240, fat 4, fiber 4, carbs 9, protein 7

Yummy Nuts Bowls

Preparation time: 10 minutes
Cooking time: 2 hours
Servings: 2
Ingredients:
- 2 tablespoons almonds, toasted
- 2 tablespoons pecans, halved and toasted
- 2 tablespoons hazelnuts, toasted and peeled
- 2 tablespoons sugar
- ½ cup coconut cream
- 2 tablespoons butter, melted
- A pinch of cinnamon powder
- A pinch of cayenne pepper

Directions:
1. In your slow cooker, mix the nuts with the sugar and the other ingredients, toss, put the lid on, cook on Low for 2 hours, divide into bowls and serve as a snack.

Nutrition: calories 125, fat 3, fiber 2, carbs 5, protein 5

Eggplant Salad

Preparation time: 10 minutes
Cooking time: 8 hours
Servings: 2
Ingredients:
- 2 eggplants, cubed
- 2 scallions, chopped
- 1 red bell pepper, chopped
- ½ teaspoon coriander, ground
- ½ cup mild salsa
- 1 teaspoon cumin, ground
- A pinch of salt and black pepper
- 1 tablespoon lemon juice

Directions:
1. In your slow cooker, combine the eggplants with the scallions, pepper and the other ingredients, toss, put the lid on, cook on Low for 8 hours, divide into bowls and serve cold as an appetizer salad.

Nutrition: calories 203, fat 2, fiber 3, carbs 7, protein 8

Yummy Lentils Dip

Preparation time: 10 minutes
Cooking time: 6 hours
Servings: 2
Ingredients:
- 2 carrots, peeled and grated
- 2 garlic cloves, minced
- A pinch of cayenne pepper
- 2 tablespoons tahini paste
- ¼ cup lemon juice
- 1 cup canned lentils, drained and rinsed
- A pinch of sea salt and black pepper
- ½ tablespoon rosemary, chopped

Directions:
1. In your slow cooker, mix the lentils with the carrots, garlic and the other ingredients, toss, put the lid on and cook on Low for 6 hours.
2. Transfer to a blender, pulse well, divide into bowls and serve.

Nutrition: calories 200, fat 2, fiber 5, carbs 8, protein 6

Turkey Meatballs

Preparation time: 10 minutes
Cooking time: 7 hours
Servings: 2
Ingredients:
- 1 pound turkey breast, skinless, boneless and ground
- 1 egg, whisked
- 6 ounces canned tomato puree
- 2 tablespoons parsley, chopped
- 1 tablespoon oregano, chopped
- 1 garlic clove, minced
- 1 small yellow onion, chopped
- Salt and black pepper to the taste

Directions:
1. In a bowl, mix the meat with the egg, parsley and the other ingredients except the tomato puree, stir well and shape medium meatballs out of it.
2. Put the meatballs in the slow cooker, add the tomato puree, put the lid on and cook on Low for 7 hours.
3. Arrange the meatballs on a platter and serve as an appetizer.

Nutrition: calories 170, fat 5, fiber 3, carbs 10, protein 7

Easy Stuffed Mushrooms

Preparation time: 10 minutes
Cooking time: 3 hours
Servings: 2
Ingredients:
- ¼ pound chorizo, chopped
- 4 Portobello mushroom caps
- 1 red onion, chopped
- Salt and black pepper to the taste
- ¼ teaspoon garlic powder
- ¼ cup tomato sauce

Directions:
1. In a bowl, mix the chorizo with the onion, garlic powder, salt and pepper, stir and stuff the mushroom caps with this mix.
2. Put the mushroom caps in the slow cooker, add the tomato sauce, put the lid on and cook on High for 3 hours.
3. Arrange the Easy Stuffed Mushrooms on a platter and serve.

Nutrition: calories 170, fat 2, fiber 3, carbs 8, protein 3

Paprika Cod Sticks
Preparation time: 10 minutes
Cooking time: 2 hours
Servings: 2
Ingredients:
- 1 eggs whisked
- ½ pound cod fillets, cut into medium strips
- ½ cup almond flour
- ½ teaspoon cumin, ground
- ½ teaspoon coriander, ground
- ½ teaspoon turmeric powder
- A pinch of salt and black pepper
- ¼ teaspoon sweet paprika
- Cooking spray

Directions:
1. In a bowl, mix the flour with cumin, coriander and the other ingredients except the fish, eggs and cooking spray.
2. Put the egg in another bowl and whisk it.
3. Dip the fish sticks in the egg and then dredge them in the flour mix.
4. Grease the slow cooker with cooking spray, add fish sticks, put the lid on, cook on High for 2 hours, arrange on a platter and serve.

Nutrition: calories 200, fat 2, fiber 4, carbs 13, protein 12

Nuts Snack
Preparation time: 10 minutes
Cooking time: 2 hours
Servings: 2
Ingredients:
- ½ pound macadamia nuts
- 1 tablespoon avocado oil
- ¼ cup water
- ½ tablespoon chili powder
- ½ teaspoon oregano, dried
- ½ teaspoon onion powder

Directions:
1. In your slow cooker, mix the macadamia nuts with the oil and the other ingredients, toss, put the lid on, cook on Low for 2 hours, divide into bowls and serve as a snack.

Nutrition: calories 108, fat 3, fiber 2, carbs 9, protein 2

Salmon Bites
Preparation time: 10 minutes
Cooking time: 2 hours
Servings: 2
Ingredients:
- 1 pound salmon fillets, boneless
- ¼ cup chili sauce
- A pinch of salt and black pepper
- ½ teaspoon turmeric powder
- 2 tablespoons grape jelly

Directions:
1. In your slow cooker, mix the salmon with the chili sauce and the other ingredients, toss gently, put the lid on and cook on High for 2 hours.
2. Serve as an appetizer.

Nutrition: calories 200, fat 6, fiber 3, carbs 15, protein 12

Spinach and Nuts Dip
Preparation time: 10 minutes
Cooking time: 2 hours
Servings: 2
Ingredients:
- ½ cup heavy cream
- ½ cup walnuts, chopped
- 1 cup baby spinach
- 1 garlic clove, chopped
- 1 tablespoon mayonnaise
- Salt and black pepper to the taste

Directions:
1. In your slow cooker, mix the spinach with the walnuts and the other ingredients, toss, put the lid on and cook on High for 2 hours.
2. Blend using an immersion blender, divide into bowls and serve as a party dip.

Nutrition: calories 260, fat 4, fiber 2, carbs 12, protein 5

Curry Pork Meatballs
Preparation time: 10 minutes
Cooking time: 4 hours
Servings: 2
Ingredients:
- ½ pound pork stew meat, ground
- 1 red onion, chopped
- 1 egg, whisked
- Salt and black pepper to the taste
- 1 tablespoon cilantro, chopped
- 5 ounces coconut milk
- ¼ tablespoon green curry paste

Directions:
1. In a bowl, mix the meat with the onion and the other ingredients except the coconut milk, stir well and shape medium meatballs out of this mix.
2. Put the meatballs in your slow cooker, add the coconut milk, put the lid on and cook on High for 4 hours.
3. Arrange the meatballs on a platter and serve them as an appetizer

Nutrition: calories 225, fat 6, fiber 2, carbs 8, protein 4

Calamari Rings
Preparation time: 10 minutes
Cooking time: 6 hours
Servings: 2
Ingredients:
- ½ pound calamari rings
- 1 tablespoon balsamic vinegar
- ½ tablespoon soy sauce
- 1 tablespoon sugar
- 1 cup veggie stock
- ½ teaspoon turmeric powder
- ½ teaspoon sweet paprika
- ½ cup chicken stock

Directions:
1. In your slow cooker, mix the calamari rings with the vinegar, soy sauce and the other ingredients, toss, put the lid on and cook on High for 6 hours.
2. Divide into bowls and serve right away as an appetizer.

Nutrition: calories 230, fat 2, fiber 4, carbs 7, protein 5

Shrimp Salad

Preparation time: 10 minutes
Cooking time: 2 hours
Servings: 2
Ingredients:
- ½ pound shrimp, peeled and deveined
- 1 green bell pepper, chopped
- ½ cup kalamata olives, pitted and halved
- 4 spring onions, chopped
- 1 red bell pepper, chopped
- ½ cup mild salsa
- 1 tablespoon olive oil
- 1 garlic clove, minced
- ¼ teaspoon oregano, dried
- ¼ teaspoon basil, dried
- Salt and black pepper to the taste
- A pinch of red pepper, crushed
- 1 tablespoon parsley, chopped

Directions:
1. In your slow cooker, mix the shrimp with the peppers and the other ingredients, toss, put the lid on and cook on High for 2 hours.
2. Divide into bowls and serve as an appetizer.

Nutrition: calories 240, fat 2, fiber 5, carbs 7, protein 2

Easy Chicken Salad

Preparation time: 10 minutes
Cooking time: 6 hours
Servings: 2
Ingredients:
- 2 chicken breasts, skinless, boneless and cubed
- ½ cup mild salsa
- ½ tablespoon olive oil
- 1 red onion, chopped
- ½ cup mushrooms, sliced
- ½ cup kalamata olives, pitted and halved
- ½ cup cherry tomatoes, halved
- 1 chili pepper, chopped
- 2 ounces baby spinach
- 1 teaspoon oregano, chopped
- ½ tablespoon lemon juice
- ½ cup veggie stock
- A pinch of salt and black pepper

Directions:
1. In your slow cooker, mix the chicken with the salsa, oil and the other ingredients except the spinach, toss, put the lid on and cook on High for 5 hours.
2. Add the spinach, cook on High for 1 more hour, divide into bowls and serve as an appetizer.

Nutrition: calories 245, fat 4, fiber 3, carbs 10, protein 6

Apple and Carrot Dip

Preparation time: 10 minutes
Cooking time: 6 hours
Servings: 2
Ingredients:
- 2 cups apples, peeled, cored and chopped
- 1 cup carrots, peeled and grated
- ¼ teaspoon cloves, ground
- ¼ teaspoon ginger powder
- 1 tablespoon lemon juice
- ½ tablespoon lemon zest, grated
- ½ cup coconut cream
- ¼ teaspoon nutmeg, ground

Directions:
1. In your slow cooker, mix the apples with the carrots, cloves and the other ingredients, toss, put the lid on and cook on Low for 6 hours.
2. Bend using an immersion blender, divide into bowls and serve.

Nutrition: calories 212, fat 4, fiber 6, carbs 12, protein 3

Easy Sweet Potato Dip

Preparation time: 10 minutes
Cooking time: 4 hours
Servings: 2
Ingredients:
- 2 sweet potatoes, peeled and cubed
- ½ cup coconut cream
- ½ teaspoon turmeric powder
- ½ teaspoon garam masala
- 2 garlic cloves, minced
- ½ cup veggie stock
- 1 cup basil leaves
- 2 tablespoons olive oil
- 1 tablespoon lemon juice
- A pinch of salt and black pepper

Directions:
1. In your slow cooker, mix the sweet potatoes with the cream, turmeric and the other ingredients, toss, put the lid on and cook on High for 4 hours.
2. Blend using an immersion blender, divide into bowls and serve as a party dip.

Nutrition: calories 253, fat 5, fiber 6, carbs 13, protein 4

Spinach, Walnuts and Calamari Salad

Preparation time: 10 minutes
Cooking time: 4 hours and 30 minutes
Servings: 2
Ingredients:
- 2 cups baby spinach
- ½ cup walnuts, chopped
- ½ cup mild salsa
- 1 cup calamari rings
- ½ cup kalamata olives, pitted and halved
- ½ teaspoons thyme, chopped
- 2 garlic cloves, minced
- 1 cup tomatoes, cubed
- A pinch of salt and black pepper
- ¼ cup veggie stock

Directions:
1. In your slow cooker, mix the salsa with the calamari rings and the other ingredients except the spinach, toss, put the lid on and cook on High for 4 hours.
2. Add the spinach, toss, put the lid on, cook on High for 30 minutes more, divide into bowls and serve.

Nutrition: calories 160, fat 1, fiber 4, carbs 18, protein 4

Delightful Chicken Meatballs
Preparation time: 10 minutes
Cooking time: 7 hours
Servings: 2
Ingredients:
- A pinch of red pepper flakes, crushed
- ½ pound chicken breast, skinless, boneless, ground
- 1 egg, whisked
- ½ cup salsa Verde
- 1 teaspoon oregano, dried
- ½ teaspoon chili powder
- ½ teaspoon rosemary, dried
- 1 tablespoon parsley, chopped
- A pinch of salt and black pepper

Directions:
1. In a bowl, mix the chicken with the egg and the other ingredients except the salsa, stir well and shape medium meatballs out of this mix.
2. Put the meatballs in the slow cooker, add the salsa Verde, toss gently, put the lid on and cook on Low for 7 hours.
3. Arrange the meatballs on a platter and serve.

Nutrition: calories 201, fat 4, fiber 5, carbs 8, protein 2

Cinnamon Pecans Snack
Preparation time: 10 minutes
Cooking time: 3 hours
Servings: 2
Ingredients:
- ½ tablespoon cinnamon powder
- ¼ cup water
- ½ tablespoon avocado oil
- ½ teaspoon chili powder
- 2 cups pecans

Directions:
1. In your slow cooker, mix the pecans with the cinnamon and the other ingredients, toss, put the lid on and cook on Low for 3 hours.
2. Divide the pecans into bowls and serve as a snack.

Nutrition: calories 172, fat 3, fiber 5, carbs 8, protein 2

Almonds and Shrimp Bowls
Preparation time: 10 minutes
Cooking time: 2 hours
Servings: 2
Ingredients:
- 1 cup almonds
- 1 pound shrimp, peeled and deveined
- ½ cup kalamata olives, pitted and halved
- ½ cup black olives, pitted and halved
- ½ cup mild salsa
- ½ tablespoon Cajun seasoning

Directions:
1. In your slow cooker, mix the shrimp with the almonds, olives and the other ingredients, toss, put the lid on and cook on High for 2 hours.
2. Divide between small plates and serve as an appetizer.

Nutrition: calories 100, fat 2, fiber 3, carbs 7, protein 3

Broccoli Dip
Preparation time: 10 minutes
Cooking time: 2 hours
Servings: 2
Ingredients:
- 1 green chili pepper, minced
- 2 tablespoons heavy cream
- 1 cup broccoli florets
- 1 tablespoon mayonnaise
- 2 tablespoons cream cheese, cubed
- A pinch of salt and black pepper
- 1 tablespoon chives, chopped

Directions:
1. In your slow cooker, mix the broccoli with the chili pepper, mayo and the other ingredients, toss, put the lid on and cook on Low for 2 hours.
2. Blend using an immersion blender, divide into bowls and serve as a party dip.

Nutrition: calories 202, fat 3, fiber 3, carbs 7, protein 6

WalYummy Nuts Bowls
Preparation time: 10 minutes
Cooking time: 2 hours
Servings: 2
Ingredients:
- Cooking spray
- 1 cup walnuts, chopped
- 2 tablespoons balsamic vinegar
- 1 tablespoon smoked paprika
- ½ tablespoon lemon zest, grated
- ½ tablespoons olive oil
- 1 teaspoon rosemary, dried

Directions:
1. Grease your slow cooker with the cooking spray, add walnuts and the other ingredients inside, toss, put the lid on and cook on Low for 2 hours.
2. Divide into bowls and serve them as a snack.

Nutrition: calories 100, fat 2, fiber 2, carbs 3, protein 2

Cauliflower Bites
Preparation time: 10 minutes
Cooking time: 4 hours
Servings: 2
Ingredients:
- 2 cups cauliflower florets
- 1 tablespoon Italian seasoning
- 1 tablespoon sweet paprika
- 2 tablespoons tomato sauce
- 1 teaspoon sweet paprika
- 1 tablespoon olive oil
- ¼ cup veggie stock

Directions:
1. In your slow cooker, mix the cauliflower florets with the Italian seasoning and the other ingredients, toss, put the lid on and cook on Low for 4 hours.
2. Divide into bowls and serve as a snack.

Nutrition: calories 251, fat 4, fiber 6, carbs 7, protein 3

Appetizing Beef Dip

Preparation time: 10 minutes
Cooking time: 4 hours
Servings: 2
Ingredients:
- 1 pound beef meat, ground
- 1 carrot, peeled and grated
- 2 spring onions, chopped
- 1 tablespoon sriracha sauce
- 3 tablespoons beef stock
- 1 teaspoon hot sauce
- 3 ounces heavy cream

Directions:
1. In your slow cooker, mix the beef meat with the stock, hot sauce and the other ingredients, whisk, put the lid on and cook on Low for 4 hours.
2. Divide the mix into bowls and serve as a party dip.

Nutrition: calories 301, fat 3, fiber 6, carbs 11, protein 5

Zucchini Spread

Preparation time: 10 minutes
Cooking time: 6 hours
Servings: 2
Ingredients:
- 1 tablespoon walnuts, chopped
- 2 zucchinis, grated
- 1 cup heavy cream
- 1 teaspoon balsamic vinegar
- 1 tablespoon tahini paste
- 1 tablespoon chives, chopped

Directions:
3. In your slow cooker, combine the zucchinis with the cream, walnuts and the other ingredients, whisk, put the lid on and cook on Low for 6 hours.
4. Blend using an immersion blender, divide into bowls and serve as a party spread.

Nutrition: calories 221, fat 6, fiber 5, carbs 9, protein 3

Appetizing Beef Dip

Preparation time: 10 minutes
Cooking time: 7 hours and 10 minutes
Servings: 2
Ingredients:
- ½ pounds beef, minced
- 3 spring onions, minced
- 1 tablespoon olive oil
- 1 cup mild salsa
- 2 ounces white mushrooms, chopped
- ¼ cup pine nuts, toasted
- 2 garlic cloves, minced
- 1 tablespoon hives, chopped
- ½ teaspoon coriander, ground
- ½ teaspoon rosemary, dried
- A pinch of salt and black pepper

Directions:
3. Heat up a pan with the oil over medium heat, add the spring onions, mushrooms, garlic and the meat, stir, brown for 10 minutes and transfer to your slow cooker.
4. Add the rest of the ingredients, toss, put the lid on and cook on Low for 7 hours.
5. Divide the dip into bowls and serve.

Nutrition: calories 361, fat 6, fiber 6, carbs 12, protein 3

Eggplant Salsa

Preparation time: 10 minutes
Cooking time: 4 hours
Servings: 2
Ingredients:
- 1 cup cherry tomatoes, cubed
- 2 cups eggplant, cubed
- 1 tablespoon capers, drained
- 1 tablespoon black olives, pitted and sliced
- 1 tablespoon lemon juice
- 1 tablespoon olive oil
- ¼ cup mild salsa
- 2 teaspoons balsamic vinegar
- 1 tablespoon basil, chopped
- 1 tablespoon chives, chopped
- Salt and black pepper to the taste

Directions:
1. In your slow cooker, mix the eggplant with the cherry tomatoes, capers, olives and the other ingredients, toss, put the lid on and cook on High for 4 hours.
2. Divide salsa into small bowls and serve.

Nutrition: calories 200, fat 6, fiber 5, carbs 9, protein 2

Appetizing Carrots Spread

Preparation time: 10 minutes
Cooking time: 7 hours
Servings: 4
Ingredients:
- 2 cups carrots, peeled and grated
- ½ cup heavy cream
- 1 teaspoon turmeric powder
- 1 teaspoon sweet paprika
- 1 cup coconut milk
- 1 teaspoon garlic powder
- ¼ teaspoon mustard powder
- A pinch of salt and black pepper

Directions:
1. In your slow cooker, mix the carrots with the cream, turmeric and the other ingredients, whisk, put the lid on and cook on Low for 7 hours.
2. Divide the mix into bowls and serve as a party spread.

Nutrition: calories 291, fat 7, fiber 4, carbs 14, protein 3

Cauliflower Dip

Preparation time: 10 minutes
Cooking time: 5 hours
Servings: 2
Ingredients:
- 1 cup cauliflower florets
- ½ cup heavy cream
- 1 tablespoon tahini paste
- ½ cup white mushrooms, chopped
- 2 garlic cloves, minced
- 2 tablespoons lemon juice
- 1 tablespoon basil, chopped
- 1 teaspoon rosemary, dried
- A pinch of salt and black pepper

Directions:
3. In your slow cooker, mix the cauliflower with the cream, tahini paste and the other ingredients, toss, put the lid on and cook on Low for 5 hours.
4. Transfer to a blender, pulse well, divide into bowls and serve as a party dip.

Nutrition: calories 301, fat 7, fiber 6, carbs 10, protein 6

Yummy Lentils Hummus

Preparation time: 10 minutes
Cooking time: 4 hours
Servings: 2
Ingredients:
- 1 cup chicken stock
- 1 cup canned lentils, drained
- 2 tablespoons tahini paste
- ¼ teaspoon onion powder
- ¼ cup heavy cream
- A pinch of salt and black pepper
- ¼ teaspoon turmeric powder
- 1 teaspoon lemon juice

Directions:
1. In your slow cooker, mix the lentils with the stock, onion powder, salt and pepper, toss, put the lid on and cook on High for 4 hours.
2. Drain the lentils, transfer to your blender, add the rest of the ingredients, pulse well, divide into bowls and serve.

Nutrition: calories 192, fat 7, fiber 7, carbs 12, protein 4

Spinach Dip

Preparation time: 10 minutes
Cooking time: 1 hour
Servings: 2
Ingredients:
- 1 cup coconut cream
- 10 ounces spinach, torn
- 2 spring onions, chopped
- 1 teaspoon rosemary, dried
- ½ teaspoon garam masala
- 1 garlic clove, minced
- A pinch of salt and black pepper

Directions:
3. In your slow cooker, mix the spinach with the cream, spring onions and the other ingredients, toss, put the lid on and cook on High for 1 hour.
4. Blend using an immersion blender, divide into bowls and serve as a party dip.

Nutrition: calories 241, fat 5, fiber 7, carbs 12, protein 5

Yummy Peppers Salsa

Preparation time: 10 minutes
Cooking time: 5 hours and 5 minutes
Servings: 2
Ingredients:
- 1 yellow onion, chopped
- 2 spring onions, chopped
- 2 teaspoons olive oil
- 1 teaspoon turmeric powder
- 1 red bell pepper, roughly cubed
- 1 green bell pepper, roughly cubed
- 1 orange bell pepper, roughly cubed
- 1 cup cherry tomatoes, halved
- 1 tablespoon chili powder
- 3 garlic cloves, minced
- ½ cup mild salsa
- 1 teaspoon oregano, dried
- A pinch of salt and black pepper

Directions:
4. Heat up a pan with the oil over medium-high heat, add the spring onions, onion and garlic, sauté for 5 minutes and transfer to the slow cooker.
5. Add the rest of the ingredients, toss, put the lid on and cook on Low for 5 hours.
6. Divide the mix into bowls and serve as a snack.

Nutrition: calories 221, fat 5, fiber 4, carbs 9, protein 3

Artichoke Dip

Preparation time: 10 minutes
Cooking time: 4 hours
Servings: 2
Ingredients:
- 1 cup canned artichoke hearts, drained and chopped
- 1 cup baby spinach
- 1 cup heavy cream
- 2 spring onions, chopped
- ½ teaspoon sweet paprika
- ½ teaspoon turmeric powder
- 2 garlic cloves, minced
- 1/3 cup mayonnaise
- 1 tablespoon lemon juice
- A pinch of salt and black pepper

Directions:
1. In your slow cooker, mix the artichoke hearts with the spinach, cream and the other ingredients, toss, put the lid on and cook on Low for 4 hours.
2. Divide into bowls and serve as a party dip.

Nutrition: calories 305, fat 14, fiber 4, carbs 9, protein 13

Yummy Mushroom Salsa
Preparation time: 10 minutes
Cooking time: 5 hours
Servings: 4
Ingredients:
- 2 cups white mushrooms, sliced
- 1 cup cherry tomatoes halved
- 1 cup spring onions, chopped
- ½ teaspoon chili powder
- ½ teaspoon rosemary, dried
- ½ teaspoon oregano, dried
- ½ cup black olives, pitted and sliced
- 3 garlic cloves, minced
- 1 cup mild salsa
- Salt and black pepper to the taste

Directions:
3. In your slow cooker, mix the mushrooms with the cherry tomatoes and the other ingredients, toss, put the lid on and cook on Low for 5 hours.
4. Divide into bowls and serve as a snack.

Nutrition: calories 205, fat 4, fiber 7, carbs 9, protein 3

Slow Cooker Poultry Recipes for 2

Chicken and Green Beans
Preparation time: 10 minutes
Cooking time: 6 hours and 10 minutes.
Servings: 2
Ingredients:
- 1 pound chicken thighs, boneless, skinless and cubed
- 1 teaspoon sweet paprika
- ½ teaspoon garam masala
- 1 cup green beans, trimmed and halved
- 1 red onion, chopped
- 2 tablespoons olive oil
- 4 garlic cloves, minced
- 1 cup chicken stock
- 1 tablespoon chives, chopped
- A pinch of salt and black pepper

Directions:
1. Heat up a pan with the oil over medium-high heat, add the chicken, onion and garlic, cook for 10 minutes and transfer to the slow cooker.
2. Add the rest of the ingredients, toss, put the lid on and cook on Low for 6 hours.
3. Divide everything into bowls and serve.

Nutrition: calories 263, fat 12, fiber 3, carbs 6, protein 14

Oregano Turkey and Tomatoes
Preparation time: 10 minutes
Cooking time: 7 hours
Servings: 4
Ingredients:
- 1 pound turkey breast, skinless, boneless and sliced
- 1 tablespoon oregano, chopped
- 1 cup chicken stock
- 1 cup cherry tomatoes, halved
- 1 teaspoon turmeric powder
- 2 tablespoons olive oil
- 1 cup scallions, chopped
- 1 teaspoon chili powder
- A pinch of salt and black pepper
- ½ cup tomato sauce

Directions:
1. In your slow cooker, mix the turkey with the oregano, stock and the other ingredients, toss, put the lid on and cook on Low for 7 hours.
2. Divide the mix between plates and serve.

Nutrition: calories 162, fat 8, fiber 2, carbs 5, protein 9

Mustard Chicken Mix
Preparation time: 10 minutes
Cooking time: 6 hours
Servings: 4
Ingredients:
- 1 tablespoon olive oil
- 1 pound chicken breast, skinless, boneless and roughly cubed
- 2 tablespoons mustard
- ¾ cup chicken stock
- 1 teaspoon sweet paprika
- 1 teaspoon rosemary, dried
- 1 tablespoon lemon juice
- A pinch of salt and black pepper
- 1 tablespoon chives, chopped

Directions:
1. In your slow cooker, mix the chicken with the oil, mustard and the other ingredients, toss, put the lid on and cook on Low for 6 hours.
2. Divide the mix into bowls and serve.

Nutrition: calories 200, fat 9, fiber 2, carbs 5, protein 10

Lemony Turkey and Spinach
Preparation time: 10 minutes
Cooking time: 7 hours
Servings: 4
Ingredients:
- 1 pound turkey breasts, skinless, boneless and roughly cubed
- 1 cup baby spinach
- Juice of ½ lemon
- 2 spring onions, chopped
- ½ teaspoon chili powder
- 1 cup chicken stock
- 1 tablespoon oregano, chopped
- A pinch of salt and black pepper
- 1 teaspoon garam masala

Directions:
1. In your slow cooker, mix the turkey with the lemon juice, spring onions and the other ingredients except the baby spinach, toss, put the lid on and cook on Low for 6 hours and 30 minutes.
2. Add the spinach, cook everything on Low for 30 minutes more, divide between plates and serve.

Nutrition: calories 258, fat 4.5, fiber 3, carbs 13.4, protein 40.1

Paprika Chicken and Artichokes
Preparation time: 10 minutes
Cooking time: 7 hours and 10 minutes
Servings: 2
Ingredients:
- 1 pound chicken breast, skinless, boneless and cut into strips
- 1 cup canned artichoke hearts, drained and halved
- 3 scallions, chopped
- 2 garlic cloves, minced
- 1 tablespoon olive oil
- 1 tablespoon sweet paprika
- 1 cup chicken stock
- ½ cup parsley, chopped

Directions:
1. Heat up a pan with the oil over medium-high heat, add the scallions, garlic and the chicken, brown for 10 minutes and transfer to the slow cooker.
2. Add the rest of the ingredients, toss, put the lid on and cook on Low for 7 hours.
3. Divide everything between plates and serve.

Nutrition: calories 350, fat 13.6, fiber 2.4, carbs 5.9, protein 50

Chicken Wings

Preparation time: 10 minutes
Cooking time: 6 hours
Servings: 2
Ingredients:
- 1 cup chicken stock
- 1 pound chicken wings
- ½ cup chives, chopped
- ½ teaspoon chili powder
- ½ teaspoon coriander, ground
- ½ teaspoon cumin, ground
- 1 teaspoon oregano, dried
- A pinch of salt and black pepper

Directions:
1. In your slow cooker, mix the chicken with the stock, chives and the other ingredients, toss, put the lid on and cook on Low for 6 hours.
2. Divide the mix between plates and serve with a side salad.

Nutrition: calories 220, fat 8, fiber 2, carbs 5, protein 11

Lime Chicken Mix

Preparation time: 10 minutes
Cooking time: 7 hours
Servings: 2
Ingredients:
- 1 pound chicken thighs, boneless and skinless
- 1 tablespoon olive oil
- Juice of 1 lime
- Zest of 1 lime, grated
- ½ cup tomato sauce
- 2 spring onions, chopped
- Salt and black pepper to the taste
- 1 tablespoon oregano, chopped

Directions:
1. In your slow cooker, mix the chicken with the oil, lime juice and the other ingredients, toss, put the lid on and cook on Low for 7 hours.
2. Divide the mix between plates and serve.

Nutrition: calories 192, fat 12, fiber 3, carbs 5, protein 12

Chicken and Olives

Preparation time: 10 minutes
Cooking time: 5 hours
Servings: 2
Ingredients:
- 1 pound chicken breasts, skinless, boneless and sliced
- 1 cup black olives, pitted and halved
- ½ cup chicken stock
- ½ cup tomato sauce
- 1 tablespoon lime juice
- 1 tablespoon lime zest, grated
- 1 teaspoon chili powder
- 2 spring onions, chopped
- 1 tablespoon chives, chopped

Directions:
1. In your slow cooker, mix the chicken with the olives, stock and the other ingredients except the chives, toss, put the lid on and cook on High for 5 hours.
2. Divide the mix into bowls, sprinkle the chives on top and serve.

Nutrition: calories 200, fat 7, fiber 1, carbs 5, protein 12

Turkey and Fennel Mix

Preparation time: 10 minutes
Cooking time: 7 hours and 10 minutes
Servings: 2
Ingredients:
- 1 pound turkey breast, skinless, boneless and cut into strips
- 1 fennel bulb, sliced
- 1 cup cherry tomatoes, halved
- ¼ cup chicken stock
- ½ cup tomato sauce
- ½ teaspoon hot paprika
- ½ teaspoon cumin, ground
- ½ teaspoon fennel seeds, crushed
- 1 tablespoon olive oil
- 1 red onion, chopped
- A pinch of salt and black pepper
- 1 tablespoon cilantro, chopped

Directions:
1. Heat up a pan with the oil over medium-high heat, add the meat, onion and fennel seeds, stir, brown for 10 minutes and transfer to the slow cooker.
2. Add the rest of the ingredients, toss, put the lid on, cook on Low for 7 hours, divide between plates and serve.

Nutrition: calories 231, fat 7, fiber 2, carbs 6, protein 12

Chicken with Tomatoes

Preparation time: 10 minutes
Cooking time: 5 hours and 10 minutes.
Servings: 2
Ingredients:
- 1 pound chicken breast, skinless, boneless and cubed
- 2 small eggplants, cubed
- 1 red onion, sliced
- 1 tablespoon olive oil
- ½ teaspoon cumin, ground
- ½ teaspoon sweet paprika
- ½ teaspoon red pepper flakes, crushed
- ½ cup canned tomatoes, crushed
- 1 cup chicken stock
- 1 teaspoon coriander, ground
- A pinch of salt and black pepper
- 1 tablespoon oregano, chopped

Directions:
1. Heat up a pan with the oil over medium-high heat, add the chicken, onion and pepper flakes, stir, brown for 10 minutes and transfer to your slow cooker.
2. Add the rest of the ingredients, toss, put the lid on and cook on High for 5 hours.
3. Divide everything between plates and serve.

Nutrition: calories 252, fat 12, fiber 4, carbs 7, protein 13

Chicken and Onions Mix
Preparation time: 10 minutes
Cooking time: 7 hours
Servings: 2
Ingredients:
- 1 pound chicken breasts, skinless, boneless and cubed
- 2 red onions, sliced
- ½ cup chicken stock
- ½ cup tomato passata
- 2 teaspoons olive oil
- A pinch of salt and black pepper
- 1 teaspoon black peppercorns, crushed
- 2 garlic cloves, minced
- 1 tablespoon chives, chopped

Directions:
1. Grease the slow cooker with the oil and mix the chicken with the onions, stock and the other ingredients inside.
2. Put the lid on, cook on Low for 7 hours, divide between plates and serve.

Nutrition: calories 221, fat 14, fiber 3, carbs 7, protein 14

Pesto Chicken
Preparation time: 10 minutes
Cooking time: 6 hours and 10 minutes
Servings: 2
Ingredients:
- 1 pound chicken breast, skinless, boneless and cut into strips
- 1 tablespoon basil pesto
- 1 tablespoon olive oil
- 4 scallions, chopped
- ½ cup kalamata olives, pitted and halved
- 1 cup chicken stock
- 1 tablespoon cilantro, chopped
- A pinch of salt and black pepper

Directions:
1. Heat up a pan with the oil over medium-high heat, add the scallions and the meat, brown for 10 minutes, transfer to the slow cooker and mix with the remaining ingredients.
2. Toss, put the lid on, cook on Low for 6 hours, divide the mix between plates and serve.

Nutrition: calories 263, fat 14, fiber 1, carbs 8, protein 12

Ginger Turkey Mix
Preparation time: 10 minutes
Cooking time: 6 hours
Servings: 2
Ingredients:
- 1 pound turkey breast, skinless, boneless and roughly cubed
- 1 tablespoon ginger, grated
- 2 teaspoons olive oil
- 1 cup tomato passata
- ½ cup chicken stock
- A pinch of salt and black pepper
- 1 teaspoon chili powder
- 2 garlic cloves, minced
- 1 tablespoon cilantro, chopped

Directions:
1. Grease the slow cooker with the oil and mix the turkey with the ginger and the other ingredients inside.
2. Put the lid on, cook on High for 6 hours, divide between plates and serve.

Nutrition: calories 263, fat 12, fiber 3, carbs 6, protein 14

Turkey and Plums
Preparation time: 10 minutes
Cooking time: 7 hours
Servings: 2
Ingredients:
- 1 pound turkey breast, skinless, boneless and sliced
- 1 cup plums, pitted and halved
- ½ cup chicken stock
- ½ teaspoon chili powder
- ½ teaspoon turmeric powder
- ½ teaspoon cumin, ground
- 1 tablespoon rosemary, chopped
- A pinch of salt and black pepper

Directions:
1. In your slow cooker, mix the turkey with the plums, stock and the other ingredients, toss, put the lid on and cook on Low for 7 hours.
2. Divide the mix between plates and serve right away.

Nutrition: calories 253, fat 13, fiber 2, carbs 7, protein 16

Creamy Turkey Mix
Preparation time: 10 minutes
Cooking time: 7 hours
Servings: 2
Ingredients:
- 1 pound turkey breast, skinless, boneless and cubed
- 1 teaspoon turmeric powder
- ½ teaspoon garam masala
- ½ cup heavy cream
- 1 red onion, chopped
- ½ cup chicken stock
- 4 garlic cloves, minced
- ¼ cup chives, chopped
- A pinch of salt and black pepper
- 1 tablespoon chives, chopped

Directions:
1. In your slow cooker, mix the turkey with turmeric, garam masala and the other ingredients except the cream, toss, put the lid on and cook on Low for 6 hours.
2. Add the cream, toss, put the lid on again, cook on Low for 1 more hour, divide everything between plates and serve.

Nutrition: calories 234, fat 14, fiber 4, carbs 7, protein 15

Chicken and Apples

Preparation time: 10 minutes
Cooking time: 7 hours
Servings: 2
Ingredients:
- 1 pound chicken breast, skinless, boneless and sliced
- 1 cup apples, cored and cubed
- 1 teaspoon olive oil
- 1 red onion, sliced
- 1 tablespoon oregano, chopped
- ½ teaspoon turmeric powder
- ½ teaspoon chili powder
- 1 cup chicken stock
- A pinch of salt and black pepper
- 1 tablespoon chives, chopped

Directions:
1. Grease the slow cooker with the oil, and mix the chicken with the apples, onion and the other ingredients inside.
2. Toss, put the lid on, cook on Low for 7 hours, divide the mix between plates and serve.

Nutrition: calories 263, fat 13, fiber 2, carbs 7, protein 15

Chicken and Endives

Preparation time: 5 minutes
Cooking time: 7 hours
Servings: 2
Ingredients:
- 1 pound chicken breasts, skinless, boneless and sliced
- 4 scallions, chopped
- 2 endives, shredded
- ½ cup tomatoes, cubed
- 1 cup chicken stock
- 1 tablespoon oregano, chopped
- A pinch of salt and black pepper

Directions:
1. In your slow cooker, combine the chicken slices with the scallions and the other ingredients except the endives and the oregano, toss, put the lid on and cook on Low for 6 hours.
2. Add the remaining ingredients, cook on Low for 1 more hour, divide everything between plates and serve.

Nutrition: calories 200, fat 13, fiber 2, carbs 5, protein 16

Basil Chicken

Preparation time: 5 minutes
Cooking time: 5 hours
Servings: 2
Ingredients:
- 1 pound chicken wings, halved
- 1 tablespoon olive oil
- 1 tablespoon honey
- 1 cup chicken stock
- A pinch of salt and black pepper
- 1 tablespoon basil, chopped
- ½ teaspoon cumin, ground

Directions:
1. In your slow cooker, mix the chicken wings with the oil, honey and the other ingredients, toss, put the lid on and cook on High for 5 hours.
2. Divide the mix between plates and serve with a side salad.

Nutrition: calories 200, fat 12, fiber 2, carbs 6, protein 15

Chicken and Broccoli

Preparation time: 10 minutes
Cooking time: 5 hours
Servings: 2
Ingredients:
- 1 pound chicken breast, skinless, boneless and sliced
- 1 cup broccoli florets
- ½ cup tomato sauce
- ½ cup chicken stock
- 1 tablespoon avocado oil
- 1 yellow onion, sliced
- 3 garlic cloves, minced
- A pinch of salt and black pepper
- 1 tablespoon cilantro, chopped

Directions:
1. In your slow cooker, mix the chicken with the broccoli, tomato sauce and the other ingredients, toss, put the lid on and cook on High for 5 hours.
2. Divide the mix between plates and serve hot.

Nutrition: calories 253, fat 14, fiber 2, carbs 7, protein 16

Flavorful Rosemary Chicken

Preparation time: 10 minutes
Cooking time: 7 hours
Servings: 2
Ingredients:
- 1 pound chicken thighs, boneless, skinless and sliced
- 1 tablespoon avocado oil
- 1 teaspoon cumin, ground
- 1 tablespoon rosemary, chopped
- 1 cup chicken stock
- A pinch of salt and black pepper
- 1 tablespoon chives, chopped

Directions:
1. In your slow cooker, mix the chicken with the oil, cumin and the other ingredients, toss, put the lid on and cook on Low for 7 hours.
2. Divide the mix between plates and serve.

Nutrition: calories 273, fat 13, fiber 3, carbs 7, protein 17

Chicken Curry

Preparation time: 10 minutes
Cooking time: 7 hours
Servings: 2
Ingredients:
- 1 pound chicken breast, skinless, boneless and cubed
- 1 tablespoon yellow curry paste
- 1 yellow onion, chopped
- 1 tablespoon olive oil
- 1 teaspoon basil, dried
- 1 teaspoon black peppercorns, crushed
- 1 cup chicken stock
- ¼ cup coconut cream
- 1 tablespoon lime juice
- 1 tablespoon cilantro, chopped

Directions:
1. In your slow cooker, mix the chicken with the curry paste, onion and the other ingredients, toss, put the lid on and cook on Low for 7 hours.
2. Divide everything into bowls and serve hot.

Nutrition: calories 276, fat 15, fiber 3, carbs 7, protein 16

Flavorful Balsamic Turkey

Preparation time: 10 minutes
Cooking time: 5 hours
Servings: 2
Ingredients:
- 1 pound turkey breast, skinless, boneless and cubed
- 1 tablespoon lemon juice
- 4 scallions, chopped
- 1 tablespoon balsamic vinegar
- 2 tablespoons avocado oil
- A pinch of salt and black pepper
- 1 tablespoon chives, chopped
- ½ cup chicken stock

Directions:
1. In your slow cooker, mix the turkey with the lemon juice, scallions and the other ingredients, toss, put the lid on and cook on High for 5 hours.
2. Divide the mix between plates and serve right away.

Nutrition: calories 252, fat 15, fiber 2, carbs 6, protein 15

Turkey and Scallions Mix

Preparation time: 10 minutes
Cooking time: 7 hours
Servings: 2
Ingredients:
- 1 pound turkey breasts, skinless, boneless and cubed
- 1 tablespoon avocado oil
- ½ cup tomato sauce
- ½ cup chicken stock
- ½ teaspoon sweet paprika
- 4 scallions, chopped
- 1 tablespoons lemon zest, grated
- 1 tablespoon lemon juice
- A pinch of salt and black pepper
- 1 tablespoon chives, chopped

Directions:
1. In your slow cooker, mix the turkey with the oil, tomato sauce and the other ingredients, toss, put the lid on and cook on Low for 7 hours.
2. Divide everything between plates and serve.

Nutrition: calories 234, fat 12, fiber 3, carbs 5, protein 7

Parsley Chicken

Preparation time: 10 minutes
Cooking time: 5 hours
Servings: 2
Ingredients:
- 1 pound chicken breast, skinless, boneless and sliced
- ½ cup parsley, chopped
- 2 tablespoons olive oil
- 1 tablespoon pine nuts
- 1 tablespoon lemon juice
- ½ cup chicken stock
- ¼ cup black olives, pitted and halved
- 1 teaspoon hot paprika
- A pinch of salt and black pepper

Directions:
1. In a blender, mix the parsley with the oil, pine nuts and lemon juice and pulse well.
2. In your slow cooker, mix the chicken with the parsley mix and the remaining ingredients, toss, put the lid on and cook on High for 5 hours.
3. Divide everything between plates and serve.

Nutrition: calories 263, fat 14, fiber 3, carbs 7, protein 16

Turkey Chili

Preparation time: 10 minutes
Cooking time: 5 hours
Servings: 2
Ingredients:
- 1 pound turkey breast, skinless, boneless and cubed
- 1 red chili, minced
- 1 teaspoon chili powder
- 1 red onion, chopped
- 1 tablespoon avocado oil
- ½ cup tomato passata
- ½ cup chicken stock
- A pinch of salt and black pepper
- 1 tablespoon cilantro, chopped

Directions:
1. In your slow cooker, mix the turkey with the chili, chili powder and the other ingredients, toss, put the lid on and cook on High for 5 hours.
2. Divide the mix into bowls and serve.

Nutrition: calories 263, fat 12, fiber 2, carbs 7, protein 18

Spicy Masala Turkey
Preparation time: 10 minutes
Cooking time: 5 hours
Servings: 2
Ingredients:
- 1 pound turkey breasts, skinless, boneless and cubed
- A pinch of salt and black pepper
- 2 scallions, chopped
- 1 teaspoon garam masala
- 1 cup coconut cream
- 1 cup chicken stock
- 1 tablespoon basil, chopped
- 1 tablespoon lime juice

Directions:
1. In your slow cooker, mix the turkey with the scallions, garam masala and the other ingredients, toss, put the lid on and cook on High for 5 hours.
2. Divide the mix into bowls and serve.

Nutrition: calories 201, fat 7, fiber 3, carbs 6, protein 8

Chicken and Beans
Preparation time: 10 minutes
Cooking time: 7 hours
Servings: 2
Ingredients:
- 1 cup canned black beans, drained and rinsed
- ½ cup canned kidney beans, drained and rinsed
- 1 pound chicken breast, skinless, boneless and cubed
- 1 red onion, chopped
- 2 garlic cloves, minced
- 1 tablespoon olive oil
- ½ teaspoon sweet paprika
- 1 tablespoon chili powder
- 1 cup tomato sauce
- A pinch of salt and black pepper
- 1 tablespoon parsley, chopped

Directions:
1. In your slow cooker, mix the chicken with the beans, onion and the other ingredients, toss, put the lid on and cook on Low for 7 hours.
2. Divide the mix into bowls and serve hot.

Nutrition: calories 263, fat 12, fiber 3, carbs 7, protein 15

Turkey and Corn
Preparation time: 10 minutes
Cooking time: 7 hours
Servings: 2
Ingredients:
- 1 red onion
- 1 cup corn
- 1 pound turkey breasts, skinless, boneless and cubed
- 1 cup heavy cream
- 2 tablespoons olive oil
- 1 tablespoon cumin, ground
- ½ cup chicken stock
- ½ teaspoon rosemary, dried
- A pinch of salt and black pepper
- 1 tablespoon cilantro, chopped

Directions:
1. In your slow cooker, mix the turkey with the corn, onion and the other ingredients, toss, put the lid on and cook on Low for 7 hours.
2. Divide everything into bowls and serve.

Nutrition: calories 214, fat 14, fiber 2, carbs 6, protein 15

Coriander Turkey
Preparation time: 10 minutes
Cooking time: 6 hours
Servings: 2
Ingredients:
- 1 pound turkey breasts, skinless, boneless and cubed
- 1 tablespoon olive oil
- 3 scallions, chopped
- 1 cup chicken stock
- 1 teaspoon sweet paprika
- 1 tablespoon coriander, chopped

Directions:
1. In your slow cooker, mix the turkey with the oil, scallions and the other ingredients, toss, put the lid on and cook Low for 6 hours.
2. Divide the mix into bowls and serve.

Nutrition: calories 311, fat 11.2, fiber 2.1, carbs 12.2, protein 39.6

Turkey with Olives and Corn
Preparation time: 10 minutes
Cooking time: 4 hours
Servings: 2
Ingredients:
- 1 pound turkey breast, skinless, boneless and cubed
- 1 tablespoon olive oil
- ½ cup kalamata olives, pitted and halved
- 1 cup corn
- 1 red onion, sliced
- 1 cup tomato passata
- 1 tablespoon parsley, chopped

Directions:
1. In your slow cooker, mix the turkey with the olives, corn and the other ingredients, toss, put the lid on and cook on High for 4 hours.
2. Divide everything between plates and serve.

Nutrition: calories 423, fat 15.3, fiber 5.6, carbs 31.4, protein 42.2

Turkey and Peas

Preparation time: 10 minutes
Cooking time: 5 hours
Servings: 2
Ingredients:
- 1 pound turkey breast, skinless, boneless and sliced
- 1 cup green peas
- ½ cup tomato sauce
- ½ cup scallions, chopped
- A pinch of salt and black pepper
- 1 cup chicken stock
- 1 teaspoon garam masala
- 1 tablespoon dill, chopped

Directions:
1. In your slow cooker, mix the turkey with the peas, tomato sauce and the other ingredients, toss, put the lid on and cook on High for 5 hours.
2. Divide the mix into bowls and serve right away.

Nutrition: calories 326, fat 4.6, fiber 6.6, carbs 26.7, protein 44.6

Turkey with Rice

Preparation time: 10 minutes
Cooking time: 7 hours
Servings: 2
Ingredients:
- 1 pound turkey breasts, skinless, boneless and cubed
- 1 cup wild rice
- 2 cups chicken stock
- 1 tablespoon cilantro, chopped
- 1 tablespoon oregano, chopped
- 2 tablespoons green onions, chopped
- ½ teaspoon coriander, ground
- ½ teaspoon rosemary, dried
- ½ teaspoon turmeric powder
- A pinch of salt and black pepper

Directions:
1. In your slow cooker, mix the turkey with the rice, stock and the other ingredients, toss, put the lid on and cook on Low for 7 hours.
2. Divide everything between plates and serve.

Nutrition: calories 232, fat 12, fiber 2, carbs 6, protein 15

Italian Turkey

Preparation time: 10 minutes
Cooking time: 6 hours
Servings: 2
Ingredients:
- 1 pound turkey breasts, skinless, boneless and roughly cubed
- 1 tablespoon olive oil
- ½ cup black olives, pitted and halved
- ½ cup pearl onions, peeled
- 1 cup chicken stock
- 1 tablespoon Italian seasoning
- A pinch of salt and black pepper

Directions:
1. In your slow cooker, mix the turkey with the olives, onions and the other ingredients, toss, put the lid on and coo on Low for 6 hours.
2. Divide the mix between plates and serve.

Nutrition: calories 263, fat 14, fiber 4, carbs 6, protein 18

Duck with Mushrooms

Preparation time: 10 minutes
Cooking time: 6 hours
Servings: 2
Ingredients:
- 1 pound duck leg, skinless, boneless and sliced
- 1 cup chicken stock
- 1 cup white mushrooms, sliced
- ½ teaspoon rosemary, dried
- ½ teaspoon cumin, ground
- ½ cup heavy cream
- 1 tablespoon olive oil
- ¼ cup chives, chopped

Directions:
1. In your slow cooker, mix the duck with the stock, mushrooms and the other ingredients, toss, put the lid on and cook on Low for 6 hours.
2. Divide everything between plates and serve.

Nutrition: calories 262, fat 16, fiber 2, carbs 8, protein 16

Turkey and Tomato Sauce

Preparation time: 10 minutes
Cooking time: 7 hours
Servings: 2
Ingredients:
- 1 cup tomato sauce
- ½ cup chicken stock
- ½ tablespoon rosemary, chopped
- 1 pound turkey breast, skinless, boneless and roughly cubed
- 1 teaspoon rosemary, dried
- 1 tablespoon cilantro, chopped
- A pinch of salt and black pepper

Directions:
1. In your slow cooker, mix the turkey with the sauce, stock and the other ingredients, toss, put the lid on and cook on Low for 7 hours.
2. Divide everything between plates and serve.

Nutrition: calories 283, fat 16, fiber 2, carbs 6, protein 17

Tomato Chicken
Preparation time: 10 minutes
Cooking time: 7 hours
Servings: 2
Ingredients:
- 1 tablespoon olive oil
- 1 red onion, chopped
- 1 cup canned chickpeas, drained
- 1 pound chicken breast, skinless, boneless and cubed
- ½ cup tomato sauce
- ½ cup cherry tomatoes, halved
- ½ teaspoon rosemary, dried
- ½ teaspoon turmeric powder
- 1 cup chicken stock
- A pinch of salt and black pepper
- 1 tablespoon chives, chopped

Directions:
1. Grease the slow cooker with the oil and mix the chicken with the onion, chickpeas and the other ingredients inside the pot.
2. Put the lid on, cook on Low for 7 hours, divide between plates and serve.

Nutrition: calories 291, fat 17, fiber 3, carbs 7, protein 16

Turkey with Leeks
Preparation time: 10 minutes
Cooking time: 6 hours
Servings: 2
Ingredients:
- 1 pound turkey breast, skinless, boneless and cubed
- 1 leek, sliced
- 1 cup radishes, sliced
- 1 red onion, chopped
- 1 tablespoon olive oil
- A pinch of salt and black pepper
- 1 cup chicken stock
- ½ teaspoon sweet paprika
- ½ teaspoon coriander, ground
- 1 tablespoon cilantro, chopped

Directions:
1. In your slow cooker, combine the turkey with the leek, radishes, onion and the other ingredients, toss, put the lid on and cook on High for 6 hours.
2. Divide everything between plates and serve.

Nutrition: calories 226, fat 9, fiber 1, carbs 6, protein 12

Coconut Turkey
Preparation time: 10 minutes
Cooking time: 5 hours
Servings: 2
Ingredients:
- 1 yellow onion, chopped
- 1 tablespoon olive oil
- 1 cup coconut cream
- ½ teaspoon curry powder
- 1 pound turkey breast, skinless, boneless and cubed
- 1 teaspoon turmeric powder
- ½ cup chicken stock
- 1 tablespoon parsley, chopped
- A pinch of salt and black pepper

Directions:
1. In your slow cooker, mix the turkey with the onion, oil and the other ingredients except the cream and the parsley, stir, put the lid on and cook on High for 4 hours and 30 minutes.
2. Add the remaining ingredients, toss, put the lid on again, cook on High for 30 minutes more, divide the mix between plates and serve.

Nutrition: calories 283, fat 11, fiber 2, carbs 8, protein 15

Chicken and Zucchinis
Preparation time: 10 minutes
Cooking time: 6 hours
Servings: 2
Ingredients:
- 1 pound chicken breasts, skinless, boneless and cubed
- 1 zucchini, cubed
- 2 garlic cloves, minced
- 1 red chili, minced
- ½ teaspoon hot paprika
- 1 red onion, chopped
- 2 tablespoons olive oil
- A pinch of salt and black pepper
- 1 cup chicken stock
- 1 tablespoon chives, chopped

Directions:
1. In your slow cooker, mix the chicken with the zucchini, garlic, chili pepper and the other ingredients, toss, put the lid on and cook on Low for 6 hours.
2. Divide everything between plates and serve.

Nutrition: calories 221, fat 12, fiber 2, carbs 5, protein 17

Turkey with Radishes
Preparation time: 10 minutes
Cooking time: 7 hours
Servings: 2
Ingredients:
- 1 tablespoon olive oil
- 2 scallions, minced
- 1 pound turkey breast, skinless, boneless and cubed
- 2 garlic cloves, minced
- 1 cup radishes, sliced
- ½ cup tomato passata
- ½ cup chicken stock
- 1 teaspoon sweet paprika
- A pinch of salt and black pepper
- ½ teaspoon coriander, ground
- 1 tablespoon parsley, chopped

Directions:
1. In your slow cooker, mix the turkey with the oil, scallions and the other ingredients, toss, put the lid on and cook on Low for 7 hours.
2. Divide the mix between plates and serve.

Nutrition: calories 227, fat 12, fiber 3, carbs 7, protein 18

Simple Chives Duck

Preparation time: 10 minutes
Cooking time: 20 minutes
Servings: 4
Ingredients:
- 1 pound duck breasts, boneless, skinless and sliced
- 1 tablespoon olive oil
- 1 red bell pepper, cut into strips
- 1 yellow onion, chopped
- 1 cup chicken stock
- ½ cup heavy cream
- A pinch of salt and black pepper
- 1 tablespoon chives, chopped

Directions:
1. Set the instant pot on Sauté mode, add the oil, heat it up, add the onion and the bell pepper and sauté for 5 minutes.
2. Add the duck and the rest of the ingredients except the chives, put the lid on and cook on High for 15 minutes.
3. Release the pressure naturally for 10 minutes, divide everything between plates, sprinkle the chives on top and serve.

Nutrition: calories 293, fat 15, fiber 4, carbs 6, protein 14

Cilantro Chicken and Eggplant Mix

Preparation time: 10 minutes
Cooking time: 7 hours
Servings: 2
Ingredients:
- 1 pound chicken breasts, skinless, boneless and sliced
- 2 eggplants, roughly cubed
- ½ cup chicken stock
- ½ cup tomato sauce
- 3 scallions, chopped
- A pinch of salt and black pepper
- 1 teaspoon chili powder
- 1 tablespoon cilantro, chopped

Directions:
1. In your slow cooker, mix the chicken with the eggplant, stock and the other ingredients, toss, put the lid on, cook on Low for 7 hours, divide the mix between plates and serve.

Nutrition: calories 223, fat 9, fiber 2, carbs 4, protein 11

Chicken and Brussels Sprouts

Preparation time: 10 minutes
Cooking time: 7 hours
Servings: 2
Ingredients:
- 1 pound chicken breasts, skinless, boneless and roughly cubed
- 1 tablespoon olive oil
- 1 cup Brussels sprouts, halved
- ½ teaspoon garam masala
- 1 cup chicken stock
- 1 tablespoon olive oil
- 1 red onion, sliced
- 1 tablespoon cilantro, chopped

Directions:
1. In your slow cooker, mix the chicken with the sprouts, oil and the other ingredients, toss, put the lid on and cook on Low for 7 hours.
2. Divide the mix between plates and serve right away.

Nutrition: calories 210, fat 11, fiber 2, carbs 7, protein 14

Chicken and Mango Mix

Preparation time: 10 minutes
Cooking time: 5 hours
Servings: 2
Ingredients:
- 1 pound chicken breast, skinless, boneless and sliced
- 1 cup mango, peeled and cubed
- 4 scallions, chopped
- 1 tablespoon avocado oil
- ½ teaspoon chili powder
- ½ teaspoon rosemary, dried
- 1 cup chicken stock
- 1 tablespoon sweet paprika
- A pinch of salt and black pepper
- 1 tablespoon chives, chopped

Directions:
1. In your slow cooker, mix the chicken with the mango, scallions, chili powder and the other ingredients, toss, put the lid on and cook on Low for 5 hours.
2. Divide the mix between plates and serve.

Nutrition: calories 263, fat 8, fiber 2, carbs 7, protein 12

Turkey with Avocado

Preparation time: 10 minutes
Cooking time: 6 hours
Servings: 2
Ingredients:
- 1 pound turkey breasts, skinless, boneless and cubed
- 1 cup avocado, peeled, pitted and cubed
- 1 cup tomatoes, cubed
- 1 tablespoon chives, chopped
- ½ teaspoon chili powder
- 4 garlic cloves, minced
- ¼ cup chicken stock

Directions:
1. In slow cooker, mix the turkey with the tomatoes, chives and the other ingredients except the avocado, toss, put the lid on and cook on Low for 5 hours and 30 minutes.
2. Add the avocado, toss, cook on Low for 30 minutes more, divide everything between plates and serve.

Nutrition: calories 220, fat 8, fiber 2, carbs 7, protein 15

Chicken and Peppers

Preparation time: 10 minutes
Cooking time: 6 hours
Servings: 2
Ingredients:
- 1 pound chicken breasts, skinless, boneless and cubed
- ¼ cup tomato sauce
- 2 red bell peppers, cut into strips
- 1 teaspoon olive oil
- ½ teaspoon rosemary, dried
- ½ teaspoon coriander, ground
- 1 teaspoon Italian seasoning
- A pinch of cayenne pepper
- 1 cup chicken stock

Directions:
1. In your slow cooker, mix the chicken with the peppers, tomato sauce and the other ingredients, toss, put the lid on and cook on Low for 6 hours.
2. divide everything between plates and serve.

Nutrition: calories 282, fat 12, fiber 2, carbs 6, protein 18

Chicken and Cabbage

Preparation time: 5 minutes
Cooking time: 7 hours
Servings: 2
Ingredients:
- 1 pound chicken breasts, skinless, boneless and halved
- 2 cups red cabbage, shredded
- 1 cup chicken stock
- ½ teaspoon rosemary, dried
- ½ teaspoon sweet paprika
- 2 teaspoons cumin, ground
- A pinch of salt and black pepper
- ¼ cup cilantro, chopped

Directions:
1. In slow cooker, mix the chicken with the cabbage, stock and the other ingredients, toss, put the lid on and cook on Low for 7 hours.
2. Divide everything between plates and serve.

Nutrition: calories 285, fat 16, fiber 4, carbs 8, protein 18

Lime Turkey and Chard

Preparation time: 10 minutes
Cooking time: 6 hours
Servings: 2
Ingredients:
- 1 pound turkey breasts, skinless, boneless and cubed
- 2 teaspoons olive oil
- 1 cup red chard, torn
- ½ teaspoon sweet paprika
- 1 cup chicken stock
- A pinch of salt and black pepper
- 2 tablespoons lime juice
- 1 tablespoon lime zest, grated
- 1 tablespoon tomato paste

Directions:
1. In your slow cooker, mix the turkey with the oil, paprika and the other ingredients, toss, put the lid on and cook on Low for 6 hours.
2. Divide everything into bowls and serve.

Nutrition: calories 292, fat 17, fiber 2, carbs 7, protein 16

BBQ Turkey

Preparation time: 10 minutes
Cooking time: 6 hours
Servings: 2
Ingredients:
- 1 pound turkey breast, skinless, boneless and sliced
- 1 teaspoon sweet paprika
- ½ teaspoon red pepper flakes, crushed
- ½ teaspoon turmeric powder
- 1 cup bbq sauce
- A pinch of salt and black pepper
- ¼ cup cilantro, chopped
- 1 cup chicken stock

Directions:
1. In slow cooker, mix the turkey with the paprika, pepper flakes and the other ingredients, toss, put the lid on and cook on Low for 6 hours.
2. Divide everything between plates and serve.

Nutrition: calories 224, fat 11, fiber 2, carbs 9, protein 11

Chicken and Asparagus

Preparation time: 10 minutes
Cooking time: 5 hours
Servings: 2
Ingredients:
- 1 pound chicken breast, skinless, boneless and cubed
- 1 cup asparagus, sliced
- 1 tablespoon olive oil
- 2 scallions, chopped
- A pinch of salt and black pepper
- 1 teaspoon garam masala
- 1 cup chicken stock
- 1 cup tomatoes, cubed
- 1 tablespoon parsley, chopped

Directions:
1. In your slow cooker, mix the chicken with the asparagus, oil and the other ingredients except the asparagus, toss, put the lid on and cook on High for 4 hours.
2. Add the asparagus, toss, cook on High for 1 more hour, divide everything between plates and serve.

Nutrition: calories 229, fat 9, fiber 4, carbs 7, protein 16

Lemony Turkey and Potatoes
Preparation time: 10 minutes
Cooking time: 7 hours
Servings: 2
Ingredients:
- 1 pound turkey breast, skinless, boneless and cubed
- 2 teaspoons olive oil
- 1 tablespoon lemon juice
- 2 gold potatoes, peeled and cubed
- 1 red onion, chopped
- ½ cup tomato sauce
- ¼ cup chicken stock
- 1 tablespoon chives, chopped
- A pinch of salt and black pepper

Directions:
1. In your slow cooker, mix the turkey with the oil, lemon juice, potatoes and the other ingredients, toss, put the lid on and cook on Low for 7 hours.
2. Divide everything between plates and serve.

Nutrition: calories 263, fat 12, fiber 3, carbs 6, protein 14

Turkey and Okra
Preparation time: 10 minutes
Cooking time: 5 hours
Servings: 2
Ingredients:
- 1 pound turkey breasts, skinless, boneless and cubed
- 1 cup okra, halved
- 1 tablespoon lime zest, grated
- ½ cup chicken stock
- 1 tablespoon lime juice
- 1 teaspoon olive oil
- ½ teaspoon sweet paprika
- ½ teaspoon coriander, ground
- ½ teaspoon oregano, dried
- 1 teaspoon chili powder
- A pinch of salt and black pepper
- 1 tablespoon cilantro, chopped

Directions:
1. In your slow cooker, mix the turkey with the okra, lime zest, juice and the other ingredients, toss, put the lid on and cook on High for 5 hours.
2. Divide everything between plates and serve.

Nutrition: calories 162, fat 8, fiber 2, carbs 5, protein 9

Spicy Duck Mix
Preparation time: 10 minutes
Cooking time: 5 hours
Servings: 2
Ingredients:
- 2 teaspoons olive oil
- 1 red onion, sliced
- 1 pound duck leg, skinless, boneless and cut into strips
- 1 tablespoon mustard
- 1 tablespoon lemon juice
- ¾ cup chicken stock
- 1 teaspoon sweet paprika
- A pinch of salt and black pepper
- 1 tablespoon coriander, chopped

Directions:
1. In your slow cooker, mix the duck with the oil, onion, mustard and the other ingredients, toss, put the lid on and cook on High for 5 hours.
2. Divide the mix between plates and serve with a side salad.

Nutrition: calories 200, fat 9, fiber 2, carbs 5, protein 10

Orange Chicken Mix
Preparation time: 10 minutes
Cooking time: 6 hours
Servings: 2
Ingredients:
- 1 pound chicken breast, skinless, boneless and cubed
- 1 cup oranges, peeled and cut into segments
- 2 teaspoons olive oil
- 1 teaspoon turmeric powder
- 1 teaspoon balsamic vinegar
- 4 scallions, minced
- 1 cup orange juice
- 1 tablespoon mint, chopped
- A pinch of salt and black pepper

Directions:
1. In your slow cooker, mix the chicken with the oranges, scallions and the other ingredients, toss, put the lid on and cook on Low for 6 hours.
2. Divide the mix between plates and serve.

Nutrition: calories 200, fat 7, fiber 2, carbs 6, protein 11

Turkey with Carrots
Preparation time: 10 minutes
Cooking time: 7 hours
Servings: 2
Ingredients:
- 1 pound turkey breasts, skinless, boneless and cubed
- 1 cup carrots, peeled and sliced
- 2 tablespoons avocado oil
- 1 tablespoon balsamic vinegar
- 2 scallions, chopped
- 1 teaspoon turmeric powder
- 1 cup chicken stock
- ½ cup chives, chopped

Directions:
1. In your slow cooker, mix the turkey with the carrots, oil, vinegar and the other ingredients, toss, put the lid on and cook on Low for 7 hours.
2. Divide the mix between plates and serve right away.

Nutrition: calories 210, fat 8, fiber 2, carbs 6, protein 11

Flavorful Rosemary Chicken Thighs

Preparation time: 10 minutes
Cooking time: 7 hours
Servings: 2
Ingredients:
- 1 pound chicken thighs, boneless
- 1 teaspoon rosemary, dried
- ½ teaspoon sweet paprika
- ½ teaspoon garam masala
- 1 tablespoon olive oil
- ½ cup chicken stock
- A pinch of salt and black pepper
- 1 tablespoon cilantro, chopped

Directions:
3. In your slow cooker, mix the chicken with the rosemary, paprika and the other ingredients, toss, put the lid on and cook on Low for 7 hours/
4. Divide the chicken between plates and serve with a side salad.

Nutrition: calories 220, fat 8, fiber 2, carbs 5, protein 11

Turkey with Kidney Beans

Preparation time: 10 minutes
Cooking time: 6 hours
Servings: 2
Ingredients:
- 1 pound turkey breasts, skinless, boneless and cut into strips
- 2 cups canned red kidney beans, drained and rinsed
- ¼ cup chicken stock
- 1 cup tomato passata
- 1 tablespoon avocado oil
- Salt and black pepper to the taste
- ½ teaspoon chili powder
- 1 tablespoon tarragon, chopped

Directions:
1. In your slow cooker, mix the turkey with the beans, stock and the other ingredients, toss, put the lid on and cook on Low for 6 hours.
2. Divide the mix between plates and serve.

Nutrition: calories 192, fat 12, fiber 3, carbs 5, protein 12

Coriander and Turmeric Chicken

Preparation time: 10 minutes
Cooking time: 6 hours
Servings: 2
Ingredients:
- 1 pound chicken breasts, skinless, boneless and cubed
- 1 tablespoon coriander, chopped
- ½ teaspoon turmeric powder
- 2 scallions, minced
- 1 tablespoon olive oil
- 1 tablespoon lime zest, grated
- 1 cup lime juice
- 1 tablespoon chives, chopped
- ¼ cup tomato sauce

Directions:
1. In your slow cooker, mix the chicken with the coriander, turmeric, scallions and the other ingredients, toss, put the lid on and cook on Low for 6 hours.
2. Divide the mix between plates and serve right away.

Nutrition: calories 200, fat 7, fiber 1, carbs 5, protein 12

Garlic Turkey

Preparation time: 10 minutes
Cooking time: 6 hours
Servings: 2
Ingredients:
- 1 pound turkey breast, skinless, boneless and cubed
- 1 tablespoon avocado oil
- ½ cup chicken stock
- 2 tablespoons tomato paste
- 2 tablespoons garlic, minced
- ½ teaspoon chili powder
- ½ teaspoon oregano, dried
- A pinch of salt and black pepper
- 1 tablespoon parsley, chopped

Directions:
1. In your slow cooker, mix the turkey with the oil, stock, tomato paste and the other ingredients, toss, put the lid on and cook on Low for 6 hours.
2. Divide the mix between plates and serve with a side salad.

Nutrition: calories 231, fat 7, fiber 2, carbs 6, protein 12

Cumin Chicken

Preparation time: 10 minutes
Cooking time: 6 hours
Servings: 2
Ingredients:
- 1 pound chicken breast, skinless, boneless and cubed
- 2 teaspoons olive oil
- ½ cup tomato sauce
- ¼ cup chicken stock
- ½ teaspoon garam masala
- ½ teaspoon chili powder
- ½ teaspoon cumin, ground
- 1 yellow onion, chopped
- ½ teaspoon sweet paprika
- A pinch of salt and black pepper
- 1 tablespoon chives, chopped

Directions:
1. In your slow cooker, mix the chicken with the oil, tomato sauce, stock and the other ingredients, toss, put the lid on and cook on Low for 6 hours.
2. Divide everything between plates and serve right away.

Nutrition: calories 252, fat 12, fiber 4, carbs 7, protein 13

Slow Cooker Meat Recipes for 2

Pork Chops and Mango
Preparation time: 10 minutes
Cooking time: 6 hours
Servings: 2
Ingredients:
- 1 pound pork chops
- 1 teaspoon sweet paprika
- ½ teaspoon chili powder
- 1 cup mango, peeled, and cubed
- 2 tablespoons ketchup
- 1 tablespoon balsamic vinegar
- ¼ cup beef stock
- 1 tablespoon cilantro, chopped

Directions:
1. In your slow cooker, mix the pork chops with the paprika, chili powder, ketchup and the other ingredients, toss, put the lid on and cook on Low for 6 hours.
2. Divide everything between plates and serve.

Nutrition: calories 345, fat 5, fiber 7, carbs 17, protein 14

Beef and Zucchinis Mix
Preparation time: 10 minutes
Cooking time: 8 hours
Servings: 2
Ingredients:
- 1 pound beef stew meat, cut into strips
- 1 tablespoon olive oil
- ¼ cup beef stock
- ½ teaspoon sweet paprika
- ½ teaspoon chili powder
- 2 small zucchinis, cubed
- 1 tablespoon balsamic vinegar
- 1 tablespoon chives, chopped

Directions:
1. In your slow cooker, mix the beef with the oil, stock and the other ingredients, toss, put the lid on and cook on Low for 8 hours.
2. Divide the mix between plates and serve.

Nutrition: calories 400, fat 12, fiber 8, carbs 18, protein 20

Pork and Olives
Preparation time: 10 minutes
Cooking time: 8 hours
Servings: 2
Ingredients:
- 1 pound pork roast, sliced
- ½ cup tomato passata
- 1 red onion, sliced
- 1 cup kalamata olives, pitted and halved
- Juice of ½ lime
- ¼ cup beef stock
- Salt and black pepper to the taste
- 1 tablespoon chives, hopped

Directions:
1. In your slow cooker, mix the pork slices with the passata, onion, olives and the other ingredients, toss, put the lid on and cook on Low for 8 hours.
2. Divide the mix between plates and serve.

Nutrition: calories 360, fat 4, fiber 3, carbs 17, protein 27

Pork and Soy Sauce Mix
Preparation time: 10 minutes
Cooking time: 8 hours
Servings: 2
Ingredients:
- 1 pound pork loin roast, boneless and roughly cubed
- 1 tablespoon soy sauce
- 3 tablespoons honey
- ½ tablespoons oregano, dried
- 1 tablespoon garlic, minced
- 1 tablespoons olive oil
- Salt and black pepper to the taste
- ½ cup beef stock
- ½ teaspoon sweet paprika

Directions:
1. In your slow cooker, mix the pork loin with the honey, soy sauce and the other ingredients, toss, put the lid on and cook on Low for 8 hours.
2. Divide everything between plates and serve.

Nutrition: calories 374, fat 6, fiber 8, carbs 29, protein 6

Beef with Sauce
Preparation time: 10 minutes
Cooking time: 8 hours
Servings: 2
Ingredients:
- 1 pound beef stew meat, cubed
- 1 teaspoon garam masala
- ½ teaspoon turmeric powder
- Salt and black pepper to the taste
- 1 cup beef stock
- 1 teaspoon garlic, minced
- ½ cup sour cream
- 2 ounces cream cheese, soft
- 1 tablespoon chives, chopped

Directions:
1. In your slow cooker, mix the beef with the turmeric, garam masala and the other ingredients, toss, put the lid on and cook on Low for 8 hours.
2. Divide everything into bowls and serve.

Nutrition: calories 372, fat 6, fiber 9, carbs 18, protein 22

Pork and Beans Mix

Preparation time: 10 minutes
Cooking time: 8 hours
Servings: 2
Ingredients:
- 1 red bell pepper, chopped
- 1 pound pork stew meat, cubed
- 1 tablespoon olive oil
- 1 cup canned black beans, drained and rinsed
- ½ cup tomato sauce
- 1 yellow onion, chopped
- 1 teaspoon Italian seasoning
- Salt and black pepper to the taste
- 1 tablespoon oregano, chopped

Directions:
1. In your slow cooker, mix the pork with the bell pepper, oil and the other ingredients, toss, put the lid on and cook on Low for 8 hours.
2. Divide the mix between plates and serve.

Nutrition: calories 385, fat 12, fiber 5, carbs 18, protein 40

Beef and Spinach

Preparation time: 10 minutes
Cooking time: 7 hours
Servings: 2
Ingredients:
- 1 red onion, sliced
- 1 pound beef stew meat, cubed
- 1 cup tomato passata
- 1 cup baby spinach
- 1 teaspoon olive oil
- Salt and black pepper to the taste
- ½ cup bee stock
- 1 tablespoon basil, chopped

Directions:
1. In your slow cooker, mix the beef with the onion, passata and the other ingredients except the spinach, toss, put the lid on and cook on Low for 6 hours and 30 minutes.
2. Add the spinach, toss, put the lid on, cook on Low for 30 minutes more, divide into bowls and serve.

Nutrition: calories 400, fat 15, fiber 4, carbs 25, protein 14

Pork and Chilies Mix

Preparation time: 10 minutes
Cooking time: 7 hours
Servings: 2
Ingredients:
- 1 pound pork stew meat, cubed
- 1 tablespoon olive oil
- ½ green bell pepper, chopped
- 1 red onion, sliced
- ½ red bell pepper, chopped
- 1 garlic clove, minced
- 2 ounces canned green chilies, chopped
- ½ cup tomato passata
- Salt and black pepper to the taste
- 1 tablespoon chili powder
- 1 tablespoon cilantro, chopped

Directions:
3. In your slow cooker, mix the pork with the oil, bell pepper and the other ingredients, toss, put the lid on and cook on Low for 7 hours.
4. Divide into bowls and serve right away.

Nutrition: calories 400, fat 14, fiber 5, carbs 29, protein 22

Hot Ribs

Preparation time: 10 minutes
Cooking time: 8 hours
Servings: 2
Ingredients:
- 2 beef short ribs, cut into individual ribs
- Salt and black pepper to the taste
- ½ cup ketchup
- 1 tablespoon balsamic vinegar
- 1 tablespoon mustard
- 1 tablespoon chives, chopped

Directions:
3. In your slow cooker, combine the ribs with the ketchup, salt, pepper and the other ingredients, toss, put the lid on and cook on Low for 8 hours.
4. Divide between plates and serve with a side salad.

Nutrition: calories 284, fat 7, 4, carbs 18, protein 20

Beef and Corn Mix

Preparation time: 10 minutes
Cooking time: 8 hours
Servings: 2
Ingredients:
- 2 teaspoons olive oil
- 3 scallions, chopped
- 1 pound beef stew meat, cubed
- 1 cup corn
- ½ cup heavy cream
- ½ cup beef stock
- 2 garlic cloves, minced
- Salt and black pepper to the taste
- 1 tablespoon soy sauce
- 1 tablespoon parsley, chopped

Directions:
1. In your slow cooker, combine the beef with the corn, oil, scallions and the other ingredients except the cream, toss, put the lid on and cook on Low for 7 hours.
2. Add the cream, toss, cook on Low for 1 more hour, divide into bowls and serve.

Nutrition: calories 400, fat 10, fiber 4, carbs 15, protein 20

Cider Beef Mix
Preparation time: 10 minutes
Cooking time: 8 hours
Servings: 2
Ingredients:
- 1 pound beef stew meat, cubed
- 1 tablespoon olive oil
- Salt and black pepper to the taste
- 3 garlic cloves, minced
- ½ yellow onion, chopped
- ½ cup beef stock
- 1 tablespoon apple cider vinegar
- 1 tablespoon lime zest, grated

Directions:
1. In your slow cooker, mix the beef with the oil, salt, pepper, garlic and the other ingredients, toss, put the lid on, and cook on Low for 8 hours.
2. Divide everything between plates and serve.

Nutrition: calories 453, fat 10, fiber 12, carbs 20, protein 36

Tarragon Pork Chops
Preparation time: 10 minutes
Cooking time: 6 hours
Servings: 2
Ingredients:
- ½ pound pork chops
- ¼ tablespoons olive oil
- 2 garlic clove, minced
- ¼ teaspoon chili powder
- ½ cup beef stock
- ½ teaspoon coriander, ground
- Salt and black pepper to the taste
- ¼ teaspoon mustard powder
- 1 tablespoon tarragon, chopped

Directions:
1. Grease your slow cooker with the oil and mix the pork chops with the garlic, stock and the other ingredients inside.
2. Toss, put the lid on, cook on Low for 6 hours, divide between plates and serve with a side salad.

Nutrition: calories 453, fat 16, fiber 8, carbs 7, protein 27

Honey Pork Chops
Preparation time: 10 minutes
Cooking time: 5 hours
Servings: 2
Ingredients:
- 2 teaspoons avocado oil
- 1 pound pork chops, bone in
- 2 tablespoons mayonnaise
- 1 tablespoon ketchup
- ½ tablespoon honey
- ¼ cup beef stock
- ½ tablespoon lime juice

Directions:
1. In your slow cooker, mix the pork chops with the oil, honey and the other ingredients, toss well, put the lid on, and cook on High for 5 hours.
2. Divide pork chops between plates and serve.

Nutrition: calories 300, fat 8, fiber 10, carbs 16, protein 16

Turmeric Lamb
Preparation time: 10 minutes
Cooking time: 5 hours
Servings: 2
Ingredients:
- 1 pound lamb chops
- 2 teaspoons avocado oil
- 1 teaspoon turmeric powder
- ½ teaspoon sweet paprika
- 1 cup beef stock
- 1 red onion, sliced
- Salt and black pepper to the taste
- 1 tablespoon chives, chopped

Directions:
1. In your slow cooker, mix the lamb chops with the oil, turmeric and the other ingredients, toss, put the lid on and cook on High for 5 hours.
2. Divide everything between plates and serve.

Nutrition: calories 254, fat 12, fiber 2, carbs 6, protein 16

Chili Lamb
Preparation time: 10 minutes
Cooking time: 4 hours
Servings: 2
Ingredients:
- 1 pound lamb chops
- 2 teaspoons avocado oil
- 2 scallions, chopped
- 1 green chili pepper, minced
- ½ teaspoon turmeric powder
- 1 teaspoon chili powder
- ½ cup veggie stock
- 2 garlic cloves, minced
- A pinch of salt and black pepper

Directions:
1. In your slow cooker, mix the lamb chops with the oil, scallions and the other ingredients, toss, put the lid on and cook on High for 4 hours.
2. Divide everything between plates and serve.

Nutrition: calories 243, fat 15, fiber 3, carbs 6, protein 20

Beef and Red Onions
Preparation time: 10 minutes
Cooking time: 7 hours
Servings: 2
Ingredients:
- 1 pound beef stew meat, cubed
- 2 teaspoons olive oil
- 2 red onions, sliced
- 1 cup heavy cream
- ¼ cup beef stock
- 1 teaspoon chili powder
- ½ teaspoon rosemary, dried
- 1 tablespoon parsley, chopped
- A pinch of salt and black pepper

Directions:
1. In your slow cooker, mix the beef with the onions, oil and the other ingredients, toss, put the lid on and cook on low for 7 hours.
2. Divide everything between plates and serve.

Nutrition: calories 263, fat 14, fiber 3, carbs 6, protein 16

Pork and Okra

Preparation time: 10 minutes
Cooking time: 6 hours
Servings: 2
Ingredients:
- 1 pound pork stew meat, cubed
- 1 cup okra, sliced
- 2 teaspoons olive oil
- 1 red onion, chopped
- ¼ cup beef stock
- ½ teaspoon chili powder
- ½ teaspoon turmeric powder
- 1 cup tomato passata
- A pinch of salt and black pepper

Directions:
1. In your slow cooker, combine the pork with the okra, oil and the other ingredients, toss, put the lid on and cook on High for 6 hours.
2. Divide the mix between plates and serve.

Nutrition: calories 264, fat 14, fiber 4, carbs 7, protein 15

Easy Chives Lamb

Preparation time: 10 minutes
Cooking time: 4 hours
Servings: 2
Ingredients:
- 1 pound lamb chops
- ½ cup chives, chopped
- ½ cup tomato passata
- 2 scallions, chopped
- 2 teaspoons olive oil
- 2 garlic cloves, minced
- ½ teaspoon sweet paprika
- 1 teaspoon cumin, ground
- A pinch of salt and black pepper

Directions:
1. In your slow cooer, mix the lamb chops with the chives, passata and the other ingredients, toss, put the lid on and cook on High for 4 hours,
2. Divide the mix between plates and serve.

Nutrition: calories 263, fat 12, fiber 4, carbs 6, protein 16

Oregano Beef

Preparation time: 10 minutes
Cooking time: 4 hours
Servings: 2
Ingredients:
- 1 pound beef stew meat, cubed
- 1 tablespoon olive oil
- 1 tablespoon balsamic vinegar
- ½ tablespoon lemon juice
- 1 tablespoon oregano, chopped
- ½ cup tomato sauce
- 1 red onion, chopped
- A pinch of salt and black pepper
- ½ teaspoon chili powder

Directions:
1. In your slow cooker, mix the beef with the oil, vinegar, lemon juice and the other ingredients, toss, put the lid on and cook on High for 4 hours.
2. Divide the mix between plates and serve right away.

Nutrition: calories 263, fat 14, fiber 4, carbs 6, protein 18

Pork with Green Beans

Preparation time: 10 minutes
Cooking time: 6 hours
Servings: 2
Ingredients:
- 1 pound pork stew meat, cubed
- 1 tablespoon balsamic vinegar
- 1 cup green beans, trimmed and halved
- 1 tablespoon lime juice
- 1 tablespoon avocado oil
- ½ teaspoon rosemary, dried
- A pinch of salt and black pepper
- 1 cup beef stock
- 1 tablespoon chives, chopped

Directions:
1. In your slow cooker, mix the pork stew meat with the green beans, vinegar and the other ingredients, toss, put the lid on and cook on Low for 6 hours.
2. Divide the mix between plates and serve.

Nutrition: calories 264, fat 14, fiber 4, carbs 6, protein 17

Lamb Chops

Preparation time: 10 minutes
Cooking time: 4 hours
Servings: 2
Ingredients:
- 2 tablespoons olive oil
- 1 pound lamb chops
- 1 tablespoon mint, chopped
- ½ teaspoon garam masala
- ½ cup coconut cream
- 1 red onion, chopped
- 2 tablespoons garlic, minced
- ½ cup beef stock
- A pinch of salt and black pepper

Directions:
1. In your slow cooker, mix the lamb chops with the oil, mint and the other ingredients, toss, put the lid on and cook on High for 4 hours.
2. Divide the mix between plates and serve warm.

Nutrition: calories 263, fat 14, fiber 3, carbs 7, protein 20

Beef and Artichokes

Preparation time: 10 minutes
Cooking time: 7 hours
Servings: 2
Ingredients:
- 1 tablespoon avocado oil
- 1 pound beef stew meat, cubed
- 2 scallions, chopped
- 1 cup canned artichoke hearts, drained and quartered
- ½ teaspoon chili powder
- A pinch of salt and black pepper
- 1 cup tomato passata
- A pinch of salt and black pepper
- ¼ tablespoon dill, chopped

Directions:
1. In your slow cooker, combine the beef with the artichokes and the other ingredients, toss, put the lid on and cook on Low for 7 hours.
2. Divide the mix between plates and serve.

Nutrition: calories 263, fat 14, fiber 5, carbs 7, protein 15

Lamb with Potatoes

Preparation time: 10 minutes
Cooking time: 4 hours
Servings: 2
Ingredients:
- 1 pound lamb stew meat, roughly cubed
- 2 sweet potatoes, peeled and cubed
- ½ cup beef stock
- ½ cup tomato sauce
- ½ teaspoon sweet paprika
- ½ teaspoon coriander, ground
- 1 tablespoon avocado oil
- 1 tablespoon balsamic vinegar
- 1 tablespoon cilantro, chopped
- A pinch of salt and black pepper

Directions:
1. In your slow cooker, mix the lamb with the potatoes, stock, sauce and the other ingredients, toss, put the lid on and cook on High for 4 hours
2. Divide everything between plates and serve.

Nutrition: calories 253, fat 14, fiber 3, carbs 7, protein 17

Lamb and Tomatoes Mix

Preparation time: 10 minutes
Cooking time: 4 hours
Servings: 2
Ingredients:
- 1 teaspoon olive oil
- 1 pound lamb stew meat, cubed
- 1 cup cherry tomatoes, halved
- 1 tablespoon basil, chopped
- ½ teaspoon rosemary, dried
- 1 tablespoon oregano, chopped
- 1 cup beef stock
- ½ teaspoon sweet paprika
- A pinch of salt and black pepper
- 1 tablespoon parsley, chopped

Directions:
1. Grease the slow cooker with the oil and mix the lamb with the tomatoes, basil and the other ingredients inside.
2. Toss, put the lid on, cook on High for 4 hours, divide the mix between plates and serve.

Nutrition: calories 276, fat 14, fiber 3, carbs 7, protein 20

Pork and Eggplant

Preparation time: 10 minutes
Cooking time: 7 hours
Servings: 2
Ingredients:
- 1 pound pork stew meat, cubed
- 1 eggplant, cubed
- 2 scallions, chopped
- 2 garlic cloves, minced
- ½ cup beef stock
- ¼ cup tomato sauce
- 1 teaspoon sweet paprika
- 1 tablespoon chives, chopped

Directions:
1. In your slow cooker, mix the pork stew meat with the scallions, eggplant and the other ingredients, toss, put the lid on and cook on Low for 7 hours.
2. Divide the mix between plates and serve right away.

Nutrition: calories 287, fat 16, fiber 4, carbs 6, protein 20

Lemon Lamb

Preparation time: 10 minutes
Cooking time: 7 hours
Servings: 2
Ingredients:
- 1 pound lamb stew meat, cubed
- 1 red onion, sliced
- ½ cup tomato sauce
- 1 tablespoon balsamic vinegar
- 1 tablespoon lemon juice
- 1 tablespoon lemon zest, grated
- 1 teaspoon olive oil
- 3 garlic cloves, chopped
- A pinch of salt and black pepper
- 1 tablespoon chives, chopped

Directions:
1. In your slow cooker, mix the lamb with the onion, tomato sauce and the other ingredients, toss, put the lid on and cook on Low for 7 hours.
2. Divide the mix between plates and serve right away.

Nutrition: calories 264, fat 8, fiber 3, carbs 6, protein 17

Lamb with Olives

Preparation time: 10 minutes
Cooking time: 4 hours
Servings: 2
Ingredients:
- 1 pound lamb chops
- 1 tablespoon olive oil
- 3 garlic cloves, minced
- 1 tablespoon rosemary, chopped
- 1 cup kalamata olives, pitted and halved
- 3 scallions, chopped
- 1 teaspoon turmeric powder
- 1 cup beef stock
- A pinch of salt and black pepper

Directions:
1. In your slow cooker, mix the lamb chops with the oil, rosemary and the other ingredients, toss, put the lid on and cook on High for 4 hours.
2. Divide the mix between plates and serve.

Nutrition: calories 275, fat 13, fiber 4, carbs 7, protein 20

Nutmeg Lamb and Squash

Preparation time: 10 minutes
Cooking time: 6 hours
Servings: 2
Ingredients:
- 1 pound lamb stew meat, roughly cubed
- 1 cup butternut squash, peeled and cubed
- ½ teaspoon nutmeg, ground
- ½ teaspoon chili powder
- ½ teaspoon coriander, ground
- 2 teaspoons olive oil
- 1 cup beef stock
- A pinch of salt and black pepper
- 1 tablespoon cilantro, chopped

Directions:
1. In your slow cooker, mix the lamb with the squash, nutmeg and the other ingredients, toss, put the lid on and cook on Low for 6 hours.
2. Divide the mix between plates and serve.

Nutrition: calories 263, fat 12, fiber 4, carbs 7, protein 12

Lamb and Fennel

Preparation time: 10 minutes
Cooking time: 4 hours
Servings: 2
Ingredients:
- 1 pound lamb stew meat, roughly cubed
- 1 fennel bulb, sliced
- 1 tablespoon lemon juice
- 1 teaspoon avocado oil
- ½ teaspoon coriander, ground
- 1 cup tomato passata
- A pinch of salt and black pepper
- 1 tablespoon cilantro, chopped

Directions:
1. In your slow cooker, combine the lamb with the fennel, lemon juice and the other ingredients, toss, put the lid on and cook on High for 4 hours.
2. Divide the mix between plates and serve.

Nutrition: calories 263, fat 12, fiber 3, carbs 7, protein 10

Creamy Lamb

Preparation time: 10 minutes
Cooking time: 6 hours
Servings: 2
Ingredients:
- 2 pounds lamb shoulder, cubed
- 1 cup heavy cream
- 1/3 cup beef stock
- 2 teaspoons avocado oil
- 1 teaspoon turmeric powder
- 1 red onion, sliced
- A pinch of salt and black pepper
- 1 tablespoon cilantro, chopped

Directions:
1. In your slow cooker, mix the lamb with the stock, oil and the other ingredients except the cream, toss, put the lid on and cook on Low for 5 hours.
2. Add the cream, toss, cook on Low for 1 more hour, divide the mix into bowls and serve.

Nutrition: calories 233, fat 7, fiber 2, carbs 6, protein 12

Beef and Capers

Preparation time: 10 minutes
Cooking time: 7 hours
Servings: 2
Ingredients:
- 1 pound beef stew meat, cubed
- 1 tablespoon capers, drained
- 1 cup heavy cream
- ½ cup beef stock
- ½ tablespoon mustard
- 3 scallions, chopped
- 2 teaspoons avocado oil
- 1 teaspoon cumin, ground
- A pinch of salt and black pepper
- 1 tablespoon parsley, chopped

Directions:
1. In your slow cooker, mix the beef with capers, stock and the other ingredients except the cream, toss, put the lid on and cook on Low for 6 hours.
2. Add the cream, toss, cook on Low for 1 more hour, divide the mix between plates and serve.

Nutrition: calories 235, fat 12, fiber 5, carbs 7, protein 10

Masala Beef with Sauce

Preparation time: 10 minutes
Cooking time: 7 hours
Servings: 2
Ingredients:
- 1 pound beef stew meat, cubed
- 1 teaspoon garam masala
- 1 tablespoon olive oil
- 1 tablespoon lime zest, grated
- 1 tablespoon lime juice
- ½ teaspoon sweet paprika
- ½ teaspoon coriander, ground
- 1 cup beef stock
- A pinch of salt and black pepper

Directions:
1. In your slow cooker, mix the beef with the garam masala, oil and the other ingredients, toss, put the lid on and cook on Low for 7 hours.
2. Divide the mix between plates and serve.

Nutrition: calories 211, fat 9, fiber 2, carbs 6, protein 12

Lamb and Cabbage

Preparation time: 10 minutes
Cooking time: 5 hours
Servings: 2
Ingredients:
- 2 pounds lamb stew meat, cubed
- 1 cup red cabbage, shredded
- 1 cup beef stock
- 1 teaspoon avocado oil
- 1 teaspoon sweet paprika
- 2 tablespoons tomato paste
- A pinch of salt and black pepper
- 1 tablespoon cilantro, chopped

Directions:
1. In your slow cooker, mix the lamb with the cabbage, stock and the other ingredients, toss, put the lid on and cook on High for 5 hours.
2. Divide everything between plates and serve.

Nutrition: calories 254, fat 12, fiber 3, carbs 6, protein 16

Pork with Lentils

Preparation time: 10 minutes
Cooking time: 7 hours
Servings: 2
Ingredients:
- 1 pound pork stew meat, cubed
- 1 cup canned lentils, drained and rinsed
- 1 tablespoon olive oil
- 1 yellow onion, chopped
- ¼ cup tomato sauce
- ¼ cup beef stock
- A pinch of salt and black pepper
- 1 tablespoon cilantro, chopped

Directions:
1. In your slow cooker, mix the pork with the lentils, oil, onion and the other ingredients, toss, put the lid on and cook on Low for 7 hours.
2. Divide the mix between plates and serve.

Nutrition: calories 232, fat 10, fiber 5, carbs 7, protein 11

Balsamic Lamb Mix

Preparation time: 10 minutes
Cooking time: 7 hours
Servings: 2
Ingredients:
- 1 pound lamb stew meat, cubed
- 2 teaspoons avocado oil
- 1 tablespoon balsamic vinegar
- ½ teaspoon coriander, ground
- A pinch of salt and black pepper
- 1 cup beef stock

Directions:
1. In your slow cooker, mix the lamb with the oil, vinegar and the other ingredients, toss, put the lid on and cook on Low for 7 hours.
2. Divide the mix between plates and serve with a side salad.

Nutrition: calories 243, fat 11, fiber 4, carbs 6, protein 10

Beef with Endives

Preparation time: 10 minutes
Cooking time: 7 hours
Servings: 2
Ingredients:
- 1 pound beef stew meat, cubed
- 2 teaspoons avocado oil
- 2 endives, shredded
- ½ cup beef stock
- ½ teaspoon sweet paprika
- ¼ cup tomato passata
- 3 garlic cloves, minced
- A pinch of salt and black pepper
- 1 tablespoon chives, chopped

Directions:
1. In your slow cooker, mix the meat with the oil, endives and the other ingredients, toss, put the lid on and cook on Low for 7 hours.
2. Divide the mix between plates and serve.

Nutrition: calories 232, fat 12, fiber 4, carbs 6, protein 9

Lamb and Lime Zucchinis

Preparation time: 10 minutes
Cooking time: 4 hours
Servings: 2
Ingredients:
- 1 pound lamb stew meat, roughly cubed
- 2 small zucchinis, cubed
- Juice of 1 lime
- ½ teaspoon rosemary, dried
- 2 tablespoons avocado oil
- 1 red onion, chopped
- ½ cup beef stock
- 1 tablespoon garlic, minced
- A pinch of salt and black pepper
- 1 tablespoon cilantro, chopped

Directions:
1. In your slow cooker, mix the lamb with the zucchinis, lime juice and the other ingredients, toss, put the lid on and cook on High for 4 hours.
2. Divide the mix between plates and serve.

Nutrition: calories 274, fat 9, fiber 5, carbs 6, protein 12

Beef with Peas

Preparation time: 10 minutes
Cooking time: 5 hours
Servings: 2
Ingredients:
- 1 pound beef stew meat, cubed
- 1 tablespoon olive oil
- ½ teaspoon coriander, ground
- ½ teaspoon sweet paprika
- ½ cup beef stock
- ½ cup tomato sauce
- 1 cup fresh peas
- 1 tablespoon lime juice
- A pinch of salt and black pepper
- 1 tablespoon dill, chopped

Directions:
1. In your slow cooker, mix the beef with the oil, coriander, peas and the other ingredients, toss, put the lid on and cook on High for 5 hours.
2. Divide everything between plates and serve.

Nutrition: calories 232, fat 9, fiber 3, carbs 6, protein 10

Maple Beef

Preparation time: 10 minutes
Cooking time: 7 hours
Servings: 2
Ingredients:
- 1 pound beef roast, sliced
- 1 tablespoon maple syrup
- 2 tablespoons balsamic vinegar
- 2 teaspoons olive oil
- ½ teaspoon Italian seasoning
- A pinch of salt and black pepper
- 1 tablespoon coriander, chopped
- ½ cup beef stock

Directions:
1. In your slow cooker, mix the roast with the maple syrup, vinegar and the other ingredients, toss, put the lid on and cook on Low for 7 hours.
2. Divide the mix between plates and serve.

Nutrition: calories 200, fat 11, fiber 3, carbs 6, protein 15

Rosemary Beef

Preparation time: 10 minutes
Cooking time: 7 hours
Servings: 2
Ingredients:
- 1 pound beef roast, sliced
- 1 tablespoon rosemary, chopped
- Juice of ½ lemon
- 1 tablespoon olive oil
- ½ cup tomato sauce
- A pinch of salt and black pepper

Directions:
1. In your slow cooker, mix the roast with the rosemary, lemon juice and the other ingredients, toss, put the lid on and cook on Low for 7 hours.
2. Divide everything between plates and serve.

Nutrition: calories 210, fat 5, fiber 3, carbs 8, protein 12

Chili Lamb

Preparation time: 10 minutes
Cooking time: 4 hours
Servings: 2
Ingredients:
- 1 pound lamb meat, roughly cubed
- 1 tablespoon avocado oil
- 2 red chilies, chopped
- ½ teaspoon chili powder
- 1 tablespoon parsley, chopped
- ½ cup tomato sauce
- ½ teaspoon oregano, dried
- Juice of 1 lime
- Salt and black pepper to the taste

Directions:
1. In your slow cooker, mix the lamb with the oil, chilies and the other ingredients, toss, put the lid on and cook on High for 4 hours.
2. Divide the mix between plates and serve right away.

Nutrition: calories 248, fat 11, fiber 3, carbs 6, protein 15

Cumin Pork Chops

Preparation time: 10 minutes
Cooking time: 5 hours
Servings: 2
Ingredients:
- 1 pound pork chops
- 2 tablespoons olive oil
- 2 tablespoons balsamic vinegar
- ½ teaspoon cumin, ground
- ½ cup beef stock
- A pinch of salt and black pepper
- 1 tablespoon chives, chopped

Directions:
1. In your slow cooker, mix the pork chops with the oil, vinegar and the other ingredients, toss, put the lid on and cook on High for 5 hours.
2. Divide everything between plates and serve.

Nutrition: calories 233, fat 9, fiber 3, carbs 7, protein 14

Paprika Lamb

Preparation time: 10 minutes
Cooking time: 4 hours
Servings: 2
Ingredients:
- 1 pound lamb chops
- 1 tablespoon sweet paprika
- ½ cup beef stock
- 2 tablespoons avocado oil
- 2 scallions, chopped
- A pinch of salt and black pepper

Directions:
1. In your slow cooker, mix the lamb chops with the paprika, stock and the other ingredients, toss, put the lid on and cook on High for 4 hours.
2. Divide the mix between plates and serve with a side salad.

Nutrition: calories 227, fat 14, fiber 4, carbs 6, protein 16

Beef and Corn

Preparation time: 10 minutes
Cooking time: 7 hours
Servings: 2
Ingredients:
- 1 pound beef stew meat, cubed
- ½ cup corn
- ½ cup fresh peas
- 2 scallions, chopped
- 1 tablespoon lime juice
- 1 cup beef stock
- 2 tablespoons tomato paste
- ½ cup chives, chopped

Directions:
1. In your slow cooker, mix the beef with the corn, peas and the other ingredients, toss, put the lid on and cook on Low for 7 hours.
2. Divide the mix between plates and serve right away.

Nutrition: calories 236, fat 12, fiber 2, carbs 7, protein 15

Lime Pork Chops

Preparation time: 10 minutes
Cooking time: 7 hours
Servings: 2
Ingredients:
- 1 pound pork chops
- 1 tablespoon lime zest, grated
- Juice of 1 lime
- ½ teaspoon turmeric powder
- 1 cup beef stock
- 2 tablespoons olive oil
- A pinch of salt and black pepper

Directions:
1. In your slow cooker, mix the pork chops with the lime juice, zest and the other ingredients, toss, put the lid on and cook on Low for 7 hours.
2. Divide the mix between plates and serve.

Nutrition: calories 273, fat 12, fiber 4, carbs 7, protein 17

Lamb and Capers

Preparation time: 10 minutes
Cooking time: 4 hours
Servings: 2
Ingredients:
- 1 pound lamb chops
- 1 tablespoon capers
- ½ cup beef stock
- ¼ cup tomato passata
- ½ teaspoon sweet paprika
- ½ teaspoon chili powder
- 2 tablespoons olive oil
- 3 scallions, chopped
- A pinch of salt and black pepper

Directions:
1. In your slow cooker, mix the lamb chops with the capers, stock and the other ingredients, toss, put the lid on and cook on High for 4 hours.
2. Divide the mix between plates and serve.

Nutrition: calories 244, fat 12, fiber 2, carbs 5, protein 16

Lamb and Appetizing Zucchini Mix

Preparation time: 10 minutes
Cooking time: 4 hours
Servings: 2
Ingredients:
- 1 pound lamb stew meat, ground
- 2 zucchinis, cubed
- 2 teaspoons olive oil
- 1 carrot, peeled and sliced
- ½ cup beef stock
- 2 tablespoons tomato paste
- ½ teaspoon cumin, ground
- 1 tablespoon chives, chopped
- A pinch of salt and black pepper

Directions:
1. In your slow cooker, mix the lamb with the zucchinis, oil, carrot and the other ingredients, toss, put the lid on and cook on High for 4 hours.
2. Divide the mix into bowls and serve hot.

Nutrition: calories 254, fat 14, fiber 3, carbs 6, protein 17

Beef with Peppers

Preparation time: 10 minutes
Cooking time: 4 hours
Servings: 2
Ingredients:
- 1 pound lamb stew meat, cubed
- 1 red bell pepper, cut into strips
- 1 green bell pepper, cut into strips
- 1 orange bell pepper, cut into strips
- 2 teaspoons olive oil
- A pinch of salt and black pepper
- 1 cup beef stock
- 1 tablespoon chives, chopped
- ½ teaspoon sweet paprika

Directions:
1. In your slow cooker, mix the lamb with the peppers and the other ingredients, toss, put the lid on and cook on High for 4 hours.
2. Divide the mix between plate sand serve.

Nutrition: calories 263, fat 14, fiber 3, carbs 6, protein 20

Cayenne Lamb

Preparation time: 10 minutes
Cooking time: 4 hours
Servings: 2
Ingredients:
- 1 pound lamb stew meat, cubed
- ½ cup tomato sauce
- ½ teaspoon cayenne pepper
- 1 red onion, sliced
- 2 teaspoons olive oil
- ½ teaspoon sweet paprika
- A pinch of salt and black pepper
- 1 tablespoon cilantro, chopped

Directions:
1. In your slow cooker, mix the lamb with the tomato sauce, cayenne and the other ingredients, toss, put the lid on and cook on High for 4 hours..
2. Divide the mix between plates and serve.

Nutrition: calories 283, fat 13, fiber 4, carbs 6, protein 16

Cinnamon Lamb

Preparation time: 10 minutes
Cooking time: 6 hours
Servings: 2
Ingredients:
- 1 pound lamb chops
- 1 teaspoon cinnamon powder
- 1 red onion, chopped
- 1 tablespoon avocado oil
- 1 tablespoon oregano, chopped
- ½ cup beef stock
- 1 tablespoon chives, chopped

Directions:
1. In your slow cooker, mix the lamb chops with the cinnamon and the other ingredients, toss, put the lid on and cook on Low for 6 hours.
2. Divide the chops between plates and serve with a side salad.

Nutrition: calories 253, fat 14, fiber 2, carbs 6, protein 18

Lamb and Kale

Preparation time: 10 minutes
Cooking time: 4 hours
Servings: 2
Ingredients:
- 1 pound lamb shoulder, cubed
- 1 cup baby kale
- 1 tablespoon olive oil
- 1 yellow onion, chopped
- ½ teaspoon coriander, ground
- ½ teaspoon cumin, ground
- ½ teaspoon sweet paprika
- A pinch of salt and black pepper
- ¼ cup beef stock
- 1 tablespoon chives, chopped

Directions:
1. In your slow cooker, mix the lamb with the kale, oil, onion and the other ingredients, toss, put the lid on and cook on High for 4 hours.
2. Divide everything between plates and serve.

Nutrition: calories 264, fat 14, fiber 3, carbs 6, protein 17

Beef with Sprouts

Preparation time: 10 minutes
Cooking time: 7 hours
Servings: 2
Ingredients:
- 1 teaspoon olive oil
- 1 pound beef stew meat, roughly cubed
- 1 cup Brussels sprouts, trimmed and halved
- 1 red onion, chopped
- 1 cup tomato passata
- A pinch of salt and black pepper
- 1 tablespoon chives, chopped

Directions:
1. In your slow cooker, mix the beef with the sprouts, oil and the other ingredients, toss, put the lid on and cook on Low for 7 hours.
2. Divide the mix between plates and serve.

Nutrition: calories 273, fat 13, fiber 2, carbs 6, protein 15

Pork Chops and Spinach

Preparation time: 10 minutes
Cooking time: 4 hours
Servings: 2
Ingredients:
- 1 pound pork chops
- 1 cup baby spinach
- ½ cup beef stock
- ¼ cup tomato passata
- ½ teaspoon sweet paprika
- ½ teaspoon coriander, ground
- 4 scallions, chopped
- 2 teaspoons olive oil
- A pinch of salt and black pepper
- 1 tablespoon chives, chopped

Directions:
1. In your slow cooker, mix the pork chops with the stock, passata and the other ingredients except the spinach, toss, put the lid on and cook on High for 3 hours and 30 minutes.
2. Add the spinach, cook on High for 30 minutes more, divide the mix between plates and serve.

Nutrition: calories 274, fat 14, fiber 2, carbs 6, protein 16

Curry Lamb

Preparation time: 10 minutes
Cooking time: 6 hours
Servings: 2
Ingredients:
- 1 pound lamb stew meat, cubed
- 2 garlic cloves, minced
- 1 tablespoon green curry paste
- A pinch of salt and black pepper
- 1 cup beef stock
- ½ teaspoon rosemary, dried
- 1 tablespoon cilantro, chopped

Directions:
1. In your slow cooker, mix the lamb with the garlic, curry paste and the other ingredients, toss, put the lid on and cook on Low for 6 hours.
2. Divide the mix between plates and serve.

Nutrition: calories 264, fat 14, fiber 2, carbs 8, protein 12

Oregano Lamb

Preparation time: 10 minutes
Cooking time: 6 hours
Servings: 2
Ingredients:
- 1 pound lamb stew meat, roughly cubed
- 1 teaspoon hot paprika
- 1 tablespoon oregano, chopped
- ½ teaspoon turmeric powder
- 4 scallions, chopped
- A pinch of salt and black pepper
- 1 cup beef stock

Directions:
1. In your slow cooker, mix the lamb with the paprika, oregano and the other ingredients, toss, put the lid on and cook on Low for 6 hours.
2. Divide the mix between plates and serve with a side salad.

Nutrition: calories 200, fat 9, fiber 2, carbs 6, protein 12

Pesto Lamb

Preparation time: 10 minutes
Cooking time: 6 hours
Servings: 2
Ingredients:
- 1 pound lamb chops
- 2 tablespoons basil pesto
- 1 tablespoon sweet paprika
- 2 tablespoons olive oil
- A pinch of salt and black pepper
- ½ cup beef stock

Directions:
1. In your slow cooker, mix the lamb chops with the pesto, paprika and the other ingredients, toss, put the lid on and cook on Low for 6 hours.
2. Divide the mix between plates and serve.

Nutrition: calories 234, fat 11, fiber 3, carbs 7, protein 15

Beef with Green Beans

Preparation time: 10 minutes
Cooking time: 7 hours
Servings: 2
Ingredients:
- 1 pound beef stew meat, cubed
- 1 cup green beans, trimmed and halved
- 1 red onion, sliced
- ½ teaspoon chili powder
- ½ teaspoon rosemary, chopped
- 2 teaspoons olive oil
- 1 cup beef stock
- 1 tablespoon cilantro, chopped

Directions:
1. In your slow cooker, mix the beef with the green beans, onion and the other ingredients, toss, put the lid on and cook on Low for 7 hours.
2. Divide the mix between plates and serve right away.

Nutrition: calories 273, fat 14, fiber 2, carbs 6, protein 15

Balsamic Lamb

Preparation time: 10 minutes
Cooking time: 6 hours
Servings: 2
Ingredients:
- 1 pound lamb chops
- 2 tablespoons balsamic vinegar
- 1 tablespoon chives, chopped
- 1 tablespoon olive oil
- 4 garlic cloves, minced
- ½ cup beef stock
- A pinch of salt and black pepper

Directions:
1. In your slow cooker, mix the lamb chops with the vinegar and the other ingredients, toss, put the lid on and cook on Low for 6 hours.
2. Divide everything between plates and serve.

Nutrition: calories 292, fat 12, fiber 3, carbs 7, protein 16

Creamy Beef
Preparation time: 10 minutes
Cooking time: 6 hours
Servings: 2
Ingredients:
- 1 pound beef stew meat, cubed
- 1 cup heavy cream
- 1 red onion, sliced
- ½ teaspoon turmeric powder
- 2 tablespoons olive oil
- 3 scallions, chopped
- 1 tablespoon chives, chopped
- A pinch of salt and black pepper

Directions:
1. In your slow cooker, mix the beef with the cream, onion and the other ingredients, toss, put the lid on and cook on Low for 6 hours.
2. Divide everything between plates and serve.

Nutrition: calories 277, fat 14, fiber 3, carbs 7, protein 17

Coconut Beef
Preparation time: 10 minutes
Cooking time: 7 hours
Servings: 2
Ingredients:
- 1 pound beef stew meat, cubed
- 2 tablespoons walnuts, chopped
- ½ cup coconut cream
- 2 scallions, chopped
- 1 cup beef stock
- ½ teaspoon Italian seasoning
- A pinch of salt and black pepper
- 1 tablespoon rosemary, chopped

Directions:
1. In your slow cooker, mix the beef with the walnuts, scallions and the other ingredients except the cream, toss, put the lid on and cook on Low for 6 hours.
2. Add the cream, toss, cook on Low for 1 more hour, divide everything between plates and serve.

Nutrition: calories 274, fat 12, fiber 4, carbs 7, protein 16

Slow Cooker Fish and Seafood Recipes for 2

Tasty Lime Shrimp

Preparation time: 10 minutes
Cooking time: 1 hour
Servings: 2
Ingredients:
- 1 pound shrimp, peeled and deveined
- Juice of 1 lime
- 2 scallions, chopped
- ½ teaspoon turmeric powder
- ¼ cup chickens stock
- A pinch of salt and black pepper
- 1 tablespoon chives, chopped

Directions:
1. In your slow cooker, mix the shrimp with the lime juice, scallions and the other ingredients, toss, put the lid on and cook on High for 1 hour.
2. Divide the mix into bowls and serve.

Nutrition: calories 198, fat 7, fiber 2, carbs 6, protein 7

Chili Salmon

Preparation time: 10 minutes
Cooking time: 3 hours
Servings: 2
Ingredients:
- 1 tablespoon avocado oil
- 1 pound salmon fillets, boneless
- 1 red chili pepper, minced
- ½ teaspoon chili powder
- 2 scallions, chopped
- ½ cup chicken stock
- A pinch of salt and black pepper

Directions:
1. In your slow cooker, mix the salmon with the chili pepper, the oil and the other ingredients, rub gently, put the lid on and cook on High for 3 hours.
2. Divide the salmon between plates and serve with a side salad.

Nutrition: calories 221, fat 8, fiber 3, carbs 6, protein 7

Herbed Shrimp

Preparation time: 10 minutes
Cooking time: 1 hour
Servings: 2
Ingredients:
- 1 pound shrimp, peeled and deveined
- 1 tablespoon avocado oil
- 1 tablespoon rosemary, chopped
- ½ teaspoon sweet paprika
- ½ teaspoon cumin, ground
- 3 garlic cloves, crushed
- 1 cup chicken stock
- A pinch of salt and black pepper

Directions:
1. In your slow cooker, mix the shrimp with the oil, rosemary and the other ingredients, toss, put the lid on and cook on High for 1 hour.
2. Divide the mix into bowls and serve.

Nutrition: calories 235, fat 8, fiber 4, carbs 7, protein 9

Paprika Cod

Preparation time: 10 minutes
Cooking time: 3 hours
Servings: 2
Ingredients:
- 1 tablespoon olive oil
- 1 pound cod fillets, boneless
- 1 teaspoon sweet paprika
- ¼ cup chicken stock
- ¼ cup white wine
- 2 scallions, chopped
- ½ teaspoon rosemary, dried
- A pinch of salt and black pepper

Directions:
1. In your slow cooker, mix the cod with the paprika, oil and the other ingredients, toss gently, put the lid on and cook on High for 3 hours.
2. Divide everything between plates and serve.

Nutrition: calories 211, fat 8, fiber 4, carbs 8, protein 8

Spicy Tuna

Preparation time: 10 minutes
Cooking time: 2 hours
Servings: 2
Ingredients:
- 1 pound tuna fillets, boneless and cubed
- ½ teaspoon red pepper flakes, crushed
- ¼ teaspoon cayenne pepper
- ½ cup chicken stock
- ½ teaspoon chili powder
- 1 tablespoon olive oil
- A pinch of salt and black pepper
- 1 tablespoon chives, chopped

Directions:
1. In your slow cooker, mix the tuna with the pepper flakes, cayenne and the other ingredients, toss, put the lid on and cook on High for 2 hours.
2. Divide the tuna mix between plates and serve.

Nutrition: calories 193, fat 7, fiber 3, carbs 6, protein 6

Herbed Ginger Tuna
Preparation time: 5 minutes
Cooking time: 2 hours
Servings: 2
Ingredients:
- 1 pound tuna fillets, boneless and roughly cubed
- 1 tablespoon ginger, grated
- 1 red onion, chopped
- 2 teaspoons olive oil
- Juice of 1 lime
- ¼ cup chicken stock
- 1 tablespoon chives, chopped
- A pinch of salt and black pepper

Directions:
1. In your slow cooker, mix the tuna with the ginger, onion and the other ingredients, toss, put the lid on and cook on High for 2 hours.
2. Divide the mix into bowls and serve.

Nutrition: calories 200, fat 11, fiber 4, carbs 5, protein 12

Chives Shrimp
Preparation time: 10 minutes
Cooking time: 1 hour
Servings: 2
Ingredients:
- 1 pound shrimp, peeled and deveined
- 1 tablespoon chives, chopped
- ½ teaspoon basil, dried
- 1 teaspoon turmeric powder
- 1 tablespoon olive oil
- ½ cup chicken stock

Directions:
1. In your slow cooker, mix the shrimp with the basil, chives and the other ingredients, toss, put the lid on and cook on High for 1 hour.
2. Divide the shrimp between plates and serve with a side salad.

Nutrition: calories 200, fat 12, fiber 3, carbs 7, protein 9

Coriander Salmon
Preparation time: 5 minutes
Cooking time: 3 hours
Servings: 2
Ingredients:
- 1 pound salmon fillets, boneless and roughly cubed
- 1 tablespoon coriander, chopped
- ½ teaspoon chili powder
- ¼ cup chicken stock
- 3 scallions, chopped
- Juice of 1 lime
- 2 teaspoons avocado oil
- A pinch of salt and black pepper

Directions:
1. In your slow cooker, mix the salmon with the coriander, chili powder and the other ingredients, toss gently, put the lid on and cook on High for 3 hours.
2. Divide the mix between plates and serve.

Nutrition: calories 232, fat 10, fiber 4, carbs 6, protein 9

Tuna and Green Beans
Preparation time: 10 minutes
Cooking time: 3 hours
Servings: 2
Ingredients:
- 1 pound tuna fillets, boneless
- 1 cup green beans, trimmed and halved
- ½ cup chicken stock
- ½ teaspoon sweet paprika
- ½ teaspoon garam masala
- 3 scallions, minced
- ½ teaspoon ginger, ground
- 1 tablespoon olive oil
- 1 tablespoon chives, chopped
- Salt and black pepper to the taste

Directions:
1. In your slow cooker, mix the tuna with the green beans, stock and the other ingredients, toss gently, put the lid on and cook on High for 3 hours.
2. Divide the mix between plates and serve.

Nutrition: calories 182, fat 7, fiber 3, carbs 6, protein 9

Cod and Corn
Preparation time: 5 minutes
Cooking time: 2 hours
Servings: 2
Ingredients:
- 1 pound cod fillets, boneless
- 1 tablespoon avocado oil
- ½ teaspoon chili powder
- ½ teaspoon coriander, ground
- 1 cup corn
- ½ tablespoon lime juice
- 1 tablespoon chives, chopped
- ¼ cup chicken stock
- A pinch of salt and black pepper

Directions:
1. In your slow cooker, mix the cod with the oil, corn and the other ingredients, toss, put the lid on and cook on High for 2 hours.
2. Divide the mix between plates and serve.

Nutrition: calories 210, fat 8, fiber 3, carbs 6, protein 14

Turmeric Salmon
Preparation time: 5 minutes
Cooking time: 2 hours
Servings: 2
Ingredients:
- 1 pound salmon fillets, boneless
- 1 red onion, chopped
- ½ teaspoon turmeric powder
- ½ teaspoon oregano, dried
- ½ cup chicken stock
- 1 teaspoon olive oil
- Salt and black pepper to the taste
- 1 tablespoon chives, chopped

Directions:
1. In your slow cooker, mix the salmon with the turmeric, onion and the other ingredients, toss gently, put the lid on and cook on High for 2 hours.
2. Divide the mix between plates and serve.

Nutrition: calories 200, fat 12, fiber 3, carbs 6, protein 11

Sea Bass with Chickpeas

Preparation time: 5 minutes
Cooking time: 3 hours
Servings: 2
Ingredients:
- 1 pound sea bass fillets, boneless
- ½ cup chicken stock
- ½ cup canned chickpeas, drained and rinsed
- 2 tablespoons tomato paste
- ½ teaspoon rosemary, dried
- ½ teaspoon oregano, dried
- 2 scallions, minced
- 1 tablespoon olive oil
- Salt and black pepper to the taste

Directions:
1. In your slow cooker, mix the sea bass with the chickpeas, stock and the other ingredients, toss, put the lid on and cook on High for 3 hours.
2. Divide everything between plates and serve.

Nutrition: calories 132, fat 9, fiber 2, carbs 5, protein 11

Creamy Shrimp

Preparation time: 10 minutes
Cooking time: 1 hour
Servings: 2
Ingredients:
- 1 pound shrimp, peeled and deveined
- 2 scallions, chopped
- ¼ cup chicken stock
- 2 tablespoons avocado oil
- ½ cup heavy cream
- 1 teaspoon garam masala
- 1 tablespoon ginger, grated
- A pinch of salt and black pepper
- 1 tablespoon parsley, chopped

Directions:
1. In your slow cooker, mix the shrimp with the scallions, stock and the other ingredients, toss, put the lid on and cook on High for 1 hour.
2. Divide the mix into bowls and serve.

Nutrition: calories 200, fat 12, fiber 2, carbs 6, protein 11

Parsley Cod

Preparation time: 5 minutes
Cooking time: 2 hours
Servings: 2
Ingredients:
- 1 pound cod fillets, boneless
- 3 scallions, chopped
- 2 teaspoons olive oil
- Juice of 1 lime
- 1 teaspoon coriander, ground
- Salt and black pepper to the taste
- 1 tablespoon parsley, chopped

Directions:
1. In your slow cooker, mix the cod with the scallions, the oil and the other ingredients, rub gently, put the lid on and cook on High for 1 hour.
2. Divide everything between plates and serve.

Nutrition: calories 200, fat 12, fiber 2, carbs 6, protein 9

Cod and Tomatoes

Preparation time: 10 minutes
Cooking time: 3 hours
Servings: 2
Ingredients:
- 1 pound cod, boneless and roughly cubed
- 2 tablespoons basil pesto
- 1 tablespoon olive oil
- 1 cup cherry tomatoes, halved
- 1 tablespoon chives, chopped
- ½ cup veggie stock
- A pinch of salt and black pepper

Directions:
1. In your slow cooker, mix the cod with the pesto, oil and the other ingredients, toss, put the lid on and cook on High for 3 hours.
2. Divide the mix between plates and serve.

Nutrition: calories 211, fat 13, fiber 2, carbs 7, protein 11

Orange Cod

Preparation time: 5 minutes
Cooking time: 3 hours
Servings: 2
Ingredients:
- 1 pound cod fillets, boneless
- Juice of 1 orange
- 1 tablespoon avocado oil
- 2 scallions, chopped
- ½ teaspoon turmeric powder
- ½ teaspoon sweet paprika
- A pinch of salt and black pepper

Directions:
1. In your slow cooker, mix the cod with the orange juice, oil and the other ingredients, toss, put the lid on and cook on High 3 hours.
2. Divide the mix between plates and serve.

Nutrition: calories 200, fat 12, fiber 4, carbs 6, protein 8

Garlic Sea Bass

Preparation time: 5 minutes
Cooking time: 4 hours
Servings: 2
Ingredients:
- 1 pound sea bass fillets, boneless
- 2 teaspoons avocado oil
- 3 garlic cloves, minced
- 1 green chili pepper, minced
- ½ teaspoon rosemary, dried
- ½ cup chicken stock
- A pinch of salt and black pepper
- 1 tablespoon cilantro, chopped

Directions:
1. In your slow cooker, mix the sea bass with the oil, garlic and the other ingredients, toss gently, put the lid on and cook on Low for 4 hours.
2. Divide the mix between plates and serve.

Nutrition: calories 232, fat 7, fiber 3, carbs 7, protein 9

Tuna with Brussels Sprouts
Preparation time: 5 minutes
Cooking time: 3 hours
Servings: 2
Ingredients:
- 1 pound tuna fillets, boneless
- ½ cup chicken stock
- 1 teaspoon sweet paprika
- ½ teaspoon chili powder
- 1 cup Brussels sprouts, trimmed and halved
- 1 red onion, chopped
- ½ teaspoon garlic powder
- A pinch of salt and black pepper
- 1 tablespoon cilantro, chopped

Directions:
1. In your slow cooker, mix the tuna with the stock, sprouts and the other ingredients, put the lid on and cook on High for 3 hours.
2. Divide the mix between plates and serve.

Nutrition: calories 232, fat 9, fiber 2, carbs 6, protein 8

Shrimp with Spinach
Preparation time: 10 minutes
Cooking time: 1 hour
Servings: 2
Ingredients:
- 1 pound shrimp, peeled and deveined
- 1 cup baby spinach
- ¼ cup tomato passata
- ½ cup chicken stock
- 3 scallions, chopped
- 1 tablespoon olive oil
- ½ teaspoon sweet paprika
- A pinch of salt and black pepper
- 1 tablespoon chives, chopped

Directions:
1. In your slow cooker, mix the shrimp with the spinach, tomato passata and the other ingredients, toss, put the lid on and cook on High for 1 hour.
2. Divide the mix between plates and serve.

Nutrition: calories 200, fat 13, fiber 3, carbs 6, protein 11

Shrimp with Avocado
Preparation time: 5 minutes
Cooking time: 1 hour
Servings: 2
Ingredients:
- 1 pound shrimp, peeled and deveined
- 1 cup avocado, peeled, pitted and cubed
- ½ cup chicken stock
- ½ teaspoon sweet paprika
- Juice of 1 lime
- 1 tablespoon olive oil
- 2 tablespoons chili pepper, minced
- A pinch of salt and black pepper
- 1 tablespoon chives, chopped

Directions:
1. In your slow cooker, mix the shrimp with the avocado, stock and the other ingredients, toss, put the lid on and cook on High for 1 hour.
2. Divide the mix into bowls and serve.

Nutrition: calories 490, fat 25.4, fiber 5.8, carbs 11.9, protein 53.6

Chives Mackerel
Preparation time: 10 minutes
Cooking time: 4 hours
Servings: 2
Ingredients:
- 1 pound mackerel fillets, boneless
- ½ teaspoon cumin, ground
- ½ teaspoon coriander, ground
- 2 garlic cloves, minced
- 1 tablespoon avocado oil
- 1 tablespoon lime juice
- ½ cup chicken stock
- A pinch of salt and black pepper
- 2 tablespoons chives, chopped

Directions:
1. In your slow cooker, mix the mackerel with the cumin, coriander and the other ingredients, put the lid on and cook on Low for 4 hours.
2. Divide the mix between plates and serve with a side salad.

Nutrition: calories 613, fat 41.6, fiber 0.5, carbs 2, protein 54.7

Dill Cod
Preparation time: 10 minutes
Cooking time: 3 hours
Servings: 2
Ingredients:
- 1 tablespoon olive oil
- 1 pound cod fillets, boneless and cubed
- 1 tablespoon dill, chopped
- ½ teaspoon sweet paprika
- ½ teaspoon cumin, ground
- 2 garlic cloves, minced
- 1 teaspoon lemon juice
- 1 cup tomato passata
- A pinch of salt and black pepper

Directions:
1. In your slow cooker, mix the cod with the oil, dill and the other ingredients, toss, put the lid on and cook on Low for 3 hours.
2. Divide the mix between plates and serve.

Nutrition: calories 192, fat 9, fiber 2, carbs 8, protein 7

Shrimp and Mango

Preparation time: 10 minutes
Cooking time: 1 hour
Servings: 2
Ingredients:
- 1 pound shrimp, peeled and deveined
- ½ cup mango, peeled and cubed
- ½ cup cherry tomatoes, halved
- ½ cup shallots, chopped
- 1 tablespoon lime juice
- ½ teaspoon rosemary, dried
- 1 tablespoon olive oil
- ½ teaspoon chili powder
- ½ cup chicken stock
- A pinch of salt and black pepper
- 1 tablespoon chives, chopped

Directions:
1. In your slow cooker, mix the shrimp with the mango, tomatoes and the other ingredients, toss, put the lid on and cook on High for 1 hour.
2. Divide the mix into bowls and serve.

Nutrition: calories 210, fat 9, fiber 2, carbs 6, protein 7

Balsamic Tuna

Preparation time: 5 minutes
Cooking time: 3 hours
Servings: 2
Ingredients:
- 1 pound tuna fillets, boneless and roughly cubed
- 1 tablespoon balsamic vinegar
- 3 garlic cloves, minced
- 1 tablespoon avocado oil
- ¼ cup chicken stock
- 1 tablespoon hives, chopped
- A pinch of salt and black pepper

Directions:
1. In your slow cooker, mix the tuna with the garlic, vinegar and the other ingredients, toss, put the lid on and cook on Low for 3 hours.
2. Divide the mix into bowls and serve.

Nutrition: calories 200, fat 10, fiber 2, carbs 5, protein 9

Lime Trout

Preparation time: 10 minutes
Cooking time: 2 hours
Servings: 2
Ingredients:
- 1 pound trout fillets, boneless
- 1 tablespoon olive oil
- ½ cup chicken stock
- 2 tablespoons lime zest, grated
- 2 tablespoons lemon juice
- 1 teaspoon garam masala
- A pinch of salt and black pepper

Directions:
1. In your slow cooker, mix the trout with the olive oil, lime juice and the other ingredients, toss, put the lid on and cook on High for 2 hours.
2. Divide everything between plates and serve.

Nutrition: calories 200, fat 13, fiber 3, carbs 6, protein 11

Creamy Tuna and Scallions

Preparation time: 10 minutes
Cooking time: 2 hours
Servings: 2
Ingredients:
- 1 pound tuna fillets, boneless and cubed
- 4 scallions, chopped
- ½ cup heavy cream
- ½ cup chicken stock
- 1 tablespoon olive oil
- 1 teaspoon turmeric powder
- A pinch of salt and black pepper
- 1 tablespoon chives, chopped

Directions:
1. In your slow cooker, mix the tuna with the scallions, cream and the other ingredients, toss, put the lid on and cook on High for 2 hours.
2. Divide the mix into bowls and serve.

Nutrition: calories 198, fat 7, fiber 2, carbs 6, protein 7

Mustard Cod

Preparation time: 10 minutes
Cooking time: 3 hours
Servings: 2
Ingredients:
- 1 tablespoon olive oil
- 1 pound cod fillets, boneless
- 2 tablespoons mustard
- ½ cup heavy cream
- ¼ cup chicken stock
- 2 garlic cloves, minced
- A pinch of salt and black pepper
- 1 tablespoon chives, chopped

Directions:
1. In your slow cooker, mix the cod with the oil, mustard and the other ingredients, toss gently, put the lid on and cook on Low for 3 hours.
2. Divide the mix between plates and serve.

Nutrition: calories 221, fat 8, fiber 3, carbs 6, protein 7

Shrimp with Pineapple Bowls

Preparation time: 5 minutes
Cooking time: 1 hour
Servings: 2
Ingredients:
- 1 pound shrimp, peeled and deveined
- 1 cup pineapple, peeled and cubed
- 1 teaspoon sweet paprika
- 1 tablespoon avocado oil
- 3 scallions, chopped
- ½ cup chicken stock
- A pinch of salt and black pepper

Directions:
1. In your slow cooker, mix the shrimp with the pineapple, paprika and the other ingredients, toss, put the lid on and cook on High for 1 hour.
2. Divide the mix into bowls and serve.

Nutrition: calories 235, fat 8, fiber 4, carbs 7, protein 9

Lime Crab
Preparation time: 10 minutes
Cooking time: 2 hours
Servings: 2
Ingredients:
- 1 tablespoon avocado oil
- 1 pound crab meat
- ¼ cup shallots, chopped
- 1 tablespoon lime juice
- ½ cup fish stock
- 1 teaspoon sweet paprika
- 1 tablespoon chives, chopped
- A pinch of salt and black pepper

Directions:
1. In your slow cooker, mix the crab with the oil, shallots and the other ingredients, toss, put the lid on and cook on High for 2 hours.
2. Divide everything into bowls and serve.

Nutrition: calories 211, fat 8, fiber 4, carbs 8, protein 8

Salmon and Carrots
Preparation time: 10 minutes
Cooking time: 3 hours
Servings: 2
Ingredients:
- 1 pound salmon fillets, boneless
- 1 cup baby carrots, peeled
- ½ teaspoon hot paprika
- ½ teaspoon chili powder
- ¼ cup chicken stock
- 2 scallions, chopped
- 1 tablespoon smoked paprika
- A pinch of salt and black pepper
- 2 tablespoons chives, chopped

Directions:
1. In your slow cooker, mix the salmon with the carrots, paprika and the other ingredients, toss, put the lid on and cook on Low for 3 hours.
2. Divide the mix between plates and serve.

Nutrition: calories 193, fat 7, fiber 3, carbs 6, protein 6

Shrimp and Eggplant
Preparation time: 5 minutes
Cooking time: 1 hour
Servings: 2
Ingredients:
- 1 pound shrimp, peeled and deveined
- 2 teaspoons avocado oil
- 1 eggplant, cubed
- 2 tomatoes, cubed
- Juice of 1 lime
- ½ cup chicken stock
- 4 garlic cloves, minced
- 1 tablespoon coriander, chopped
- 1 tablespoon chives, chopped
- A pinch of salt and black pepper

Directions:
1. In your slow cooker, mix the shrimp with the oil, eggplant, tomatoes and the other ingredients, toss, put the lid on and cook on High for 1 hour.
2. Divide the mix into bowls and serve.

Nutrition: calories 200, fat 11, fiber 4, carbs 5, protein 12

Sea Bass with Squash
Preparation time: 10 minutes
Cooking time: 3 hours
Servings: 2
Ingredients:
- 1 pound sea bass, boneless and cubed
- 1 cup butternut squash, peeled and cubed
- 1 teaspoon olive oil
- ½ teaspoon turmeric powder
- ½ teaspoon Italian seasoning
- 1 cup chicken stock
- 1 tablespoon cilantro, chopped

Directions:
1. In your slow cooker, mix the sea bass with the squash, oil, turmeric and the other ingredients, toss, the lid on and cook on Low for 3 hours.
2. Divide everything between plates and serve.

Nutrition: calories 200, fat 12, fiber 3, carbs 7, protein 9

Coconut Mackerel
Preparation time: 5 minutes
Cooking time: 3 hours
Servings: 2
Ingredients:
- 1 pound mackerel fillets, boneless, skinless and cubed
- 1 tablespoon avocado oil
- 1 cup coconut cream
- ½ teaspoon cumin, ground
- 2 scallions, chopped
- A pinch of salt and black pepper
- ½ teaspoon garam masala
- 1 tablespoon cilantro, chopped

Directions:
1. In your slow cooker, mix the mackerel with the oil, cream and the other ingredients, toss, put the lid on and cook on Low for 3 hours.
2. Divide the mix into bowls and serve.

Nutrition: calories 232, fat 10, fiber 4, carbs 6, protein 9

Salmon with Peas
Preparation time: 10 minutes
Cooking time: 2 hours
Servings: 2
Ingredients:
- 1 pound salmon fillets, boneless and cubed
- 1 tablespoon olive oil
- 1 cup sugar snap peas
- 1 tablespoon lemon juice
- ½ cup tomato passata
- 1 tablespoon chives, chopped
- Salt and black pepper to the taste

Directions:
1. In your slow cooker, mix the salmon with the peas, oil and the other ingredients, toss, put the lid on and cook on High for 2 hour.
2. Divide the mix between plates and serve.

Nutrition: calories 182, fat 7, fiber 3, carbs 6, protein 9

Chili Shrimp with Zucchinis
Preparation time: 10 minutes
Cooking time: 1 hour
Servings: 4
Ingredients:
- 1 pound shrimp, peeled and deveined
- 1 zucchini, cubed
- 2 scallions, minced
- 1 cup tomato passata
- 2 green chilies, chopped
- A pinch of salt and black pepper
- 1 tablespoon chives, chopped

Directions:
1. In your slow cooker, mix the shrimp with the zucchini and the other ingredients, toss, put the lid on and cook on High for 1 hour.
2. Divide the shrimp mix into bowls and serve.

Nutrition: calories 210, fat 8, fiber 3, carbs 6, protein 14

Italian Shrimp
Preparation time: 5 minutes
Cooking time: 1 hour
Servings: 2
Ingredients:
- 1 pound shrimp, peeled and deveined
- 1 tablespoon avocado oil
- ½ teaspoon sweet paprika
- 1 teaspoon Italian seasoning
- Salt and black pepper to the taste
- Juice of 1 lime
- ¼ cup chicken stock
- 1 tablespoon chives, chopped

Directions:
1. In your slow cooker, mix the shrimp with the oil, seasoning and the other ingredients, toss, put the lid on and cook on High for 1 hour.
2. Divide the mix into bowls and serve.

Nutrition: calories 200, fat 12, fiber 3, carbs 6, protein 11

Basil Cod with Olives
Preparation time: 5 minutes
Cooking time: 3 hours
Servings: 2
Ingredients:
- 1 pound cod fillets, boneless
- 1 cup black olives, pitted and halved
- ½ tablespoon tomato paste
- 1 tablespoon basil, chopped
- ¼ cup chicken stock
- 1 red onion, sliced
- 1 tablespoon lime juice
- 1 tablespoon chives, chopped
- Salt and black pepper to the taste

Directions:
1. In your slow cooker, mix the cod with the olives, basil and the other ingredients, toss, put the lid on and cook on Low for 3 hours.
2. Divide everything between plates and serve.

Nutrition: calories 132, fat 9, fiber 2, carbs 5, protein 11

Tuna and Fennel
Preparation time: 10 minutes
Cooking time: 2 hours
Servings: 2
Ingredients:
- 1 pound tuna fillets, boneless and cubed
- 1 fennel bulb, sliced
- ½ cup chicken stock
- ½ teaspoon sweet paprika
- ½ teaspoon chili powder
- 1 red onion, chopped
- A pinch of salt and black pepper
- 2 tablespoons cilantro, chopped

Directions:
1. In your slow cooker, mix the tuna with the fennel, stock and the other ingredients, toss, put the lid on and cook on High for 2 hour.
2. Divide the mix between plates and serve.

Nutrition: calories 200, fat 12, fiber 2, carbs 6, protein 11

Shrimp with Mushrooms
Preparation time: 10 minutes
Cooking time: 1 hour
Servings: 2
Ingredients:
- 1 pound shrimp, peeled and deveined
- 1 cup white mushrooms, halved
- 1 tablespoon avocado oil
- ½ tablespoon tomato paste
- 4 scallions, minced
- ½ cup chicken stock
- Juice of 1 lime
- Salt and black pepper to the taste
- 1 tablespoon chives, minced

Directions:
1. In your slow cooker, mix the shrimp with the mushrooms, oil and the other ingredients, toss, put the lid on and cook on High for 1 hour.
2. Divide the mix into bowls and serve.

Nutrition: calories 200, fat 12, fiber 2, carbs 6, protein 9

Salmon and Berries
Preparation time: 10 minutes
Cooking time: 3 hours
Servings: 2
Ingredients:
- 1 pound salmon fillets, boneless and roughly cubed
- ½ cup blackberries
- Juice of 1 lime
- 1 tablespoon avocado oil
- 2 scallions, chopped
- ½ teaspoon Italian seasoning
- ½ cup fish stock
- A pinch of salt and black pepper

Directions:
1. In your slow cooker, mix the salmon with the berries, lime juice and the other ingredients, toss, put the lid on and cook on Low for 3 hours.
2. Divide the mix between plates and serve.

Nutrition: calories 211, fat 13, fiber 2, carbs 7, protein 11

Cod with Artichokes
Preparation time: 5 minutes
Cooking time: 3 hours
Servings: 2
Ingredients:
- 1 pound cod fillets, boneless and roughly cubed
- 1 cup canned artichoke hearts, drained and quartered
- 2 scallions, chopped
- 1 tablespoon olive oil
- ½ cup chicken stock
- 1 tablespoon lime juice
- 1 tablespoon cilantro, chopped
- A pinch of salt and black pepper

Directions:
1. In your slow cooker, mix the cod with the artichokes, scallions and the other ingredients, toss, put the lid on and cook on Low for 3 hours.
2. Divide the mix between plates and serve.

Nutrition: calories 200, fat 12, fiber 4, carbs 6, protein 8

Salmon, Tomatoes and Green Beans
Preparation time: 5 minutes
Cooking time: 2 hours
Servings: 2
Ingredients:
- 1 pound salmon fillets, boneless and cubed
- 1 cup cherry tomatoes, halved
- 1 cup green beans, trimmed and halved
- 1 cup tomato passata
- ½ cup chicken stock
- A pinch of salt and black pepper
- 1 tablespoon parsley, chopped

Directions:
1. In your slow cooker, mix the salmon with the tomatoes, green beans and the other ingredients, toss, put the lid on and cook on High for 2 hours.
2. Divide the mix into bowls and serve.

Nutrition: calories 232, fat 7, fiber 3, carbs 7, protein 9

Shrimp and Rice
Preparation time: 5 minutes
Cooking time: 1 hour and 30 minutes
Servings: 2
Ingredients:
- 1 pound shrimp, peeled and deveined
- 1 cup chicken stock
- ½ cup wild rice
- ½ cup carrots, peeled and cubed
- 1 green bell pepper, cubed
- ½ teaspoon turmeric powder
- ½ teaspoon coriander, ground
- 1 tablespoon olive oil
- 1 red onion, chopped
- A pinch of salt and black pepper
- 1 tablespoon cilantro, chopped

Directions:
1. In your slow cooker, mix the stock with the rice, carrots and the other ingredients except the shrimp, toss, put the lid on and cook on High for 1 hour.
2. Add the shrimp, toss, put the lid back on and cook on High for 30 minutes.
3. Divide the mix between plates and serve.

Nutrition: calories 232, fat 9, fiber 2, carbs 6, protein 8

Shrimp with Red Chard
Preparation time: 5 minutes
Cooking time: 1 hour
Servings: 2
Ingredients:
- 1 pound shrimp, peeled and deveined
- Juice of 1 lime
- 1 cup red chard, torn
- ½ cup tomato sauce
- 2 garlic cloves, minced
- 1 red onion, sliced
- 1 tablespoon olive oil
- ½ teaspoon sweet paprika
- A pinch of salt and black pepper
- 1 tablespoon parsley, chopped

Directions:
1. In your slow cooker, mix the shrimp with the lime juice, chard and the other ingredients, toss, put the lid on and cook on High for 1 hour.
2. Divide the mix into bowls and serve.

Nutrition: calories 200, fat 13, fiber 3, carbs 6, protein 11

Chives Mussels
Preparation time: 5 minutes
Cooking time: 1 hour
Servings: 2
Ingredients:
- 1 pound mussels, debearded
- ½ teaspoon coriander, ground
- ½ teaspoon rosemary, dried
- 1 tablespoon lime zest, grated
- Juice of 1 lime
- 1 cup tomato passata
- ¼ cup chicken stock
- A pinch of salt and black pepper
- 1 tablespoon chives, chopped

Directions:
1. In your slow cooker, mix the mussels with the coriander, rosemary and the other ingredients, toss, put the lid on and cook on High for 1 hour.
2. Divide the mix into bowls and serve.

Nutrition: calories 200, fat 12, fiber 2, carbs 6, protein 9

Calamari with Sauce
Preparation time: 10 minutes
Cooking time: 2 hours
Servings: 2
Ingredients:
- 1 pound calamari rings
- 2 scallions, chopped
- 2 garlic cloves, minced
- ½ cup heavy cream
- ½ cup chicken stock
- 1 tablespoon lime juice
- ½ cup black olives, pitted and halved
- A pinch of salt and black pepper
- 2 tablespoons chives, chopped

Directions:
1. In your slow cooker, mix the calamari with the scallions, garlic and the other ingredients except the cream, toss, put the lid on and cook on High for 1 hour.
2. Add the cream, toss, cook on High for 1 more hour, divide into bowls and serve.

Nutrition: calories 200, fat 12, fiber 2, carbs 5, protein 6

Salmon Salad
Preparation time: 5 minutes
Cooking time: 3 hours
Servings: 2
Ingredients:
- 1 pound salmon fillets, boneless and cubed
- ¼ cup chicken stock
- 1 zucchini, cut with a spiralizer
- 1 carrot, sliced
- 1 eggplant, cubed
- ½ cup cherry tomatoes, halved
- 1 red onion, sliced
- ½ teaspoon turmeric powder
- ½ teaspoon chili powder
- ½ tablespoon rosemary, chopped
- A pinch of salt and black pepper
- 1 tablespoon chives, chopped

Directions:
1. In your slow cooker, mix the salmon with the zucchini, stock, carrot and the other ingredients,, toss , put the lid on and cook on High for 3 hours.
2. Divide the mix into bowls and serve.

Nutrition: calories 424, fat 15.1, fiber 12.4, carbs 28.1, protein 49

Walnut Tuna
Preparation time: 10 minutes
Cooking time: 3 hours
Servings: 2
Ingredients:
- 1 pound tuna fillets, boneless
- ½ tablespoon walnuts, chopped
- ½ cup chicken stock
- ½ teaspoon chili powder
- ½ teaspoon sweet paprika
- 1 red onion, sliced
- 2 tablespoons parsley, chopped
- A pinch of salt and black pepper

Directions:
3. In your slow cooker, mix the tuna with the walnuts, stock and the other ingredients, toss, put the lid on and cook on High for 3 hours.
4. Divide everything between plates and serve.

Nutrition: calories 200, fat 10, fiber 2, carbs 5, protein 9

Almond Shrimp and Cabbage
Preparation time: 5 minutes
Cooking time: 1 hour
Servings: 2
Ingredients:
- 1 pound shrimp, peeled and deveined
- 1 cup red cabbage, shredded
- 1 tablespoon almonds, chopped
- 1 cup cherry tomatoes, halved
- 1 tablespoon balsamic vinegar
- 2 tablespoons olive oil
- ½ cup tomato passata
- A pinch of salt and black pepper

Directions:
1. In your slow cooker, mix the shrimp with the cabbage, almonds and the other ingredients, toss, put the lid on and cook on High for 1 hour.
2. Divide everything into bowls and serve.

Nutrition: calories 200, fat 13, fiber 3, carbs 6, protein 11

Spicy Shrimp
Preparation time: 5 minutes
Cooking time: 1 hours
Servings: 2
Ingredients:
- 4 scallions, chopped
- 1 tablespoon olive oil
- 1 pound shrimp, peeled and deveined
- ½ teaspoon garam masala
- ½ teaspoon coriander, ground
- ½ teaspoon turmeric powder
- 1 tablespoon lime juice
- ½ cup chicken stock
- ¼ cup lime leaves, torn

Directions:
1. In your slow cooker, mix the shrimp with the oil, scallions, masala and the other ingredients, toss, put the lid on and cook on High for 1 hour.
2. Divide the mix into bowls and serve.

Nutrition: calories 211, fat 12, fiber 3, carbs 6, protein 7

Tomatoes and Kale

Preparation time: 5 minutes
Cooking time: 1 hour
Servings: 2
Ingredients:
- 1 pound shrimp, peeled and deveined
- ½ cup cherry tomatoes, halved
- 1 cup baby kale
- ½ cup chicken stock
- 1 tablespoon olive oil
- Salt and black pepper to the taste
- Juice of 1 lime
- ½ teaspoon sweet paprika
- 1 tablespoon cilantro, chopped

Directions:
1. In your slow cooker, mix the shrimp with the cherry tomatoes, kale and the other ingredients, toss, put the lid on and cook on High for 1 hour.
2. Divide the mix into bowls and serve.

Nutrition: calories 200, fat 12, fiber 3, carbs 6, protein 11

Trout Bowls

Preparation time: 5 minutes
Cooking time: 3 hours
Servings: 2
Ingredients:
- 1 pound trout fillets, boneless, skinless and cubed
- 1 cup kalamata olives, pitted and chopped
- 1 cup baby spinach
- 2 garlic cloves, minced
- 1 tablespoon olive oil
- Juice of ½ lime
- Salt and black pepper to the taste
- 1 tablespoon parsley, chopped

Directions:
1. In your slow cooker, mix the trout with the olives, spinach and the other ingredients, toss, put the lid on and cook on Low for 3 hours.
2. Divide everything into bowls and serve.

Nutrition: calories 132, fat 9, fiber 2, carbs 5, protein 11

Curry Calamari

Preparation time: 10 minutes
Cooking time: 3 hours
Servings: 2
Ingredients:
- 1 pound calamari rings
- ½ tablespoon yellow curry paste
- 1 cup coconut milk
- ½ teaspoon turmeric powder
- ½ cup chicken stock
- 2 garlic cloves, minced
- ½ tablespoon coriander, chopped
- A pinch of salt and black pepper
- 2 tablespoons lemon juice

Directions:
1. In your slow cooker, mix the rings with the curry paste, coconut milk and the other ingredients, toss, put the lid on and cook on High for 3 hours.
2. Divide the curry into bowls and serve.

Nutrition: calories 200, fat 12, fiber 2, carbs 6, protein 11

Balsamic Trout

Preparation time: 10 minutes
Cooking time: 3 hours
Servings: 2
Ingredients:
- 1 pound trout fillets, boneless
- ½ cup chicken stock
- 2 garlic cloves, minced
- 2 tablespoons balsamic vinegar
- ½ teaspoon cumin, ground
- Salt and black pepper to the taste
- 1 tablespoon parsley, chopped
- 1 tablespoon olive oil

Directions:
1. In your slow cooker, mix the trout with the stock, garlic and the other ingredients, toss gently, put the lid on and cook on High for 3 hours.
2. Divide the mix between plates and serve.

Nutrition: calories 200, fat 12, fiber 2, carbs 6, protein 9

Oregano Shrimp

Preparation time: 10 minutes
Cooking time: 1 hour
Servings: 2
Ingredients:
- 1 pound shrimp, peeled and deveined
- ½ cup cherry tomatoes, halved
- ½ cup baby spinach
- 1 tablespoon lime juice
- 1 tablespoon oregano, chopped
- ¼ cup fish stock
- ½ teaspoon sweet paprika
- 2 garlic cloves, chopped
- A pinch of salt and black pepper

Directions:
1. In your slow cooker, mix the shrimp with the cherry tomatoes, spinach and the other ingredients, toss, put the lid on and cook on High for 1 hour.
2. Divide everything between plates and serve.

Nutrition: calories 211, fat 13, fiber 2, carbs 7, protein 11

Salmon and Strawberries Mix

Preparation time: 10 minutes
Cooking time: 2 hours
Servings: 2
Ingredients:
- 1 pound salmon fillets, boneless
- 1 cup strawberries, halved
- ½ cup orange juice
- Zest of 1 lemon, grated
- 4 scallions, chopped
- 1 teaspoon balsamic vinegar
- 1 tablespoon chives, chopped
- A pinch of salt and black pepper

Directions:
1. In your slow cooker, mix the salmon with the strawberries, orange juice and the other ingredients, toss, put the lid on and cook on High for 2 hours.
2. Divide everything into bowls and serve.

Nutrition: calories 200, fat 12, fiber 4, carbs 6, protein 8

Salmon and Tomatoes

Preparation time: 5 minutes
Cooking time: 1 hour and 30 minutes
Servings: 2
Ingredients:
- 1 pound shrimp, peeled and deveined
- ½ pound salmon fillets, boneless and cubed
- 1 cup cherry tomatoes, halved
- ½ cup chicken stock
- ½ teaspoon chili powder
- ½ teaspoon rosemary, dried
- A pinch of salt and black pepper
- 1 tablespoon parsley, chopped
- 2 tablespoons tomato sauce
- 2 garlic cloves, minced

Directions:
1. In your slow cooker, combine the shrimp with the salmon, tomatoes and the other ingredients, toss gently, put the lid on and cook on High for 1 hour and 30 minutes.
2. Divide the mix into bowls and serve.

Nutrition: calories 232, fat 7, fiber 3, carbs 7, protein 9

Shrimp and Cauliflower Bowls

Preparation time: 5 minutes
Cooking time: 2 hours
Servings: 2
Ingredients:
- 1 pound shrimp, peeled and deveined
- ½ cup chicken stock
- 1 cup cauliflower florets
- ½ teaspoon turmeric powder
- ½ teaspoon coriander, ground
- ½ cup tomato passata
- A pinch of salt and black pepper
- 1 tablespoon cilantro, chopped

Directions:
1. In your slow cooker, mix the cauliflower with the stock, turmeric and the other ingredients except the shrimp, toss, put the lid on and cook on High for 1 hour.
2. Add the shrimp, toss, cook on High for 1 more hour, divide into bowls and serve.

Nutrition: calories 232, fat 9, fiber 2, carbs 6, protein 8

Cod with Broccoli

Preparation time: 10 minutes
Cooking time: 3 hours
Servings: 2
Ingredients:
- 1 pound cod fillets, boneless
- 1 cup broccoli florets
- ½ cup veggie stock
- 2 tablespoons tomato paste
- 2 garlic cloves, minced
- 1 red onion, minced
- ½ teaspoon rosemary, dried
- A pinch of salt and black pepper
- 1 tablespoon chives, chopped

Directions:
1. In your slow cooker, mix the cod with the broccoli, stock, tomato paste and the other ingredients, toss, put the lid on and cook on Low for 3 hours.
2. Divide the mix between plates and serve.

Nutrition: calories 200, fat 13, fiber 3, carbs 6, protein 11

Cinnamon Trout

Preparation time: 5 minutes
Cooking time: 3 hours
Servings: 2
Ingredients:
- 1 pound trout fillets, boneless
- 1 tablespoon cinnamon powder
- ¼ cup chicken stock
- 2 tablespoons chili pepper, minced
- A pinch of salt and black pepper
- A pinch of cayenne pepper
- 1 tablespoon chives, chopped

Directions:
1. In your slow cooker, mix the trout with the cinnamon, stock and the other ingredients, toss gently, put the lid on and cook on Low for 3 hours.
2. Divide the mix between plates and serve with a side salad.

Nutrition: calories 200, fat 12, fiber 2, carbs 6, protein 9

Slow Cooker Dessert Recipes for 2

Apples with Cinnamon
Preparation time: 10 minutes
Cooking time: 2 hours
Servings: 2
Ingredients:
- 2 tablespoons brown sugar
- 1 pound apples, cored and cut into wedges
- 1 tablespoon cinnamon powder
- 2 tablespoons walnuts, chopped
- A pinch of nutmeg, ground
- ½ tablespoon lemon juice
- ¼ cup water
- 2 apples, cored and tops cut off

Directions:
1. In your slow cooker, mix the apples with the sugar, cinnamon and the other ingredients, toss, put the lid on and cook on High for 2 hours.
2. Divide the mix between plates and serve.

Nutrition: calories 189, fat 4, fiber 7, carbs 19, protein 2

Vanilla Pears
Preparation time: 10 minutes
Cooking time: 2 hours
Servings: 2
Ingredients:
- 2 tablespoons avocado oil
- 1 teaspoon vanilla extract
- 2 pears, cored and halved
- ½ tablespoon lime juice
- 1 tablespoon sugar

Directions:
1. In your slow cooker combine the pears with the sugar, oil and the other ingredients, toss, put the lid on and cook on High for 2 hours.
2. Divide between plates and serve.

Nutrition: calories 200, fat 4, fiber 6, carbs 16, protein 3

Easy Avocado Cake
Preparation time: 10 minutes
Cooking time: 2 hours
Servings: 2
Ingredients:
- ½ cup brown sugar
- 2 tablespoons coconut oil, melted
- 1 cup avocado, peeled and mashed
- ½ teaspoon vanilla extract
- 1 egg
- ½ teaspoon baking powder
- 1 cup almond flour
- ¼ cup almond milk
- Cooking spray

Directions:
1. In a bowl, mix the sugar with the oil, avocado and the other ingredients except the cooking spray and whisk well.
2. Grease your slow cooker with cooking spray, add the cake batter, spread, put the lid on and cook on High for 2 hours.
3. Leave the cake to cool down, slice and serve.

Nutrition: calories 300, fat 4, fiber 4, carbs 27, protein 4

Coconut Cream
Preparation time: 10 minutes
Cooking time: 1 hour
Servings: 2
Ingredients:
- 2 ounces coconut cream
- 1 cup coconut milk
- ½ teaspoon almond extract
- 2 tablespoons sugar

Directions:
1. In your slow cooker, mix the cream with the milk and the other ingredients, whisk, put the lid on, cook on High for 1 hour, divide into bowls and serve cold.

Nutrition: calories 242, fat 12, fiber 6, carbs 9, protein 4

Rice Pudding
Preparation time: 10 minutes
Cooking time: 1 hour
Servings: 2
Ingredients:
- 2 tablespoons almonds, chopped
- 1 cup white rice
- 2 cups almond milk
- 1 tablespoon sugar
- 1 tablespoons maple syrup
- ¼ teaspoon cinnamon powder
- ¼ teaspoon ginger, grated

Directions:
1. In your slow cooker, mix the milk with the rice, sugar and the other ingredients, toss, put the lid on and cook on High for 1 hour.
2. Divide the pudding into bowls and serve cold

Nutrition: calories 205, fat 2, fiber 7, carbs 11, protein 4

Cherry Bowls
Preparation time: 10 minutes
Cooking time: 1 hour
Servings: 2
Ingredients:
- 1 cup cherries, pitted
- 1 tablespoon sugar
- ½ cup red cherry juice
- 2 tablespoons maple syrup

Directions:
1. In your slow cooker, mix the cherries with the sugar and the other ingredients, toss gently, put the lid on, cook on High for 1 hour, divide into bowls and serve.

Nutrition: calories 200, fat 1, fiber 4, carbs 5, protein 2

Flavorful Berry Cream
Preparation time: 10 minutes
Cooking time: 2 hours
Servings: 2
Ingredients:
- 2 tablespoons cashews, chopped
- 1 cup heavy cream
- ½ cup blueberries
- ½ cup maple syrup
- ½ tablespoon coconut oil, melted

Directions:
1. In your slow cooker, mix the cream with the berries and the other ingredients, whisk, put the lid on and cook on Low for 2 hours.
2. Divide the mix into bowls and serve cold.

Nutrition: calories 200, fat 3, fiber 5, carbs 12, protein 3

Simple Maple Pudding
Preparation time: 10 minutes
Cooking time: 1 hour
Servings: 2
Ingredients:
- ¼ cup cashew butter
- 1 tablespoon coconut oil, melted
- ½ cup white rice
- 1 cup almond milk
- 2 tablespoons lemon juice
- ½ teaspoon lemon zest, grated
- 1 tablespoon maple syrup

Directions:
1. In your slow cooker, mix the rice with the milk, coconut oil and the other ingredients, whisk, put the lid on and cook on High for 1 hour.
2. Divide into bowls and serve.

Nutrition: calories 202, fat 4, fiber 5, carbs 14, protein 1

Chia and Orange Pudding
Preparation time: 10 minutes
Cooking time: 1 hour
Servings: 2
Ingredients:
- 1 tablespoon chia seeds
- ½ cup almond milk
- ½ cup oranges, peeled and cut into segments
- 1 tablespoon sugar
- ½ teaspoon cinnamon powder
- 1 tablespoon coconut oil, melted
- 2 tablespoons pecans, chopped

Directions:
1. In your slow cooker, mix the chia seeds with the almond milk, orange segments and the other ingredients, toss, put the lid on and cook on High for 1 hour.
2. Divide the pudding into bowls and serve cold.

Nutrition: calories 252, fat 3, fiber 3, carbs 7, protein 3

Berries Mix
Preparation time: 10 minutes
Cooking time: 1 hour
Servings: 2
Ingredients:
- ½ teaspoon nutmeg, ground
- ½ teaspoon vanilla extract
- ½ cup blackberries
- ½ cup blueberries
- ¼ cup whipping cream
- 1 tablespoon sugar
- 2 tablespoons walnuts, chopped

Directions:
1. In your slow cooker, combine the berries with the cream and the other ingredients, toss gently, put the lid on, cook on High for 1 hour, divide into bowls, and serve.

Nutrition: calories 260, fat 3, fiber 2, carbs 14, protein 3

Apple Compote
Preparation time: 10 minutes
Cooking time: 1 hour
Servings: 2
Ingredients:
- 1 pound apples, cored and cut into wedges
- ½ cup water
- 1 tablespoon sugar
- 1 teaspoon vanilla extract
- ½ teaspoon almond extract

Directions:
1. In your slow cooker, mix the apples with the water and the other ingredients, toss, put the lid on and cook on High for 1 hour.
2. Divide into bowls and serve cold.

Nutrition: calories 203, fat 0, fiber 1, carbs 5, protein 4

Easy Plums Stew
Preparation time: 10 minutes
Cooking time: 1 hour
Servings: 2
Ingredients:
- 1 pound plums, pitted and halved
- ½ teaspoon nutmeg, ground
- 1 cup water
- 1 and ½ tablespoons sugar
- 1 tablespoon vanilla extract

Directions:
1. In your slow cooker, mix the plums with the water and the other ingredients, toss gently, put the lid on and cook on High for 1 hour.
2. Divide the mix into bowls and serve.

Nutrition: calories 200, fat 2, fiber 1, carbs 5, protein 4

Cinnamon Peach

Preparation time: 10 minutes
Cooking time: 2 hours
Servings: 2
Ingredients:
- 2 cups peaches, peeled and halved
- 3 tablespoons sugar
- ½ teaspoon cinnamon powder
- ½ cup heavy cream
- 1 teaspoon vanilla extract

Directions:
1. In your slow cooker, mix the peaches with the sugar and the other ingredients, toss, put the lid on and cook on High for 2 hours.
2. Divide the mix into bowls and serve.

Nutrition: calories 212, fat 4, fiber 4, carbs 7, protein 3

Strawberry Cake

Preparation time: 10 minutes
Cooking time: 1 hour
Servings: 2
Ingredients:
- ¼ cup coconut flour
- ¼ teaspoon baking soda
- 1 tablespoon sugar
- ¼ cup strawberries, chopped
- ½ cup coconut milk
- 1 teaspoon butter, melted
- ½ teaspoon lemon zest, grated
- ¼ teaspoon vanilla extract
- Cooking spray

Directions:
1. In a bowl, mix the coconut flour with the baking soda, sugar and the other ingredients except the cooking spray and stir well.
2. Grease your slow cooker with the cooking spray, line it with parchment paper, pour the cake batter inside, put the lid on and cook on High for 1 hour.
3. Leave the cake to cool down, slice and serve.

Nutrition: calories 200, fat 4, fiber 4, carbs 10, protein 4

Ginger Pears

Preparation time: 10 minutes
Cooking time: 2 hours
Servings: 2
Ingredients:
- 2 pears, peeled and cored
- 1 cup apple juice
- ½ tablespoon brown sugar
- 1 tablespoon ginger, grated

Directions:
1. In your slow cooker, mix the pears with the apple juice and the other ingredients, toss, put the lid on and cook on Low for 2 hour.
2. Divide the mix into bowls and serve warm.

Nutrition: calories 250, fat 1, fiber 2, carbs 12, protein 4

Raisin Cookies

Preparation time: 10 minutes
Cooking time: 2 hours and 30 minutes
Servings: 2
Ingredients:
- 1 tablespoon coconut oil, melted
- 2 eggs, whisked
- ¼ cup brown sugar
- ½ cup raisins
- ¼ cup almond milk
- ¼ teaspoon vanilla extract
- ¼ teaspoon baking powder
- 1 cup almond flour

Directions:
1. In a bowl, mix the eggs with the raisins, almond milk and the other ingredients and whisk well.
2. Line your slow cooker with parchment paper, spread the cookie mix on the bottom of the pot, put the lid on, cook on Low for 2 hours and 30 minutes, leave aside to cool down, cut with a cookie cutter and serve.

Nutrition: calories 220, fat 2, fiber 1, carbs 6, protein 6

Easy Blueberries Jam

Preparation time: 10 minutes
Cooking time: 4 hours
Servings: 2
Ingredients:
- 2 cups blueberries
- ½ cup water
- ¼ pound sugar
- Zest of 1 lime

Directions:
1. In your slow cooker, combine the berries with the water and the other ingredients, toss, put the lid on and cook on High for 4 hours.
2. Divide into small jars and serve cold.

Nutrition: calories 250, fat 3, fiber 2, carbs 6, protein 1

Orange Bowls

Preparation time: 10 minutes
Cooking time: 3 hours
Servings: 2
Ingredients:
- ½ pound oranges, peeled and cut into segments
- 1 cup heavy cream
- ½ tablespoon almonds, chopped
- 1 tablespoon chia seeds
- 1 tablespoon sugar

Directions:
1. In your slow cooker, mix the oranges with the cream and the other ingredients, toss, put the lid on and cook on Low for 3 hours.
2. Divide into bowls and serve.

Nutrition: calories 170, fat 0, fiber 2, carbs 7, protein 4

Quinoa Pudding

Preparation time: 10 minutes
Cooking time: 2 hours
Servings: 2
Ingredients:
- 1 cup quinoa
- 2 cups almond milk
- ½ cup sugar
- ½ tablespoon walnuts, chopped
- ½ tablespoon almonds, chopped

Directions:
1. In your slow cooker, mix the quinoa with the milk and the other ingredients, toss, put the lid on and cook on High for 2 hours.
2. Divide the pudding into cups and serve.

Nutrition: calories 213, fat 4, fiber 6, carbs 10, protein 4

Chia with Avocado Pudding

Preparation time: 10 minutes
Cooking time: 3 hours
Servings: 2
Ingredients:
- ½ cup almond flour
- 1 tablespoon lime juice
- 2 tablespoons chia seeds
- 1 cup avocado, peeled, pitted and cubed
- 1 teaspoons baking powder
- ¼ teaspoon nutmeg, ground
- ¼ cup almond milk
- 2 tablespoons brown sugar
- 1 egg, whisked
- 2 tablespoons coconut oil, melted
- Cooking spray

Directions:
1. Grease your slow cooker with the cooking spray and mix the chia seeds with the flour, avocado and the other ingredients inside.
2. Put the lid on, cook on High for 3 hours, leave the pudding to cool down, divide into bowls and serve

Nutrition: calories 220, fat 4, fiber 4, carbs 9, protein 6

Almond and Cherries Pudding

Preparation time: 10 minutes
Cooking time: 3 hours
Servings: 2
Ingredients:
- ½ cup almonds, chopped
- ½ cup cherries, pitted and halved
- ½ cup heavy cream
- ½ cup almond milk
- 1 tablespoon butter, soft
- 1 egg
- 2 tablespoons sugar
- ½ cup almond flour
- ½ teaspoon baking powder
- Cooking spray

Directions:
1. Grease the slow cooker with the cooking spray and mix the almonds with the cherries, cream and the other ingredients inside.
2. Put the lid on, cook on High for 3 hours, divide into bowls and serve.

Nutrition: calories 200, fat 4, fiber 2, carbs 8, protein 6

Peach Cream

Preparation time: 10 minutes
Cooking time: 3 hours
Servings: 2
Ingredients:
- ¼ teaspoon cinnamon powder
- 1 cup peaches, pitted and chopped
- ¼ cup heavy cream
- Cooking spray
- 1 tablespoon maple syrup
- ½ teaspoons vanilla extract
- 2 tablespoons sugar

Directions:
1. In a blender, mix the peaches with the cinnamon and the other ingredients except the cooking spray and pulse well.
2. Grease the slow cooker with the cooking spray, pour the cream mix inside, put the lid on and cook on Low for 3 hours.
3. Divide the cream into bowls and serve cold.

Nutrition: calories 200, fat 3, fiber 4, carbs 10, protein 9

Cinnamon Plums

Preparation time: 10 minutes
Cooking time: 2 hours
Servings: 2
Ingredients:
- ½ pound plums, pitted and halved
- 2 tablespoons sugar
- 1 teaspoon cinnamon, ground
- ½ cup orange juice

Directions:
1. In your slow cooker, mix the plums with the cinnamon and the other ingredients, toss, put the lid on and cook on Low for 2 hours.
2. Divide into bowls and serve as a dessert.

Nutrition: calories 180, fat 2, fiber 1, carbs 8, protein 8

Delightful Cardamom Apples

Preparation time: 10 minutes
Cooking time: 2 hours
Servings: 2
Ingredients:
- 1 pound apples, cored and cut into wedges
- ½ cup almond milk
- ¼ teaspoon cardamom, ground
- 2 tablespoons brown sugar

Directions:
1. In your slow cooker, mix the apples with the cardamom and the other ingredients, toss, put the lid on and cook on High for 2 hours.
2. Divide the mix into bowls and serve cold.

Nutrition: calories 280, fat 2, fiber 1, carbs 10, protein 6

Cherry and Rhubarb Mix
Preparation time: 10 minutes
Cooking time: 2 hours
Servings: 2
Ingredients:
- 2 cups rhubarb, sliced
- ½ cup cherries, pitted
- 1 tablespoon butter, melted
- ¼ cup coconut cream
- ½ cup sugar

Directions:
1. In your slow cooker, mix the rhubarb with the cherries and the other ingredients, toss, put the lid on and cook on High for 2 hours.
2. Divide the mix into bowls and serve cold.

Nutrition: calories 200, fat 2, fiber 3, carbs 6, protein 1

Peaches and Wine Sauce
Preparation time: 10 minutes
Cooking time: 2 hours
Servings: 2
Ingredients:
- 3 tablespoons brown sugar
- 1 pound peaches, pitted and cut into wedges
- ½ cup red wine
- ½ teaspoon vanilla extract
- 1 teaspoon lemon zest, grated

Directions:
1. In your slow cooker, mix the peaches with the sugar and the other ingredients, toss, put the lid on and cook on High for 2 hours.
2. Divide into bowls and serve.

Nutrition: calories 200, fat 4, fiber 6, carbs 9, protein 4

Apricot and Peaches Cream
Preparation time: 10 minutes
Cooking time: 2 hours
Servings: 2
Ingredients:
- 1 cup apricots, pitted and chopped
- 1 cup peaches, pitted and chopped
- 1 cup heavy cream
- 3 tablespoons brown sugar
- 1 teaspoon vanilla extract

Directions:
1. In a blender, mix the apricots with the peaches and the other ingredients, and pulse well.
2. Put the cream in the slow cooker, put the lid on, cook on High for 2 hours, divide into bowls and serve.

Nutrition: calories 200, fat 4, fiber 5, carbs 10, protein 4

Vanilla Grapes Mix
Preparation time: 10 minutes
Cooking time: 2 hours
Servings: 2
Ingredients:
- 1 cup grapes, halved
- ½ teaspoon vanilla extract
- 1 cup oranges, peeled and cut into segments
- ¼ cup water
- 1 and ½ tablespoons sugar
- 1 teaspoon lemon juice

Directions:
1. In your slow cooker, mix the grapes with the oranges, water and the other ingredients, toss, put the lid on and cook on Low for 2 hours.
2. Divide into bowls and serve.

Nutrition: calories 100, fat 3, fiber 6, carbs 8, protein 3

Pomegranate and Mango Bowls
Preparation time: 10 minutes
Cooking time: 3 hours
Servings: 2
Ingredients:
- 2 cups pomegranate seeds
- 1 cup mango, peeled and cubed
- ½ cup heavy cream
- 1 tablespoon lemon juice
- ½ teaspoon vanilla extract
- 2 tablespoons white sugar

Directions:
1. In your slow cooker, combine the mango with the pomegranate seeds and the other ingredients, toss, put the lid on and cook on Low for 3 hours.
2. Divide into bowls and serve cold.

Nutrition: calories 162, fat 4, fiber 5, carbs 20, protein 6

Mandarin Cream
Preparation time: 10 minutes
Cooking time: 2 hours
Servings: 2
Ingredients:
- 1 tablespoon ginger, grated
- 3 tablespoons sugar
- 3 mandarins, peeled and chopped
- 2 tablespoons agave nectar
- ½ cup coconut cream

Directions:
1. In your slow cooker, mix the ginger with the sugar, mandarins and the other ingredients, whisk, put the lid on and cook on High for 2 hours.
2. Blend the cream using an immersion blender, divide into bowls and serve cold.

Nutrition: calories 100, fat 4, fiber 5, carbs 6, protein 7

Cranberries Cream
Preparation time: 10 minutes
Cooking time: 1 hour
Servings: 2
Ingredients:
- 3 cups cranberries
- ½ cup water
- ½ cup coconut cream
- ½ teaspoon vanilla extract
- ½ teaspoon almond extract
- ½ cup sugar

Directions:
1. In your slow cooker, mix the cranberries with the water, cream and the other ingredients, whisk, put the lid on and cook on High for 1 hour.
2. Transfer to a blender, pulse well, divide into bowls and serve cold.

Nutrition: calories 100, fat 3, fiber 6, carbs 7, protein 3

Buttery Pineapple
Preparation time: 10 minutes
Cooking time: 2 hours
Servings: 2
Ingredients:
- 2 cups pineapple, peeled and roughly cubed
- 1 and ½ tablespoons butter
- ½ cup heavy cream
- 2 tablespoons brown sugar
- ½ teaspoon cinnamon powder
- ½ teaspoon ginger, grated

Directions:
1. In your slow cooker, mix the pineapple with the butter, cream and the other ingredients, toss, put the lid on and cook on High for 2 hours.
2. Divide into bowls and serve cold.

Nutrition: calories 152, fat 3, fiber 1, carbs 17, protein 3

Strawberry and Orange Mix
Preparation time: 10 minutes
Cooking time: 1 hour
Servings: 2
Ingredients:
- 2 tablespoons sugar
- 1 cup orange segments
- 1 cup strawberries, halved
- A pinch of ginger powder
- ½ teaspoon vanilla extract
- ½ cup orange juice
- 1 tablespoon chia seeds

Directions:
1. In your slow cooker, mix the oranges with the berries, ginger powder and the other ingredients, toss, put the lid on and cook on High for 1 hour.
2. Divide into bowls and serve cold.

Nutrition: calories 100, fat 2, fiber 2, carbs 10, protein 2

Maple Plums and Mango
Preparation time: 10 minutes
Cooking time: 1 hour
Servings: 2
Ingredients:
- 2 teaspoons orange zest
- 1 tablespoon orange juice
- 1 cup plums, pitted and halved
- 1 cup mango, peeled and cubed
- 1 tablespoon maple syrup
- 3 tablespoons sugar

Directions:
1. In your slow cooker, mix the plums with the mango and the other ingredients, toss, put the lid on and cook on High for 1 hour.
2. Divide into bowls and serve cold

Nutrition: calories 123, fat 1, fiber 2, carbs 20, protein 3

Cantaloupe Cream
Preparation time: 5 minutes
Cooking time: 1 hour
Servings: 2
Ingredients:
- 2 cups cantaloupe, peeled and cubed
- 2 tablespoons sugar
- 1 cup coconut cream
- 1 tablespoon butter
- 1 tablespoon lemon zest, grated
- Juice of ½ lemon

Directions:
1. In your slow cooker, mix the cantaloupe with the sugar, cream and the other ingredients, toss, put the lid on and cook on High for 1 hour.
2. Blend using an immersion blender, divide into bowls and serve cold.

Nutrition: calories 100, fat 2, fiber 3, carbs 6, protein 1

Yogurt Cheesecake
Preparation time: 1 hour
Cooking time: 3 hours
Servings: 2
Ingredients:
For the crust:
- 1 tablespoon coconut oil, melted
- ½ cup graham cookies, crumbled

For the filling:
- 3 ounces cream cheese, soft
- 1 cup Greek yogurt
- ½ tablespoon cornstarch
- 3 tablespoons sugar
- 1 egg, whisked
- 1 teaspoon almond extract
- Cooking spray

Directions:
1. In a bowl mix the cookie crumbs with butter and stir well.
2. Grease your slow cooker with the cooking spray, line it with parchment paper and press the crumbs on the bottom.
3. In a bowl, mix the cream cheese with the yogurt and the other ingredients, whisk well and spread over the crust.
4. Put the lid on, cook on Low for 3 hours, cool down and keep in the fridge for 1 hour before serving.

Nutrition: calories 276, fat 12, fiber 3, carbs 20, protein 4

Chocolate Mango

Preparation time: 10 minutes
Cooking time: 1 hour
Servings: 2
Ingredients:
- 1 cup crème fraiche
- ¼ cup dark chocolate, cut into chunks
- 1 cup mango, peeled and chopped
- 2 tablespoons sugar
- ½ teaspoon almond extract

Directions:
1. In your slow cooker, mix the crème fraiche with the chocolate and the other ingredients, toss, put the lid on and cook on Low for 1 hour.
2. Blend using an immersion blender, divide into bowls and serve.

Nutrition: calories 200, fat 12, fiber 4, carbs 7, protein 3

Lemon Jam

Preparation time: 10 minutes
Cooking time: 3 hours
Servings: 2
Ingredients:
- ½ cup lemon juice
- 1 orange, peeled and cut into segments
- 1 lemon, peeled and cut into segments
- ½ cup water
- 2 tablespoons lemon zest, grated
- ¼ cup sugar
- A pinch of cinnamon powder
- ½ tablespoon cornstarch

Directions:
1. In your slow cooker, mix the lemon juice with the sugar, water and the other ingredients, whisk, put the lid on and cook on Low for 3 hours.
2. Divide into small jars and serve cold.

Nutrition: calories 70, fat 1, fiber 3, carbs 13, protein 1

Lemon Peach

Preparation time: 10 minutes
Cooking time: 3 hours
Servings: 2
Ingredients:
- 1 cup peaches, peeled and halved
- 2 tablespoons sugar
- ½ tablespoon lemon juice
- ½ cup heavy cream
- 1 tablespoon lemon zest, grated

Directions:
1. In your slow cooker, mix the peaches with the sugar and the other ingredients, toss gently, put the lid on and cook on Low for 3 hours.
2. Divide into cups and serve cold.

Nutrition: calories 50, fat 0, fiber 2, carbs 10, protein 0

Rhubarb Stew

Preparation time: 10 minutes
Cooking time: 2 hours
Servings: 2
Ingredients:
- ½ pound rhubarb, roughly sliced
- 2 tablespoons sugar
- ½ teaspoon vanilla extract
- ½ teaspoon lemon extract
- 1 tablespoon lemon juice
- ¼ cup water

Directions:
1. In your slow cooker, mix the rhubarb with the sugar, vanilla and the other ingredients, toss, put the lid on and cook on Low for 2 hours.
2. Divide the mix into bowls and serve cold.

Nutrition: calories 60, fat 1, fiber 0, carbs 10, protein 1

Strawberry with Blackberry Jam

Preparation time: 10 minutes
Cooking time: 3 hours
Servings: 2
Ingredients:
- ½ pound strawberries, halved
- 1 cup blackberries
- 1 tablespoon lemon zest, grated
- ½ teaspoon almond extract
- 2 tablespoons lemon juice
- 1 cup sugar

Directions:
1. In your slow cooker, combine the berries with the lemon zest and the other ingredients, toss, put the lid on and cook on Low for 3 hours.
2. Stir the mix well, divide into bowls and serve cold.

Nutrition: calories 451, fat 0.8, fiber 6.3, carbs 112, protein 2

Pear Cream

Preparation time: 10 minutes
Cooking time: 3 hours
Servings: 2
Ingredients:
- ½ pound pears, peeled and chopped
- ½ cup heavy cream
- ½ cup honey
- 1 tablespoon lemon zest, grated
- Juice of ½ lemon

Directions:
1. In your slow cooker, mix the pears with the cream and the other ingredients, whisk, put the lid on and cook on Low for 3 hours.
2. Blend using an immersion blender, divide into cups and serve cold.

Nutrition: calories 429, fat 11.3, fiber 3.9, carbs 88.6, protein 1.4

Simple Rhubarb Jam
Preparation time: 10 minutes
Cooking time: 2 hours
Servings: 2
Ingredients:
- ½ pound rhubarb, sliced
- ½ tablespoon cornstarch
- ¼ cup sugar
- 1 tablespoon lemon juice
- 1 cup water

Directions:
1. In your slow cooker, mix the rhubarb with the sugar and the other ingredients, toss, put the lid on and cook on High for 2 hours.
2. Whisk the jam, divide into bowls and serve cold.

Nutrition: calories 40, fat 0, fiber 1, carbs 10, protein 1

Apricot Marmalade
Preparation time: 10 minutes
Cooking time: 3 hours
Servings: 2
Ingredients:
- 1 cup apricots, chopped
- ½ cup water
- 1 teaspoon vanilla extract
- 2 tablespoons lemon juice
- 1 teaspoon fruit pectin
- 2 cups sugar

Directions:
1. In your slow cooker, mix the apricots with the water, vanilla and the other ingredients, whisk, put the lid on and cook on High for 3 hours.
2. Stir the marmalade, divide into bowls and serve cold.

Nutrition: calories 100, fat 1, fiber 2, carbs 20, protein 1

Avocado and Mango Bowls
Preparation time: 10 minutes
Cooking time: 2 hours
Servings: 2
Ingredients:
- 1 cup avocado, peeled, pitted and cubed
- 1 cup mango, peeled and cubed
- 1 apple, cored and cubed
- 2 tablespoons brown sugar
- 1 cup heavy cream
- 1 tablespoon lemon juice

Directions:
1. In your slow cooker, combine the avocado with the mango and the other ingredients, toss gently, put the lid on and cook on Low for 2 hours.
2. Divide the mix into bowls and serve.

Nutrition: calories 60, fat 1, fiber 2, carbs 20, protein 1

Tomato Jam
Preparation time: 10 minutes
Cooking time: 3 hours
Servings: 2
Ingredients:
- ½ pound tomatoes, chopped
- 1 green apple, grated
- 2 tablespoons red wine vinegar
- 4 tablespoons sugar

Directions:
1. In your slow cooker, mix the tomatoes with the apple and the other ingredients, whisk, put the lid on and cook on Low for 3 hours.
2. Whisk the jam well, blend a bit using an immersion blender, divide into bowls and serve cold.

Nutrition: calories 70, fat 1, fiber 1, carbs 18, protein 1

Cinnamon Peaches
Preparation time: 10 minutes
Cooking time: 2 hours
Servings: 2
Ingredients:
- 4 peaches, stoned and halved
- 1 tablespoon cinnamon powder
- 1 tablespoon cocoa powder
- 2 tablespoons coconut oil, melted
- 2 tablespoons sugar
- 1 cup heavy cream

Directions:
1. In your slow cooker, mix the peaches with the cinnamon, cocoa and the other ingredients, toss, put the lid on and cook on Low for 2 hours.
2. Divide the mix into bowls and serve cold.

Nutrition: calories 40, fat 1, fiber 1, carbs 5, protein 0

Coconut Jam
Preparation time: 10 minutes
Cooking time: 3 hours
Servings: 2
Ingredients:
- ½ cup coconut flesh, shredded
- 1 cup coconut cream
- ½ cup heavy cream
- 3 tablespoons sugar
- 1 tablespoon lemon juice

Directions:
1. In your slow cooker, mix the coconut cream with the lemon juice and the other ingredients, whisk, put the lid on and cook on Low for 3 hours.
2. Whisk well, divide into bowls and serve cold.

Nutrition: calories 50, fat 1, fiber 1, carbs 10, protein 2

Bread Pudding
Preparation time: 10 minutes
Cooking time: 3 hours
Servings: 2
Ingredients:
- 2 cups white bread, cubed
- 1 cup blackberries
- 2 tablespoons butter, melted
- 2 tablespoons white sugar
- 1 cup almond milk
- ¼ cup heavy cream
- 2 eggs, whisked
- 1 tablespoon lemon zest, grated
- ¼ teaspoon vanilla extract

Directions:
1. In your slow cooker, mix the bread with the berries, butter and the other ingredients, toss gently, put the lid on and cook on Low for 3 hours.
2. Divide pudding between dessert plates and serve.

Nutrition: calories 354, fat 12, fiber 4, carbs 29, protein 11

Tapioca and Chia Pudding
Preparation time: 10 minutes
Cooking time: 3 hours
Servings: 2
Ingredients:
- 1 cup almond milk
- ¼ cup tapioca pearls
- 2 tablespoons chia seeds
- 2 eggs, whisked
- ½ teaspoon vanilla extract
- 3 tablespoons sugar
- ½ tablespoon lemon zest, grated

Directions:
1. In your slow cooker, mix the tapioca pearls with the milk, eggs and the other ingredients, whisk, put the lid on and cook on Low for 3 hours.
2. Divide the pudding into bowls and serve cold.

Nutrition: calories 180, fat 3, fiber 4, carbs 12, protein 4

Dates Pudding
Preparation time: 10 minutes
Cooking time: 3 hours
Servings: 2
Ingredients:
- 1 cup dates, chopped
- ½ cup white rice
- 1 cup almond milk
- 2 tablespoons brown sugar
- 1 teaspoon almond extract

Directions:
1. In your slow cooker, mix the rice with the milk and the other ingredients, whisk, put the lid on and cook on Low for 3 hours.
2. Divide the pudding into bowls and serve.

Nutrition: calories 152, fat 5, fiber 2, carb 6, protein 3

Walnuts and Mango Bowls
Preparation time: 10 minutes
Cooking time: 2 hours
Servings: 2
Ingredients:
- 1 cup walnuts, chopped
- 2 tablespoons almonds, chopped
- 1 cup mango, peeled and roughly cubed
- 1 cup heavy cream
- ½ teaspoon vanilla extract
- 1 teaspoon almond extract
- 1 tablespoon brown sugar

Directions:
1. In your slow cooker, mix the nuts with the mango, cream and the other ingredients, toss, put the lid on and cook on High for 2 hours.
2. Divide the mix into bowls and serve.

Nutrition: calories 220, fat 4, fiber 2, carbs 4, protein 6

Berries Salad
Preparation time: 10 minutes
Cooking time: 1 hour
Servings: 2
Ingredients:
- 2 tablespoons brown sugar
- 1 tablespoon lime juice
- 1 tablespoon lime zest, grated
- 1 cup blueberries
- ½ cup cranberries
- 1 cup blackberries
- 1 cup strawberries
- ½ cup heavy cream

Directions:
1. In your slow cooker, mix the berries with the sugar and the other ingredients, toss, put the lid on and cook on High for 1 hour.
2. Divide the mix into bowls and serve.

Nutrition: calories 262, fat 7, fiber 2, carbs 5, protein 8

Pears and Apples
Preparation time: 10 minutes
Cooking time: 2 hours
Servings: 2
Ingredients:
- 1 teaspoon vanilla extract
- 2 pears, cored and cut into wedges
- 2 apples, cored and cut into wedges
- 1 tablespoon walnuts, chopped
- 2 tablespoons brown sugar
- ½ cup coconut cream

Directions:
1. In your slow cooker, mix the pears with the apples, nuts and the other ingredients, toss, put the lid on and cook on Low for 2 hours.
2. Divide the mix into bowls and serve cold.

Nutrition: calories 120, fat 2, fiber 2, carbs 4, protein 3

Creamy Rhubarb and Plums Bowls
Preparation time: 10 minutes
Cooking time: 2 hours
Servings: 2
Ingredients:
- 1 cup plums, pitted and halved
- 1 cup rhubarb, sliced
- 1 cup coconut cream
- ½ teaspoon vanilla extract
- ½ cup sugar
- ½ tablespoon lemon juice
- 1 teaspoon almond extract

Directions:
1. In your slow cooker, mix the plums with the rhubarb, cream and the other ingredients, toss, put the lid on and cook on High for 2 hours.
2. Divide the mix into bowls and serve.

Nutrition: calories 162, fat 2, fiber 2, carbs 4, protein 5

Cheese Pudding
Preparation time: 5 minutes
Cooking time: 2 hours
Servings: 2
Ingredients:
- 1 cup cream cheese, soft
- ½ cup Greek yogurt
- 2 eggs, whisked
- ½ teaspoon baking soda
- 1 cup almonds, chopped
- 1 tablespoon sugar
- ½ teaspoon almond extract
- ½ teaspoon cinnamon powder

Directions:
1. In your slow cooker, mix the cream cheese with the yogurt, eggs and the other ingredients, whisk, put the lid on and cook on Low for 2 hours.
2. Divide the pudding into bowls and serve.

Nutrition: calories 172, fat 2, fiber 3, carbs 4, protein 5

Greek Cream
Preparation time: 10 minutes
Cooking time: 1 hour
Servings: 2
Ingredients:
- 1 cup heavy cream
- 1 cup Greek yogurt
- 2 tablespoons brown sugar
- ½ teaspoon vanilla extract
- ½ teaspoon ginger powder

Directions:
1. In your slow cooker, mix the cream with the yogurt and the other ingredients, whisk, put the lid on and cook on High for 1 hour.
2. Divide the cream into bowls and serve cold.

Nutrition: calories 200, fat 5, fiber 3, carbs 4, protein 5

Easy Ginger Cream
Preparation time: 10 minutes
Cooking time: 1 hour
Serving: 2
Ingredients:
- 1 cup coconut cream
- 1 tablespoon ginger, grated
- 2 eggs, whisked
- 1 cup Greek yogurt
- 2 tablespoons brown sugar
- 1 tablespoon lemon juice

Directions:
1. In your slow cooker, mix the cream with the ginger, eggs and the other ingredients, whisk, put the lid on and cook on High for 1 hour.
2. Cool the cream down and serve.

Nutrition: calories 384, fat 33.2, fiber 3, carbs 17.9, protein 8.6

Quinoa Pudding
Preparation time: 10 minutes
Cooking time: 3 hours
Servings: 2
Ingredients:
- 1 cup quinoa
- 1 cup bread, cubed
- 2 cups almond milk
- 2 tablespoons honey
- 1 teaspoon cinnamon powder
- 1 teaspoon nutmeg, ground

Directions:
1. In your slow cooker, mix the quinoa with the milk and the other ingredients, whisk, put the lid on and cook on Low for 3 hours.
2. Divide the pudding into bowls and serve.

Nutrition: calories 981, fat 63.4, fiber 11.9, carbs 94.6, protein 19

Melon Pudding
Preparation time: 10 minutes
Cooking time: 2 hours
Servings: 2
Ingredients:
- 1 cup melon, peeled and cubed
- ½ cup white rice
- 1 cup coconut milk
- 2 tablespoons honey
- 1 teaspoon vanilla extract
- 1 teaspoon ginger powder
- ½ tablespoon lime zest, grated

Directions:
1. In your slow cooker, mix the rice with the melon, milk and the other ingredients, whisk, put the lid on and cook on High for 2 hours.
2. Divide the pudding into bowls and serve cold.

Nutrition: calories 545, fat 29.1, fiber 4.3, carbs 68.4, protein 6.9

Appendix : Recipes Index

A

Almond and Cherries Pudding 97
Almond and Quinoa Bowls 13
Almond Shrimp and Cabbage 91
Almonds and Shrimp Bowls 55
Appetizing Almond Bowls 51
Appetizing Almond Spread 51
Appetizing Beef Dip 56
Appetizing Beef Dip 56
Appetizing Beets Salad 50
Appetizing Carrots Spread 56
Appetizing Corn Sauté 34
Appetizing Zucchini Mix 35
Appetizing Zucchini Mix 40
Apple and Carrot Dip 54
Apple Compote 95
Apple Spread 16
Apple with Chia Mix 10
Apples with Cinnamon 94
Apricot and Peaches Cream 98
Apricot Marmalade 101
Artichoke Dip 47
Artichoke Dip 57
Artichoke Soup 28
Asparagus Casserole 19
Asparagus Mix 43
Avocado and Mango Bowls 101

B

Baby Spinach Rice Mix 19
Bacon Potatoes 40
Balsamic Cauliflower 34
Balsamic Lamb 81
Balsamic Lamb Mix 77
Balsamic Okra Mix 42
Balsamic Trout 92
Balsamic Tuna 87
Banana Oatmeal 9
Barley Mix 38
Basil Chicken 62
Basil Cod with Olives 89
Basil Sausage and Broccoli Mix 17
BBQ Turkey 68
BBQ-Beans 39
Beans and Mushroom 29
Beans Bowls 17
Beans Chili 26
Beans Mix 38
Beans Salad 16
Beef and Artichokes 32
Beef and Artichokes 75
Beef and Cabbage 31
Beef and Capers 76
Beef and Cauliflower 22
Beef and Celery 24
Beef and Corn 79
Beef and Corn Mix 72
Beef and Red Onions 73
Beef and Spinach 72
Beef and Zucchinis Mix 71

Beef Curry 31
Beef Soup 32
Beef Stew 23
Beef Stew 31
Beef with Endives 77
Beef with Green Beans 81
Beef with Peas 78
Beef with Peppers 79
Beef with Sauce 71
Beef with Sprouts 80
Berries Mix 95
Berries Quinoa 10
Berries Salad 102
Black Beans Mix 34
Black Beans Mix 37
Bread Pudding 102
Broccoli Casserole 11
Broccoli Dip 55
Brussels Sprouts and Cauliflower 44
Bulgur and Beans Salsa 50
Butter Green Beans 34
Buttery Pineapple 99
Buttery Spinach 40

C

Cabbage and Kale Mix 44
Cabbage and Onion 42
Cabbage Mix 39
Calamari Rings 53
Calamari with Sauce 91
Cantaloupe Cream 99
Carrots and Parsnips 44
Carrots and Spinach Mix 36
Carrots Casserole 13
Cashew Butter 16
Cauliflower and Almonds 36
Cauliflower and Potatoes 43
Cauliflower Bites 55
Cauliflower Casserole 15
Cauliflower Dip 57
Cauliflower Mash 40
Cauliflower Spread 48
Cauliflower with Eggs 11
Cayenne Lamb 80
Cheddar Potatoes 34
Cheese Pudding 103
Cheesy Eggs 13
Cherry and Rhubarb Mix 98
Cherry Bowls 94
Chia and Orange Pudding 95
Chia Oatmeal 9
Chia with Avocado Pudding 97
Chicken and Apples 62
Chicken and Asparagus 68
Chicken and Beans 64
Chicken and Broccoli 62
Chicken and Brussels Sprouts 32
Chicken and Brussels Sprouts 67
Chicken and Cabbage 68
Chicken and Eggplant Stew 29

Chicken and Endives 62
Chicken and Green Beans 59
Chicken and Mango Mix 67
Chicken and Olives 60
Chicken and Onions Mix 61
Chicken and Peach Mix 28
Chicken and Peppers 68
Chicken and Rice 30
Chicken and Tomato Mix 22
Chicken and Zucchinis 66
Chicken Curry 63
Chicken Drumsticks 28
Chicken Soup 25
Chicken Soup 25
Chicken Wings 60
Chicken with Corn 27
Chicken with Tomatoes 60
Chickpeas Salsa 50
Chickpeas Spread 48
Chickpeas Stew 24
Chickpeas Stew 32
Chili Eggs Mix 12
Chili Lamb 73
Chili Lamb 78
Chili Salmon 83
Chili Shrimp with Zucchinis 89
Chives Mackerel 86
Chives Mussels 90
Chives Shrimp 84
Chocolate Bread 13
Chocolate Mango 100
Cider Beef Mix 73
Cilantro Chicken and Eggplant Mix 67
Cinnamon French Toast 9
Cinnamon Lamb 80
Cinnamon Oatmeal 8
Cinnamon Peach 96
Cinnamon Peaches 101
Cinnamon Pecans Snack 55
Cinnamon Plums 97
Cinnamon Pork Ribs 29
Cinnamon Squash 39
Cinnamon Trout 93
Cocoa Oats 16
Coconut Beef 82
Coconut Bok Choy 42
Coconut Cream 94
Coconut Jam 101
Coconut Mackerel 88
Coconut Potatoes 36
Coconut Turkey 66
Cod and Corn 84
Cod and Tomatoes 85
Cod Stew 21
Cod with Artichokes 90
Cod with Broccoli 93
Coriander and Turmeric Chicken 70
Coriander Salmon 84
Coriander Turkey 64
Corn Dip 49

Crab Dip 47
Cranberries Cream 99
Cranberry Oatmeal 14
Creamy Beans 38
Creamy Beef 82
Creamy Lamb 76
Creamy Rhubarb and Plums Bowls 103
Creamy Shrimp 85
Creamy Tuna and Scallions 87
Creamy Turkey Mix 61
Cumin Chicken 70
Cumin Pork Chops 78
Cumin Quinoa Pilaf 41
Curry Broccoli Mix 43
Curry Calamari 92
Curry Lamb 81
Curry Pork Meatballs 53
Curry Savory Veggie Mix 36

D

Dates Pudding 102
Delightful Cardamom Apples 97
Delightful Chicken Meatballs 55
Delish Carrots Oatmeal 9
Delish Spinach Spread 47
Dill Cod 86
Dill Mushroom Sauté 35
Duck with Mushrooms 65

E

Easy Avocado Cake 94
Easy Blueberries Jam 96
Easy Buttery Oatmeal 9
Easy Chicken Salad 54
Easy Chives Lamb 74
Easy Ginger Cream 103
Easy Plums Stew 95
Easy Stuffed Mushrooms 52
Easy Sweet Potato Dip 54
Egg Scramble 19
Eggplant Curry 32
Eggplant Salad 52
Eggplant Salsa 51
Eggplant Salsa 56
Eggs and Sweet Potato 15
Eggs Mix 12

F

Farro Mix 41
Fennel Soup 28
Flavorful Balsamic Turkey 63
Flavorful Berry Cream 95
Flavorful Coconut Quinoa 8
Flavorful Rosemary Chicken 62
Flavorful Rosemary Chicken Thighs 70
Flavorful Spinach Frittata 12
Flavory Beans Spread 48
Flavory Mushroom Dip 48

G

Garlic Carrots 43
Garlic Risotto 36
Garlic Sea Bass 85
Garlic Squash Mix 43

Garlic Turkey 70
Ginger Bowls 14
Ginger Pears 96
Ginger Raisins Oatmeal 10
Ginger Salmon 20
Ginger Turkey Mix 61
Granola Bowls 14
Greek Cream 103
Green Beans and Zucchinis 45

H

Ham Omelet 18
Hash Brown with Bacon 8
Herbed Ginger Tuna 84
Herbed Shrimp 83
Honey Lamb Roast 24
Honey Pork Chops 73
Hot Lentils 37
Hot Ribs 72

I

Italian Eggplant 42
Italian Shrimp 89
Italian Turkey 65

K

Kale Mix 40

L

Lamb and Appetizing Zucchini Mix 79
Lamb and Cabbage 77
Lamb and Capers 79
Lamb and Eggs 14
Lamb and Fennel 76
Lamb and Kale 80
Lamb and Lime Zucchinis 77
Lamb and Onion 23
Lamb and Tomatoes Mix 75
Lamb Chops 74
Lamb with Olives 76
Lamb with Potatoes 75
Leek Casserole 15
Lemon Jam 100
Lemon Lamb 75
Lemon Peach 100
Lemony Artichokes 42
Lemony Kale 44
Lemony Shrimp Dip 47
Lemony Turkey and Potatoes 69
Lemony Turkey and Spinach 59
Lentils Salsa 51
Lime Chicken 25
Lime Chicken Mix 60
Lime Crab 88
Lime Pork Chops 79
Lime Trout 87
Lime Turkey and Chard 68

M

Mandarin Cream 98
Mango Rice 42
Maple Beef 78
Maple Chicken 21
Maple Plums and Mango 99
Marjoram Rice Mix 38

Masala Beef Mix 33
Masala Beef with Sauce 77
Mashed Potatoes 38
Melon Pudding 103
Mint Farro Pilaf 41
Mixed Pork and Beans 27
Mushroom Casserole 14
Mushroom Quiche 18
Mushroom Soup 27
Mushroom Spread 50
Mushroom Stew 26
Mustard Chicken Mix 59
Mustard Cod 87
Mustard Pork Chops 28
Mustard Short Ribs 26

N

Nutmeg Lamb and Squash 76
Nuts Snack 53

O

Onion Dip 51
Orange Bowls 96
Orange Carrots Mix 37
Orange Chicken Mix 69
Orange Cod 85
Oregano Beef 74
Oregano Lamb 81
Oregano Shrimp 92
Oregano Turkey and Tomatoes 59

P

Paprika Chicken and Artichokes 59
Paprika Cod 83
Paprika Cod Sticks 53
Paprika Lamb 78
Parmesan Quinoa 11
Parmesan Rice 41
Parmesan Spinach Mix 45
Parsley Chicken 26
Parsley Chicken 63
Parsley Cod 85
Parsley Mushroom 39
Peach Cream 97
Peach, Vanilla and Oats Mix 12
Peaches and Wine Sauce 98
Pear Cream 100
Pears and Apples 102
Peas and Rice Bowls 19
Peas and Tomatoes 46
Peppers and Eggs 18
Peppers Rice 16
Pesto Chicken 61
Pesto Lamb 81
Pineapple and Tofu 50
Piquant Creamy Brisket 27
Pomegranate and Mango Bowls 98
Pork and Beans Mix 72
Pork and Chickpeas 31
Pork and Chilies Mix 72
Pork and Cranberries 23
Pork and Eggplant 15
Pork and Eggplant 75

Pork and Mushroom 30
Pork and Okra 74
Pork and Olives 71
Pork and Soy Sauce Mix 71
Pork and Tomatoes Mix 30
Pork Chili 29
Pork Chops 28
Pork Chops and Mango 71
Pork Chops and Spinach 80
Pork Roast and Olives 23
Pork Shanks 30
Pork Soup 26
Pork with Green Beans 74
Pork with Lentils 77
Potato and Ham Mix 12
Potato Salad 49
Potato Soup 27
Potato Stew 30
Potatoes and Leeks Mix 37
Pumpkin and Berries 17
Pumpkin and Quinoa Mix 10

Q

Quinoa and Chia Pudding 17
Quinoa and Veggies Casserole 10
Quinoa Pudding 103
Quinoa Pudding 97

R

Raisin Cookies 96
Rhubarb Stew 100
Rice and Corn 43
Rice Bowls 48
Rice Pudding 94
Rosemary Beef 78
Rosemary Leeks 37

S

Saffron Risotto 41
Sage Peas 35
Sage Sweet Potatoes 36
Salmon and Berries 89
Salmon and Carrots 88
Salmon and Strawberries Mix 93
Salmon and Tomatoes 93
Salmon Bites 53
Salmon Salad 91
Salmon Stew 31
Salmon with Peas 88
Salmon, Tomatoes and Green Beans 90
Salsa Beans Dip 49
Salsa Chicken 21
Sausage and Eggs Mix 11
Sausage and Potato Mix 8
Savory Lentils Soup 25
Savory Veggie Mix 40
Savoy Cabbage Mix 46
Scallions Quinoa and Carrots 18
Sea Bass with Chickpeas 85
Sea Bass with Squash 88
Seafood Soup 20
Sesame Salmon 20
Shrimp and Cauliflower Bowls 93

Shrimp and Eggplant 88
Shrimp and Mango 87
Shrimp and Rice 90
Shrimp and Spinach 20
Shrimp Bowls 11
Shrimp Gumbo 25
Shrimp Salad 54
Shrimp Stew 20
Shrimp with Avocado 86
Shrimp with Mushrooms 89
Shrimp with Pineapple Bowls 87
Shrimp with Red Chard 90
Shrimp with Spinach 86
Simple Chives Duck 67
Simple Maple Pudding 95
Simple Rhubarb Jam 101
Soy Pork Chops 23
Spicy Brussels Sprouts 37
Spicy Brussels Sprouts 45
Spicy Duck Mix 69
Spicy Masala Turkey 64
Spicy Shrimp 91
Spicy Tuna 83
Spinach and Nuts Dip 53
Spinach Dip 49
Spinach Dip 57
Spinach Mix 38
Spinach Rice 41
Spinach, Walnuts and Calamari Salad 54
Squash and Eggplant Mix 35
Squash Bowls 14
Squash Salsa 47
Strawberry and Orange Mix 99
Strawberry Cake 96
Strawberry with Blackberry Jam 100
Stuffed Peppers 49
Sweet Potato and Cauliflower 39
Sweet Potato and Clam Chowder 21

T

Tacos 51
Tapioca and Chia Pudding 102
Tarragon Pork Chops 73
Tarragon Sweet Potatoes 45
Tasty Lime Shrimp 83
Thyme Chicken 22
Thyme Hash Browns 9
Thyme Mushrooms 44
Tomato and Corn 35
Tomato and Mushroom 49
Tomato and Zucchini Eggs Mix 13
Tomato Chicken 66
Tomato Jam 101
Tomato Pasta Mix 24
Tomatoes and Kale 92
Trout Bowls 92
Tuna and Fennel 89
Tuna and Green Beans 84
Tuna with Brussels Sprouts 86
Turkey and Corn 64
Turkey and Fennel Mix 60

Turkey and Figs 22
Turkey and Mushrooms 21
Turkey and Okra 69
Turkey and Peas 65
Turkey and Plums 61
Turkey and Scallions Mix 63
Turkey and Tomato Sauce 65
Turkey and Walnuts 22
Turkey Chili 63
Turkey Meatballs 52
Turkey Stew 33
Turkey with Avocado 67
Turkey with Carrots 69
Turkey with Kidney Beans 70
Turkey with Leeks 66
Turkey with Olives and Corn 64
Turkey with Radishes 66
Turkey with Rice 65
Turmeric Lamb 73
Turmeric Salmon 84
Turmeric Stew 29

V

Vanilla Grapes Mix 98
Vanilla Pears 94
Veggie Hash Brown Mix 8
Veggie Medley 45
Veggie Soup 33

W

Walnut Tuna 91
Walnuts and Mango Bowls 102
WalYummy Nuts Bowls 55
White Beans Mix 39
Worcestershire Beef 24

Y

Yogurt Cheesecake 99
Yummy Beef Meatloaf 15
Yummy Lentils Dip 52
Yummy Lentils Hummus 57
Yummy Mushroom Salsa 58
Yummy Nuts Bowls 52
Yummy Peppers Salsa 57

Z

Zucchini and Cauliflower Eggs 17
Zucchini Spread 56

www.ingramcontent.com/pod-product-compliance
Lightning Source LLC
LaVergne TN
LVHW060047030325
804929LV00015B/1781